ECONOMIC DEMOCRACY

ECONOMIC DEMOCRACY

The Politics of Feasible Socialism

ROBIN ARCHER

CLARENDON PRESS · OXFORD

1995

Oxford University Press, Walton Street, Oxford OX2 6DP
Oxford New York
Athens Auckland Bangkok Bombay
Calcutta Cape Town Dar es Salaam Delhi
Florence Hong Kong Istanbul Karachi
Kuala Lumpur Madras Madrid Melbourne
Mexico City Nairobi Paris Singapore
Taipei Tokyo Toronto
and associated companies in
Berlin Ibadan

Oxford is a trade mark of Oxford University Press

Published in the United States
by Oxford University Press Inc., New York

British Library Cataloguing in Publication Data
Data available

Library of Congress Cataloging in Publication Data
Archer, Robin.
Economic democracy : the politics of feasible socialism / Robin
Archer.
Includes bibliographical references.
1. Employee ownership. 2. Socialism. 3. Corporate state.
4. Management—Employee participation. I. Title.
HD5650.A682 1995 335—dc20 94-38333
CIP
ISBN 0–19–827891–8

1 3 5 7 9 10 8 6 4 2

Typeset by Best-set Typesetter Ltd., Hong Kong
Printed in Great Britain
on acid-free paper by
Bookcraft (Bath) Ltd.
.Midsomer Norton, Avon

*For
my parents*

Acknowledgements

I have accumulated a great many debts of gratitude in the course of writing this book. The book began life as a doctoral thesis at Balliol College, Oxford. But I would not have come to Oxford at all without the financial backing of the Commonwealth Scholarship Commission and the unfailing support of Stephen Gaukroger and Gyorgy Markus, my old teachers at Sydney University.

I am also grateful to friends and colleagues in the Australian labour movement. Many of my ideas about socialism, democracy and industrial relations were first tested in discussion with them.

On coming to Oxford I learnt a great deal from Colin Crouch and Steven Lukes, who supervised my original research. Steven's influence is strongest where I deal with political theory, while Colin's is strongest where I deal with political economy and industrial relations. I am very grateful to them both.

Many other people also helped me to produce this book. Alon Harel, Anton Hemerijck, Paul Hirst, Les Jacobs and Joe Liscio helped to clarify a number of key issues. G. A. Cohen and David Miller wrote detailed comments on a number of the chapters. And, collectively, members of the Oxford University Socialist Discussion Group provided an important forum for numerous formal and informal debates.

Special thanks are due to Hanjo Glock and Adam Steinhouse, who read through the entire final draft; and to Bronte Adams, who rescued me from my diagrams and, both literally and figuratively, stood by me to the end.

Thanks are also due to my parents and my brothers. I am particularly grateful to my father, Richard Douglas Archer, whose weekly letters and news cuttings ensured that, in matters Australian, I was the world's best-informed expatriate. Without his help Chapter 9 would not have been possible.

Finally, I owe an especially great debt of thanks to Terry Shakinovsky. Throughout the process of writing this book she has offered constant support and invaluable assistance.

R. A.

Contents

List of Figures	x
List of Tables	xi
Introduction	1
1. Freedom and Authority	12
2. Economic Democracy	38
3. Feasibility	61
4. Industrial Relations	68
5. Potentials and Dangers of Corporatism	85
6. The Corporatist Trade-off Strategy	103
7. Stagflation	145
8. Structural Adjustment	170
9. An Unexpected Case of Corporatism	191
10. Into the Next Century	230
Bibliography	237
Index	259

Figures

1. Programmatic goals of socialism   7
2. Individual freedom   15
3. Subject and non-subject individuals   31
4. The dimensions of labour freedom   58
5. Union centralization   73
6. The six dimensions of an industrial relations system   78
7. Stephens's levels of controls   104
8. The maximum control that capitalists are prepared to trade off for any given profit-threat   119
9. A simple bargaining game   122
10. The effect of increased workers' power on a simple bargaining game   138
11. The effect of control stickiness on cyclical externally produced changes in workers' power   141
12. Unemployment and inflation in the large OECD economies, 1960–1990   146
13. Key events in Australian national wage fixation, 1904–1983   204
14. Terms of trade in Australia, 1970–1990   210
15. Net external debt in Australia, 1981–1991   210
16. Balance on current account in Australia, 1974–1992   211
17. Consumer price inflation in Australia and major trading partners, 1981–1991   213
18. Labour market aggregates in Australia, 1981–1991   214
19. Real commodity prices, 1960–1990   222

Tables

1. Australian wage-fixing systems since the onset of
   stagflation   212
2. Growth of real GDP in Australia and the OECD,
   1982–1992   214
3. Employment and unemployment in Australia and the
   OECD, 1982–1992   215
4. Wages and household income in Australia, 1982–1988   218

Introduction

Socialism is both a theory and a movement. At the core of the theory are certain values. At the core of the movement are organized workers.

Socialist theory emerged in the wake of the French Revolution as a response to the failed promise of the Enlightenment.[1] It was not a reaction against the values of the Enlightenment, but rather an attempt to develop them and to apply them more consistently. The Enlightenment had promised a society of individual freedom and equality, and so socialism took these values as its basic moral reference point.[2] In this respect it was similar to other Enlightenment-influenced theories, and, in particular, it was similar to liberalism.[3]

Marx and Engels clearly acknowledged this lineage.[4] But their ambiguous attitude to moral concepts[5] led some socialists to deny its importance. As a result two distinct traditions of socialist thought had emerged by the end of the nineteenth century. According to the first, socialist theory continued to be based, as it originally was, on the fundamental values of the Enlightenment. According to the second, socialist theory was either based on

[1] There is some contention about when the word 'socialism' was first used in its modern sense. The invention of the term was claimed by Pierre Leroux who used it in *Le Globe* in 1832 to describe the theory of Saint-Simon (Kolakowski, 1978, 183). But in 1827 the term 'socialist' had already been used in the *Co-operative Magazine* to describe the followers of Robert Owen (Cole, 1953, 1).

[2] See, for example, Cole (1953, 11), Engels (1975, 45–51), Hobsbawm (1962, 35; 1982, 4–5), Kolakowski (1978, 182) and Wright (1986, 25–9, 33–4).

[3] '. . . with respect to liberalism as a great historical movement, socialism is its legitimate heir, not only in chronological sequence, but also in its spiritual qualities' (Bernstein, 1961, 149).

[4] Here is Engels (1975, 45) attempting to summarize their position: 'In its theoretical form', he says, modern socialism 'originally appears as a more developed and allegedly more consistent extension of the principles laid down by the French philosophers of the Enlightenment in the eighteenth century.' For an interpretation of Marx and Engels' work that emphasizes their ongoing liberal credentials see Hunt (1974 and 1984).

[5] See Buchanan (1982), Lukes (1984) and chapter 4 of Elster (1985).

quite different values or else it was based on no values at all. This
work falls squarely in the first tradition.

The socialist movement emerged in the wake of the Industrial
Revolution in response to the potential for collective action that
was offered by capitalist development.[6] Between 1890 and 1914
this movement took on the characteristic form of a mature labour
movement. A mature movement has two wings: an industrial
wing consisting of trade unions and a political wing consisting
of a pro-labour party.[7] From time to time—especially, but not
exclusively, in the last two decades—movements of women and
of racially oppressed people also played an important role in the
socialist movement. But, for better or worse, the industrial and
political wings of the labour movement have remained the core
constituents of the socialist movement in the advanced capitalist
world.

At various times and in various countries this socialist-cum-
labour movement has been able to adopt a co-ordinated strategy
and to take united action. But in recent years some have argued
that the changing nature of work may be making this sort of unity
impossible.[8] There is no doubt that significant changes are taking
place and that they have the potential to undermine labour movement unity. However, since the onset of industrialization, there
have *always* been various waxing and waning divisions in the
workforce which have carried this potential.[9] But there has also
always been the possibility of overcoming these divisions. In this
work I will assume that that possibility remains.

The rise of the labour movement produced a powerful constituency with an interest in pursuing the universal application
of the universal values of the Enlightenment. But in order to
realize these values, the labour movement first had to translate
them into policies which it had a feasible strategy for achieving.
In other words, the labour movement had to translate these
values into what we can call for short 'strategically feasible'
policies.

---

[6] There is a wealth of historical literature on the emergence of working class
organization. For an excellent fully-annotated comparative discussion see chapter
2, 'The Emergence of Organized Protest', in Geary (1981). See especially pp. 31–5.
[7] See chapter 3 in Geary (1981).
[8] See, for example, Lash and Urry (1987).
[9] See, for example, Hyman (1992).

Strategically feasible policies are often grouped together into larger 'programmatic goals'. A programmatic goal is the kind of goal which a political party might make the centre-piece of its election manifesto over a number of years. It is a middle order integrating framework or meta-policy which links morally desirable values on the one hand and strategically feasible policies on the other. Thus a socialist programmatic goal must be not just morally ordained by the values of socialist theory. It must also be strategically feasible for the movement that is pursuing those values.

In the course of their history the labour movements of the advanced capitalist world have pursued a variety of programmatic goals. These can be divided into two categories: participation goals and welfare goals.[10] Both can be derived from the fundamental Enlightenment values of individual freedom and equality. Participation goals can be derived from the idea that each individual's actions must be governed by his or her own choices to the maximum possible extent: even when the individual is participating in an association. Welfare goals can be derived from the idea that each individual needs to be provided with the means to enable this to take place.

Some of the programmatic goals which the labour movement has pursued fall into both categories. For example, nationalization and central planning were supposed both to increase participation by making enterprises accountable to parliament and to increase welfare by improving economic efficiency. Other programmatic goals fall clearly into one category or the other. For example, participatory goals like universal suffrage and parliamentary government were almost always the main programmatic goals of the labour movement if they had not already been established.[11] Welfare goals like the improvement of wages and working conditions have also played an important role.

After the Second World War, the labour movements of the advanced capitalist world opted for a new programmatic goal. Universal suffrage and parliamentary government had by now

[10] Compare these with the two 'equality assumptions' which Amy Gutmann (1980, 18) identifies in classical liberal theories. Gutmann sees these two assumptions reappearing in 'the two faces of democratic socialism' (1980, 78).

[11] The proto-socialist Chartist movement in Britain which lasted from about 1838 to 1848 is the earliest example of this (Cole, 1953).

been established, and the importance of nationalization and central planning was increasingly being questioned.[12] Instead the labour movement opted for a welfare goal. This goal was the establishment of a welfare state, and throughout the advanced capitalist world this became the main programmatic goal of the labour movement. Indeed, so successful was this goal that a commitment to some sort of welfare state programme became a feature of almost every electorally significant party: whether socialist or non-socialist. In this way, socialism, or at least its programmatic goal, came to dominate the advanced capitalist countries in the post-war world.

By the 1980s, however, the dominance of the welfare state pro-gramme had come to an end. The basic institutions of the welfare state were now in place and widely accepted. But the need for a tight fiscal policy meant that, whatever a government's political complexion, reduction rather than expansion of the welfare state was the order of the day.[13]

Of course there are still important additions and alterations that need to be made to the institutions of the welfare state. New measures are needed, for example, to assist the poverty-plagued underclass which continues to exist on the margins of many countries. In just the same way there are still important additions and alterations that need to be made to the institutions of parlia-mentary democracy. Electoral reform and greater freedom of in-formation are topical in some countries.[14] In both cases important

---

[12] Of course some socialists had always questioned the wisdom of these goals. Sceptics included prominent social democrats as well as those who had been influenced by syndicalism. For example, writing in 1898, Eduard Bernstein denied that nationalization has 'the fundamental importance commonly ascribed to it' and argued that 'there can be more socialism in a good factory act than in the nationalization of a whole group of factories' (Tudor and Tudor, 1988, 168). Similarly, writing in 1917, G. D. H. Cole (1972, 151) argued that it is not appropri-ate for socialists 'either to advocate or to oppose nationalization'. With a few exceptions, notably in Britain, most pro-labour parties made little effort to nation-alize their industries when they eventually came to power. For example, in Sweden, which is often considered the most 'socialist' country in the capitalist world, there has been almost no attempt to implement nationalization as an ideological goal.

[13] Even if this was not always achieved.

[14] For example, during the late 1980s and early 1990s pressure for electoral reform grew in both Britain and Italy. Ironically, while Italian reformers were pressing for an electoral system more like that of the British, British reformers were pressing for an electoral system more like that of the Italians.

changes are demanded. But they are changes that can be built on to well developed existing institutions. In neither case do the required changes challenge the fundamental principles underlying the organization of advanced capitalist societies. Thus, in spite of the need for further change, the welfare state programme, like the demand for parliamentary democracy, no longer poses a radical challenge to the advanced capitalist world.

Indeed, many argue that socialism itself no longer poses such a challenge. According to the proponents of this argument the socialist challenge has run its course. Some of its programmatic goals—like parliamentary democracy, decent wages and conditions, and a welfare state—have largely been achieved. Its other programmatic goals—like nationalization and central planning—have been abandoned as at best unhelpful and at worst counter-productive. If there *is* a radical challenge to the principles underlying the organization of advanced capitalist societies, it comes, so the argument goes, not from socialism but rather from environmentalism. Socialists can now do no more than fine-tune the *status quo*. In conclusion, then, the proponents of this argument claim that there is no longer a programmatic goal with which the socialist movement can pose a radical challenge to the political and economic institutions of advanced capitalism.

I believe that this claim is false. And I want to prove that it is false by showing that 'economic democracy' is just such a goal. Perhaps I could also show that the sceptics are wrong by showing that *international* welfare and democracy provide the socialist movement with radical programmatic goals. Here, however, I will restrict myself to *intra*-national goals, since it is still everywhere the case that the socialist movement can only succeed where it has the support of a national constituency.

By economic democracy I mean an economic system in which firms operate in a market but are governed by those who work for them. Since there is nowhere in the advanced capitalist world where the government of firms is based on this principle, economic democracy certainly provides a radical challenge to the institutions of advanced capitalism. But does it provide a programmatic goal with which the socialist movement can pose this challenge? To show that it does I need to show both that economic democracy is a morally desirable goal in terms of socialist theory,

and that it is a strategically feasible goal for the socialist movement. These are the primary tasks of my book.

This is not to say that economic democracy is a new concern for
socialists. Indeed something like it was the principal goal of many
of the earliest socialists. And this was especially true of those who
were influenced by the co-operative doctrines of Robert Owen
and Charles Fourier. In fact, the establishment of workers' co-
operatives remained the principal goal of socialists until the late
nineteenth century (Hobsbawm, 1982, 25; Bernstein, 1961, 110). A
new wave of interest in economic democracy arose in the early
twentieth century, and during this period there was some particularly interesting and innovative socialist thought. Economic
democracy found powerful advocates in Britain, Germany,
Sweden, Austria, and elsewhere. Especially noteworthy are two
seminal essays: *Self-Government in Industry*, published by G. D. H.
Cole in 1917; and *The Conditions of Economic Liberty*, published
by R. H. Tawney in 1918. Each of these essays foreshadows both
my attempt to justify economic democracy and my attempt to
propose a gradual union-based strategy for achieving it.[15]

Of course there are vast differences between the early and late
decades of the twentieth century. After the First World War,
socialism seemed unstoppable and economic democracy had to
compete with a great many other pressing socialist goals. The
most important competitors were welfare goals.[16] But, as we have
seen, this is no longer the case. Figure 1 lists the intra-national
programmatic goals of socialism which I believe have proved to
be of enduring significance. By the 1980s all the goals in the
hatched area had been more or less achieved.[17] That leaves just
economic democracy. The problem now is not competition between programmatic goals, but rather the possibility that there

[15] On the latter point see Cole (1972, 103–6, 149) and Tawney (1964, 103–10).

[16] Here is Cole in 1917: 'What, I want to ask, is the fundamental evil in our
modern Society which we should set out to abolish? There are two possible
answers to that question, and I am sure that very many well-meaning people
would make the wrong one. They would answer POVERTY, when they ought to
answer SLAVERY. Face to face with the shameful contrasts of riches and destitution,
high dividends and low wages, and painfully conscious of the futility of trying to
adjust the balance by means of charity, private or public, they would answer
unhesitatingly that they stand for the ABOLITION OF POVERTY' (Cole, 1972, 40).

[17] Note, however, that in Europe, political participation goals may have to be
re-won, albeit at an international level, as more and more powers are given to
multinational authorities like the European Union.

	POLITICAL INSTITUTIONS	ECONOMIC INSTITUTIONS
WELFARE GOALS	The welfare state	Decent wages and conditions
PARTICIPATION GOALS	Parliamentary democracy	Economic democracy

FIG. 1. *Programmatic goals of socialism that have been of enduring importance (divided according to the type of goal and the principal institutions through which the goal has been pursued)*

may not even be this *one* goal. By showing that economic democracy is indeed a programmatic goal which the socialist movement can and should achieve, I hope to contribute something to a renewal of the socialist tradition.

It may be that it is a mistake for me to identify my project with the socialist tradition. Perhaps I should identify it with the social democratic tradition instead. After all, the term 'social democracy' has certain advantages over the term 'socialism'. First, it has the advantage of better conveying the programmatic goal that I am advocating: namely, the establishment, not just of political democracy, but also of social, and in particular economic, democracy. It also better suggests the Enlightenment values of the intellectual tradition that I have been discussing, and is less likely to be confused with opposition to moral individualism. Second, 'social democracy' has the advantage of identifying the historical allegiance to the Second International of most (though not all) of the political parties with which I will be concerned. Third and finally, 'social democracy' has the advantage of clearly distinguishing my goals from those of Soviet socialism, which is now mercifully defunct. 'Social democracy' thus also serves to retain the interest of people in Eastern Europe. At present advocates of socialism receive the same response amongst people in Eastern Europe that *laissez-faire* advocates once received amongst those recovering from the Great Depression.

Despite these advantages, I have chosen to continue to identify my project with the socialist tradition. Here are some of the reasons. First, the social democratic tradition has not always been as sympathetic to the goal of economic democracy as its name suggests, and for some people 'social democracy' has become associated with a form of paternalistic state-centred socialism. In any case the social democratic tradition is part of a larger Western socialist tradition, which, as we have seen, has been concerned with economic democracy since its earliest days. Second, the term 'socialism' enables me to encompass more unambiguously not just the social democratic parties of Germanic Europe, but also the socialist (and where relevant the ex-communist) parties of Latin Europe, as well as the labour parties of the Anglo-Saxon world. And third, there is a danger of imposing a false unity on the beliefs of those who opposed Soviet socialism. Long before 1989, long before 1956, indeed long before the Cold War, the over-whelming majority of Western socialists opposed the Soviet system. But not all of them saw themselves as social democrats. Some of the most innovative—including Cole and the Austro-Marxists—insisted on remaining outside both the Soviet and the social democratic camp (Cole, 1960, 337; Bottomore and Goode, 1978, 1). For there have been periods when social democracy itself has hardened into orthodoxy.

To repeat, then, I want to try to convince those who feel some affinity with this broader socialist tradition—be they social democrats or not—that economic democracy is a programmatic goal which the socialist movement can and should achieve.

But I do not want to address myself solely to socialists. On the contrary, I want to try to convince all those who have been influenced by the values of the Enlightenment that economic democracy is both morally desirable and strategically feasible. Despite its brevity, this last introductory remark is the most important of all.

Thus my book has two main aims. First, it seeks to justify the claim that firms operating in a market economy should be governed by those who work for them. Second, it seeks to show that a gradual transition to such a system is feasible in the advanced capitalist countries. Chapters 1 and 2 deal with the first aim and the remaining chapters deal with the second.

In Chapter 1 I try to explain and justify two propositions. The first proposition is the 'principle of equal liberty': the principle that every human individual should have the maximum liberty that is compatible with an equal liberty for all other individuals.

In a separate argument I show that this principle forms the basis for a 'constitutive morality' of socialism. The second proposition is a weak version of the 'axiom of sociality': the axiom that human individuals are inherently social in nature. By looking at the relationship between these two propositions I derive the 'all-affected principle' and the 'all-subjected principle' which I take to be the fundamental principles of democracy. According to the all-subjected principle, all those, and only those, who are subject to the authority of an association should exercise direct decision-making control over that association. Other affected individuals should exercise indirect control, such as that which consumers exercise through the market.

Capitalist firms are associations that exercise authority. In Chapter 2 I argue that since the exercise of some authority by firms is unavoidable, and since workers are the only people subject to that authority, therefore it is workers (and not capitalists) who should exercise direct decision-making control over those firms. Like all other affected individuals, capitalists should only exercise indirect control: in their case, through capital and stock markets. This is my main argument for economic democracy, and it leads to the formulation of a 'basic model'. However, there are alternative criticisms of capitalism which, like mine, are also ultimately based on the claim that workers in a capitalist system are unfree. The most important alternative is the argument that workers are unfree because they are not free to move from class to class. I argue that economic democracy is also a solution to this sort of unfreedom, and show that the freedom of labour under different regimes is best represented on a multi-dimensional continuum. On this continuum the main difference between advanced capitalism and socialism is the absence of economic democracy.

Chapter 3 seeks to clarify the concept of feasibility. In particular I separate out questions about the viability (or efficiency) of economic democracy and argue that although these questions are important, there are legitimate grounds for setting them to one side. Instead I focus on the strategic feasibility of economic democracy. In particular, I focus on the question of whether or not there is at least one feasible strategy which would enable the labour movement to move step by step towards the attainment of this goal given the circumstances that exist at present. In order to make this question more manageable I limit myself to considering the advanced capitalist countries, and, in particular, those advanced capitalist countries that have politically significant labour movements. In effect this limits me to Western Europe and Australasia.

In Chapter 4 I identify the unions, the capitalist employers, and the government as the three actors in an advanced capitalist country who have the most influence over the feasibility of any strategy for achieving economic democracy. I consider the different ways in which these actors can organize both themselves and relations between themselves. Each of the actors can be more or less centralized, there can be more or less class co-operation between the unions and the employers, and the government and the two class actors can be more or less involved in each other's affairs. These dimensions of intra- and inter-actor organization can be used to specify the wide variety of industrial relations systems that are possible in advanced capitalist societies.

In Chapter 5 I focus on corporatist industrial relations systems. These are characterized by centralized actors and society-wide bargaining. I argue that while corporatism poses some serious dangers, it also offers the prospect for making some headway towards economic democracy. Corporatism has three key advantages over other industrial relations systems. First, it maximizes the workers' strength and enables them to have a sustained power advantage over the capitalist employers. Second, it enables workers to exchange goods (such as wages and restrictive work practices) over which they have a great deal of influence for goods (such as greater control) over which their direct influence is weaker. And third, it enables the goods which are obtained to be distributed to *all* workers.

Chapter 6 shows how these advantages provide the labour movement with the basis for a feasible strategy for achieving economic democracy. I argue that workers in a corporatist system can gradually accumulate greater and greater control through a series of 'control trade-offs' in which they exchange profit-threatening goods (such as wage rises) for incremental increases in control. However, given what we know about the nature of parliamentary elections, and if we assume the worst of the capitalists, then this strategy will only be feasible if a series of conditions are met. In order to establish these conditions I argue

that we should treat the workers, the capitalists, and the government as rational collective actors. Given this assumption it turns
out that three conditions are sufficient to establish the feasibility
of a single control trade-off: the workers must have a profit-
threatening exchangeable good, the trade-off must be compatible
with the requirements of national economic management, and the
corporatist system itself must be compatible with the requirements of national economic management. To repeat these trade-
offs and compound their effect, a further three conditions must
be met.

In Chapter 7 I show that the conditions for a single control
trade-off were in fact met during the stagflationary economic
environment which lasted from the mid 1970s to the early 1980s.
In Chapter 8 I show that these conditions are still being met in the
environment of structural adjustment which lasted from the mid
1980s to the early 1990s and perhaps beyond. In both chapters I
also consider whether a control trade-off is still feasible if we
assume that workers are solely concerned with their material
well-being. This discussion leads me to some conclusions about
the kinds of control trade-offs that are most likely in each of the
two periods. Again in both chapters, I then briefly point to the
recurring nature of the problems that emerged during the two
periods and to the potential for further control trade-offs in the
future.

In Chapter 9 I support the conclusions of Chapters 7 and 8 with
more detailed evidence from a case study of Australia. The
evidence shows that, both during the period of stagflation and
during the period of structural adjustment, the conditions for a
control trade-off were met and the predicted kind of control
trade-off took place. I also use the case study to address an out-
standing issue. Until now I have simply assumed that where a
corporatist system does not already exist, its initial establishment
is itself a feasible goal. The case study shows that this assumption
was justified in the case of Australia. This is of more than local
interest because it seems to belie the oft-repeated claim that an
Anglo-Saxon industrial relations tradition makes it impossible for
a country to establish a corporatist system.

Finally, in Chapter 10 I conclude by considering whether the
main arguments of this book will still be tenable as we move into
the next century.

1

Freedom and Authority

As a theory, socialism rests on two propositions about human individuals. One is a commitment to the maximum individual liberty that is compatible with an equal liberty for others. Let me call this the principle of equal liberty. The other is a recognition of the inherently social nature of individuals. Let me call this the axiom of sociality. The first is a moral claim about the value of human individuals. The second is a sociological claim about the nature of individuals. In this chapter I will elaborate and justify each of these propositions. I will then look at the relationship between the two propositions and derive what I take to be the two fundamental principles of democracy.

No doubt many readers will already be wondering what is so socialist about these two propositions. It is certainly true that the version of the axiom of sociality on which I will rely is shared by many non-socialist theories. To some extent this is a virtue. If socialist conclusions can be drawn from more widely accepted premisses then they should be able to command concomitantly wider support. I do believe, however, that the principle of equal liberty is distinctively socialist. It is not distinctively socialist simply because it deals with liberty and equality. These concepts are common to all Enlightenment influenced theories.[1] Rather, it is the interpretation of these concepts, and, in particular, that of liberty, which is distinctive.[2] At the end of this chapter I hope to be able to show that the principle of equal liberty is distinctively socialist by demonstrating that it forms the basis for what Ronald Dworkin (1986, 186) would call a 'constitutive morality' of socialism.

---

[1] It has even been argued that there is a universal commitment to these values presupposed in the use of speech (Habermas, 1976, 107–8).

[2] Thus, while John Rawls's first principle of justice seems similar to the principle of equal liberty, he relies, as we shall see, on a different interpretation of liberty. According to Rawls's first principle, 'each person is to have an equal right to the most extensive total system of equal basic liberties compatible with a similar system of liberty for all' (1972, 302).

In a sense, however, this is a task of secondary importance. For demonstrating the socialist credentials of a constitutive morality does not provide a reason for preferring it. On the contrary, it is the constitutive political morality which provides a reason for preferring socialism. Those who established a tradition of socialist theory could not do so by arguing about how 'socialist' their theory was, and nor can those who seek to renew that tradition.

I will begin, then, by elaborating and justifying the principle of equal liberty. Clearly this principle has two key concepts. I will deal first with liberty or freedom (which I will use interchangeably) and then with equality.

Even a casual perusal of writings on liberty will confirm that there are many competing interpretations of the concept. Why is this? John Rawls has pointed out that even when there is agreement about the meaning of a moral or political 'concept', there can still be different 'conceptions' of it. In the case of justice, for example, there is a 'concept' of justice which specifies the 'role' (or functional meaning) which all the competing 'conceptions' of justice have in common (Rawls, 1972, 5–6, 9–10). But in the case of freedom there is not even this much in common.[3] Hence disagreements tend to focus on arguments for and against giving freedom certain defining features (Gray, 1984a, 2–3). So what are the appropriate defining features of individual liberty?

Freedom is a composite concept (Lukes, 1973, 127): a compound made up of a number of more simple elements. A variety of different compounds can be formed from one or more of these simple elements. And each of these compounds represents at least one different interpretation of freedom.[4]

While there is no one compound which encompasses the functional meaning of all the various interpretations of freedom, there is, in the modern European tradition, one element which is common to almost all the competing compounds. This common element is the idea that I am free only if I can act in the absence of constraints imposed by others. This idea delimits the concept of freedom in two ways. Freedom is limited to the realm of action,

---

[3] Although Rawls, following MacCallum, implicitly suggests that there is (1972, 201–3). Against this see Gray (1984b, 325–8, 331), Gould (1988, 38), Berlin (1969, pp. xliii, 135), and Steiner (1974/75).

[4] 'At least', since each compound may represent more than one 'conception' in Rawls's sense.

and freedom of action is limited to the absence of humanly imposed constraint.[5] Freedom of action as lack of constraint has not
always been a ubiquitous element of individual liberty. For example, the Greeks sometimes used freedom to describe the status of
a man who was not a slave. Hence, on this interpretation, even
while Socrates was imprisoned, it would make sense to call him a
free man (Gray, 1984b, 328). But it is almost always present in
modern interpretations of freedom, and may even be a distinctively modern idea (Berlin, 1969, 129, p. xl; Lukes, 1973, 59).[6] In
particular, freedom of action as lack of constraint is at the centre
of modern liberalism. For modern liberalism is paradigmatically
concerned with privacy: that is, with the maintenance of a space
in which public, especially governmental, authorities cannot in-
terfere with or impose constraints on the individual.

Indeed, for a number of contemporary liberals, freedom of
action as lack of constraint is the only appropriate defining feature of individual liberty. Typical are the advocates of so-called
'negative liberty'. Hillel Steiner is a good example. According to
Steiner, 'An individual is unfree if, and only if, his doing of any
action is rendered impossible by the action of another individual'
(1974/75, 33). At times Isaiah Berlin also seems to be saying this,
although his position is more nuanced. Consider how he opens
his section on negative liberty: 'I am normally said to be free to the
degree to which no man or body of men interferes with my
activity. Political liberty in this sense is simply the area within
which a man can act unobstructed by others' (1969, 122).[7]

However, as I have said, I believe that freedom is a more complex concept. To demonstrate this I propose to build a compound
around the one common element that we have identified. My
strategy will be to provide arguments as to why certain elements
must (and certain other elements must not) be added to this
common element in order to provide an adequate interpretation
of freedom. In this way we should end up with a compound
concept that specifies the appropriate defining features of individual liberty. I will first argue for a fuller, compound concept of
freedom of action. I will then argue that freedom of action alone

---

[5] Although this humanly imposed constraint need not be *deliberate*. Compare
Macpherson (1973, 97–100) with Berlin (1969, 122–3).

[6] A usage similar to that of the Greeks can sometimes be found in the work of
seventeenth-century English thinkers like Harrington (Macpherson, 1973, 214),
who stand at the threshold of the modern world of political ideas.

[7] He also equates 'individual liberty' with 'a free area for action' (1969, 130–1).

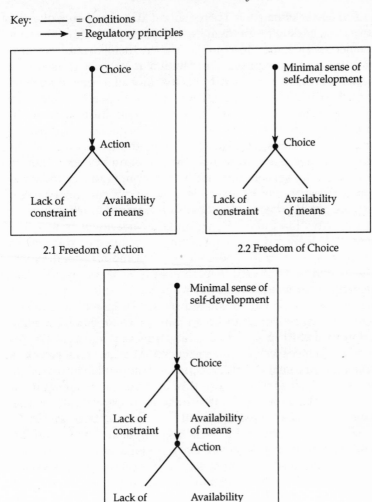

Key: ——— = Conditions
⟶ = Regulatory principles

2.1 Freedom of Action

2.2 Freedom of Choice

2.3 The Full Compound Concept of Individual Freedom

Fig. 2. *Individual freedom*

is only half of the story, and that a complete interpretation of individual liberty must also include another compound concept: freedom of choice. The structure of these compounds is represented graphically in Figure 2.

16 *Freedom and Authority*

Advocates of negative liberty simply define freedom of action as lack of constraint. But why is 'lack of constraint' an important element of freedom of action? To answer this we must recognize that freedom is a value. We value lack of constraints on our actions because we value the possibility of taking alternative courses of action.[8] An individual's freedom depends on the range of options for action that are open to that individual.[9] A constraint limits an individual's freedom of action because it makes it impossible for him or her to act in a certain way. But a constraint is not the only thing that can do this. To be able to undertake the action the individual must also have certain means or resources. Unless these means are available he or she will still not be free to act, even in the absence of any humanly imposed constraints. Some basic means, like food, clothing, and shelter, are a prerequisite for undertaking almost any action. Other more specialized means are only a prerequisite for undertaking particular actions. It may be that nobody is permitted to intervene to stop a poor person from taking a grievance to court. But without access to legal resources he or she will still be unable to do so. The freedom to take a grievance to court requires both the absence of constraints (like arbitrary arrest) and the availability of means (like legal aid).[10]

So it seems that there is not one but at least two elements to freedom of action: lack of constraint and the availability of means. Of course, just as it is only constraints that can be humanly imposed that count as limits to freedom, so it is only means that can be humanly distributed[11] that count as limits to freedom (Berlin, 1969, 122–3; Macpherson, 1973, 97). The offending impositions and distributions must be humanly remediable.

Two criticisms can been raised against expanding 'freedom of action' to include the 'availability of means' as a second element. Both, however, fail.

[8] Note that to value the possibility of acting in a certain way is different from valuing acting in a certain way. Hence I can demand the right to join the Communist Party even though I would never join myself.

[9] Cf. Crocker (1981, 38): 'Freedom is not the absence of constraint but rather the presence of alternatives.' See also Norman (1987, 38) and Cunningham (1987, 182).

[10] Hence the standard socialist complaint that many liberals—namely those who equate freedom of action with lack of constraint—only support purely 'abstract' as opposed to 'concrete' freedom.

[11] This rules out, e.g., special aptitudes that people are born with or means that are (at present) technologically impossible. Note that this last point implies that what counts as a limitation of freedom will have to be continually reassessed as

The first argues that while the availability of means is important, it is not a part of the concept of freedom. According to this argument there is a sharp distinction between what Berlin (1969, p. liii) calls 'liberty' and the 'conditions of liberty', and Rawls calls 'liberty' and the 'worth of liberty' (1972, 204). For both, the availability of means comes under the latter heading. C. B. Macpherson (1973, 101–4) and Norman Daniels (1975, 159–263) have attacked this distinction. They argue, correctly I think, that the same reasons that lead us to include absence of constraint in the definition of freedom, lead us also to include the availability of means.[12] In both cases the reason for inclusion is the same: the value that we place on the possibility of taking alternative courses of action. This possibility exists only if constraints on action are absent and the means for action are available. So it is not the case that one of these elements is constitutive of liberty and the other of the conditions of liberty. Rather, both elements are conditions for freedom of action, and these conditions define freedom of action. Hence it would be morally arbitrary to identify freedom of action with only one of these conditions. Only when all the conditions are fulfilled is an action free.

The second criticism argues that while the availability of means is a part of the concept of liberty, it is not a separate element. Both Macpherson and Daniels propose versions of this argument.[13] Macpherson, for example, agrees that 'access to the means of life and labour' (1973, 101) is a condition for freedom, but argues that lack of access to these means is just another sort of constraint. So on this view, the poverty that leaves the potential litigant unable to go to court is just as much of a constraint as arbitrary arrest. It is a humanly imposed constraint because it is the (perhaps unintended) consequence of an economic system which is subject to the control of human beings. Now there *is* a sense of constraint which can cover both of the conditions that we are discussing, but it is not the sense which typical advocates of negative liberty have in mind. For when these advocates talk about constraint they usually focus on 'interference' (Berlin, 1969, 122) whose absence requires 'privacy' (Berlin, 1969, 124, 129; Lukes, 1973, 62): a realm

technologies develop. Think, for example, of medical technologies that allow life to be prolonged.

[12] Cf. Daniels's 'relative rationality proof' (1975, 264).

[13] Other versions appear in Crocker (1980) and Miller (1983).

where the public—that is, outside agents and authorities—are not permitted to act. This suggests an important difference between 'absence of constraint' and the 'availability of means'. If constraint necessarily involves interfering action by outside agents and authorities, then the 'absence of constraint' condition (or privacy) requires forbearance from action (Gould, 1988, 38). On the other hand, if adequate means are not available to an individual, and if we value that individual's freedom of action, then the 'availability of means' condition will require action by outside agents and authorities to provide these means. One condition requires public inaction, the other public action. Of course not all individuals will require public action to provide them with adequate means. Wealthy individuals, for example, may have all the means they need to act freely. For these individuals a narrow negative concept of liberty as absence of constraint may well be quite satisfactory, if only because the availability of means condition can be tacitly assumed to have been satisfied already.

So the absence of constraint and the availability of means are two distinct elements of freedom of action. But there is still one further element. Consider two situations (Benn and Weinstein, 1971, 209–10). In the first an insane individual acts in a bizarre and random way. In the second a hypnotized individual acts at the behest of another. In both situations, even when the individuals are both unconstrained and have the means to act, we do not think of them as acting freely. We draw a distinction between situations in which individuals, like wild animals, have the power to act, and situations in which they are free to act. What distinguishes the power to act from freedom to act is human choice. The first example shows that, to be free, my actions must result from choices. The second example shows that, to be free, my actions must result from choices of my own. Thus, 'underlying and presupposed by the concept of freedom of action' is the concept of 'the free man as chooser' (Benn and Weinstein, 1971, 194).

The idea of the individual as chooser is at the heart of the concept of autonomy. Individuals are autonomous if their actions are regulated by self-determined decisions and choices (Lukes, 1973, 127). This concept of autonomy is closely related to Berlin's concept of 'positive liberty'. According to this concept, I am free if I am 'self-directed . . . conceiving goals and policies of my own and realizing them' (Berlin, 1969, 131). Now Berlin focuses his criticisms on one 'monstrous impersonation' (133) of this concept, but that is no reason to abandon the concept itself. Indeed, the idea that our ability to choose is a fundamentally important aspect of human nature, is the real value underlying even the most minimal negative concept of freedom. We saw earlier that we value the absence of constraints because we value the possibility of taking alternative courses of action. Now we can see the reason why. We value this possibility because it enables us to exercise our faculty for choice and implement the outcome. The concept of freedom is underwritten by the concept of autonomy. The latter determines the extent of the former's complexity.

So freedom of action has three elements.[14] Two conditions— absence of constraint and the availability of means—must be fulfilled, and the action must be regulated by choice. But, with the introduction of this third element, it becomes clear that an adequate concept of freedom cannot be limited to the concept of freedom of action; it must also include the concept of freedom of choice. Freedom demands that action be regulated by choice. But, as the example of hypnosis demonstrates, this cannot be just any choice: it must be an individual's own choice. The requirement that free actions must be regulated by free choices brings a number of conditions with it. In fact, it turns out that freedom of choice is a compound concept very similar to freedom of action. Indeed, the first two elements of freedom of choice are analogous to the two conditions that are elements of freedom of action. A choice can only be fully my own if there are no constraints like hypnosis or the application of mind-bending drugs which limit my ability to choose. The first condition for freedom of choice is the absence of such constraints. But, just as in the case of freedom of action, and for the same reasons, the means for choice must also be available. Thus, again, there is a second condition: the availability of means. The means for choice include both information and skills to analyse it. Access to education and to the media will be especially important. As before, the first condition will tend to require public inaction, the second public action.

Note that just as an adequate concept of freedom cannot be limited to the concept of freedom of action, but must also include

14 See Figure 2.

the concept of freedom of choice, so, too, an adequate concept of freedom cannot be limited to the concept of freedom of choice but must also include the concept of freedom of action. For a concept of freedom that is limited to the concept of freedom of choice falls foul of the 'free slave paradox'. If an individual is free whenever he is able to act in accordance with his own choices, then a slave could make himself free by desisting from making choices which he would not be able to pursue (Berlin, 1969, 139, pp. xxxviii–xxxix). The conditions for freedom of choice rightly focus on the process by which choices made. But the 'free slave' is not free because his choices are a function of the constraints on his action. Thus the paradox simply serves to emphasize that an individual is only free if both the conditions for freedom of choice and the conditions for freedom of action are fulfilled.

But why not take the analogy between freedom of action and freedom of choice the whole way? If freedom of choice has conditions which are analogous to freedom of action, does it not also have an analogous regulative principle? For example, I could argue that just as you must act in accordance with your own choice in order to act freely, so you must choose in accordance with your own nature in order to choose freely. On this view freedom would involve some form of self-development or self-realization (Lukes, 1973, 67, 130): you would only be free if you chose to develop or realize those capacities that are an essential part of your nature.[15] Marx seems to believe something like this, as do a number of other thinkers who are influenced by a Romantic view of human individuality.[16] It is worth noting that, *contra* Berlin (1969, 133–4), adding a self-realization element to the concept of freedom need not necessarily lead us to accept that people

---

[15] Of course there are plenty of other candidates for regulatory principles which place the object to be developed outside the individual: the nation and the glory of God have been popular. But by attributing value to supra-individual entities, these regulative principles fit uneasily with the Enlightenment impulse (to attribute value solely to individuals) which underlies the value of choice and autonomy.

[16] 'Marx calls man's freedom "the positive power to assert his true individuality". This "true individuality" is man at the height of his powers and needs. . . . Free activity is activity that fulfils such powers, and freedom, therefore, is the condition of man whose human powers are thus fulfilled; it passes beyond the absence of restraint to the active unfolding of all his potentials' (Ollman, 1971, 117). For the roots of these ideas in German Romanticism see Lukes (1973, 17–22, 67–72).

can be forced to be free. Charles Taylor makes this point clearly. 'We may hold a self-realization view of freedom, and hence believe that there are certain conditions on my motivation necessary to my being free, but also believe that there are other necessary conditions which rule out my being forcibly led towards some definition of my self-realization by external authority' (1985b, 216). Taylor attempts to defend self-realization as a regulative principle governing free choices. He argues that freedom is a function, not just of the number of choices that are open to one, but also of their significance (1985b, 229), where their significance depends on whether or not they are 'truly mine' (224). But what choices does this rule out? Taylor thinks that Charles Manson's murderous choices were clearly not free. But how can we know that they were not an expression of his 'true self'?[17] Macpherson faces a similar problem. He picks up the gist of Marx's position and pursues it more systematically, arguing for a 'developmental concept' of freedom as the ability to exercise and develop one's 'essentially human capacities' (1973, 52, 95). However, as Lukes points out, there is no uncontroversial way of specifying what these 'essentially human capacities' are (1979, 147). But the fundamental problem with these attempts is not just that they fail to adequately specify a regulative principle. Rather, they confuse the extent of our freedom to choose with the relative significance of particular choices.[18] Obviously we value some choices more than others. For example, we value our choice of religion more than we value our choice of ice creams. But to include these values in the concept of freedom is to confuse them with the value we place on being able to choose *per se*. As Norman points out, it 'is wrong to infer that freedom is valuable only insofar as it enables us to do something valuable' (1987, 37).

There is, however, one 'essential human capacity' which a concept of freedom as autonomy does presuppose: namely, the capacity for choice itself. And unless we make the psychologically

---

[17] Taylor's emphasis on the significance of choices is similar to that of T. H. Green, for whom freedom is 'a positive power or capacity of doing or enjoying something worth doing or enjoying' (Norman, 1987, 27).

[18] Interestingly, in spite of his hostility to these attempts, at one point Berlin also seems to confuse these things. In a lengthy footnote (1969, 130) he claims that the extent of an individual's freedom depends, amongst other things, on the importance or value which both he and society place on the various possibilities that are open to him.

untenable assumption that this capacity exists fully-formed rather than as a potential, then, if we are to utilize it fully, it must be developed (Taylor, 1985a, 197). If freedom is a function of our capacity for choice, then the greater that capacity the freer we are. And so some sort of minimal sense of self-development must indeed regulate all free choices. This minimal regulative principle has two implications. First, it rules out certain regressive choices like suicide. In such a case limited intervention by others would be justified in order to protect the individual's capacity to make choices in the future. Second, it calls for the development of a critical consciousness. This involves an open and questioning attitude to our own previous choices and a preparedness to re-assess them. In particular it calls for an ability to adjudicate between one's own choices when they conflict. That is, it calls for us to develop the capacity to make choices about choices or 'second order choices'. It does not tell us what criteria we should use to make these second order choices. That would be to return with Taylor to a less minimal version of regulation by self-development. With the addition of this minimal regulative principle our compound concept is finally complete.[19]

Let me now turn to the other key concept in the principle of equal liberty: equality.

We have seen that underpinning the concept of freedom is the value of autonomy: that is, the value we place on making our own choices and being able to act on them. One of the main reasons why we value autonomy is because the potential to do these things is common to all humans and distinguishes us from other beings (Williams, 1962, 114; Rawls, 1972, 505; Lukes, 1974, 77). As a criterion for judging the moral desirability of social institutions, my autonomy is important not because it is *mine*, but rather because it is an expression of the fact that I am an individual who has this potential and who thus shares a common humanity. But if it is because I am an individual who has this potential that I value my autonomy, then consistency demands that I value the autonomy of all other individuals who have this potential (Graham, 1982, 130; 1986, 89). But, just because this potential is a common and distinctive human potential, all other individuals have it. And so I must value the autonomy, and hence the liberty, of every human individual.

[19] See Figure 2.

Now it is possible to argue that while all individuals have this potential they have it to different degrees, and hence that while we should value the liberty of every individual we should not value it equally. Presumably the potential in question—namely, the potential to make choices and act on them—does vary from individual to individual. But this is not a reason for placing less value on some individuals' liberty. For what we value is what we all (bar some mad people) share: that is, the presence of this potential to at least some minimum degree. Focusing on this minimum potential allows us to draw the stronger conclusion that we should *equally* value the autonomy of every human individual, and hence that all individuals should be equally free. 'While individuals presumably have varying capacities . . . this is not a reason for depriving those with a lesser capacity. . . . Once a certain minimum is met, a person is entitled to equal liberty on a par with everyone else' (Rawls, 1972, 506).

But if every individual is to be equally free (indeed, even if everyone is to be just a little bit free), then no individual's freedom can be unlimited. For the exercise of one individual's freedom can sometimes adversely affect the freedom of another. At the most extreme, no individual can be allowed to kill another individual, for that would completely preclude the latter's freedom. But nor is an unduly Spartan equal distribution of freedom acceptable. Rather, each individual must have the *maximum* freedom that is compatible with an equal freedom for all the others. And so here at last we have the principle of equal liberty.

What about the second proposition: the axiom of sociality? To say that human individuals have an inherently social nature is to say that their nature is in some sense determined by their relationship to the society in which they live.

One of the most important proponents of this proposition is Karl Marx. 'Man', says Marx, 'is not an abstract being squatting outside the world' (1975, 244). Rather, he is, 'in the most literal sense of the word, a *zoon politikon*, not merely a gregarious animal, but an animal that can develop into an individual only in society' (1973, 84). Just what Marx means by this is somewhat ambiguous. He is often interpreted as making a maximal claim about both the *extent* to which human individuals are socially determined and the *nature* of that determination. Regarding the extent of social determination, Marx can be read as claiming that the means for achieving all of our ends, and even the ends themselves, are socially determined.[20] Regarding the nature of social determination, he can be read as claiming that we are totally constituted by our social relations.[21]

A case can be made for each of these claims. However, here I want to restrict myself to defending a far weaker version of the proposition that individuals have an inherently social nature. It is weaker both in regard to the extent of social determination, which is limited to the means needed to achieve only *some* of our ends; and in regard to the nature of social determination, which consists in the need for co-operation with others. Thus, here, the proposition that human individuals have an inherently social nature amounts only to the proposition that in order to achieve some of our ends we require the co-operation of others. This is borne out by a host of everyday activities. Even apparently solitary activities like writing a book depend, at the very least, on the co-operation of those who produce pencils and paper.

Individuals that are co-operating with each other need to co-ordinate their activities. They can do this by either market co-ordination or associative (or bureaucratic) co-ordination, or by a combination of these two 'pure' alternatives (Lindblom, 1977, 12; Coase, 1986, 73; Williamson, 1985, 4). Now there are those who believe that market co-ordination should be adopted wherever possible. But even these believers would have to agree that associative co-ordination is either the only or at least the best way to co-ordinate certain activities.[22] Later we will look more closely at the reasons for this in the case of economic firms. In these sorts of cases, if co-operation must be maintained over time in order to achieve a common end, then the co-operators will form an association. Each association has a purpose (drawn from the com-

---

[20] This is because 'it is not the consciousness of men that determines their existence, but their social existence that determines their consciousness' (Marx, 1975, 425), and 'consciousness is . . . from the very beginning a social product, and remains so as long as men exist at all' (Marx and Engels, 1976, 49–50).

[21] 'The human essence is no abstraction inherent in each single individual. In its reality it is the ensemble of the social relations' (Marx, 1975, 423). However, it is also possible to interpret Marx as making a less maximal claim in this regard. In the *German Ideology* he argues that human life is social, where 'social' means that it involves 'the co-operation of several individuals, no matter under what conditions, in what manner and to what end' (Marx and Engels, 1976, 49). Gyorgy Markus (1978, 16–25) argues against the maximal interpretation in his extensive discussion of Marx's concept of human sociality.

[22] Nozick, for example, acknowledges that individuals cannot always operate as a 'miniature firm' (1974, 186).

mon end or ends of the individuals who founded it), and a set of rules which govern how it will pursue that purpose (Cole, 1920a, 37).

Because of the wide range of purposes about which individuals will need to co-operate, there will inevitably be a large number of different associations. In Anglo-American political philosophy there have been two schools of thought that have taken the existence of a plurality of associations as a serious starting-point. In the early decades of the twentieth century an English pluralist school flourished which was based on the works of John Figgis and others who emphasized their rejection of John Austin's then influential notion of state sovereignty (Nicholls, 1974). An American school of pluralism, which had roots in the works of Montesquieu, Tocqueville, and Madison and emphasized the role of interest groups, became something of an orthodoxy in the 1950s and 1960s (Held, 1987). Both of these schools developed in socialist directions, in the first case in the 'guild socialism' of G. D. H. Cole (1972, 1920a and 1920b) and in the works of Harold Laski (1967), and in the second case in the 'critical pluralism' of Robert Dahl (1970 and 1985) and Charles Lindblom (1977).[23] I will draw on the work of both Cole and Dahl later in this chapter.

I now want to consider two consequences that flow from the relationship between the principle of equal liberty and the axiom of sociality. The first concerns why we value fraternity. The second concerns why we value democracy.

The point about fraternity can be made briefly enough. Since there are times when we need associative forms of co-operation with others in order to be able to act on our choices (according to the axiom of sociality), and since we value being able to act on our choices (according to the principle of equal freedom), therefore, at least at those times, we must value associative forms of co-operation with others. This helps to explain why fraternity is not just a fact but is also a value alongside liberty and equality. It also helps to show where the 'social' comes from in 'socialism'. It is not that there is some supra-individual social entity which is valued *per se*, in the way that the nation is valued by the nationalist, or tradition is valued by the conservative. For the socialist, the value

[23] There has also been some convergence between critical pluralism and 'neo-Marxism', especially where the latter has been influenced by the legacy of the Frankfurt School (McLennan, 1984, 107; Held, 1987, 224).

of social co-operation can be derived from the fundamental value attached to the freedom of all human individuals. Social co-operation, including associative forms of social co-operation, is valued because at times it is a necessary condition for individual freedom.[24]

The point about democracy is central to my argument, and so I will spend a little longer on it. We know (from the axiom of sociality) that, in order to realize their choices, individuals will at times require the co-operation of others, and that at times this will require the formation of associations. The point of forming these associations is to co-ordinate the activities of the co-operating individuals. But in order to do this an association itself must be able to make choices. How should these collective choices be made? We know that (if they are to be compatible with the principle of equal liberty) collective choices should be made so as to maximize individual freedom. And (from our interpretation of that principle) we know that I am free when I can make my own individual choices and act on them.

Now clearly the decisions of an association, or rather the actions that result from these decisions, will affect various individuals. If I am one of these individuals then the only way that I can maximize my freedom is to ensure that the choices, and hence the actions, of the association are in accord with my own choices. And the only way to ensure that is to control the association's decision-making process. In order to control an association's decision-making process I must ensure that nobody who disagrees with me can affect the outcome of that process. Setting myself up as a dictator would be one way of achieving this. Ensuring that I was part of a permanent majority would be another. Either way I would guarantee that I had the maximum individual freedom, but only by denying a similar freedom to other individuals.

But the principle of equal liberty commits us to attach as much importance to every other individual's freedom as we do to our own. This means that each affected individual must be prepared to accept less than maximum individual freedom, since it is clearly not possible for each individual who is affected by an association simultaneously to exercise complete control over it. If the freedom we gain from controlling an association's decision-making process is to be compatible with an equal freedom for

---

[24] This is not to deny that many socialists also value social co-operation independently of the value that they attach to individual freedom.

every other individual who is affected by that process, then that control can only be partial and must be shared with every other affected individual. In other words: all individuals whose ability to make choices and act on them is affected by the decisions of an association should share control over the process by which those decisions are made. I will call this the 'all-affected principle'. Versions of the all-affected principle can be found in both Cole (1920b, 33–5) and Dahl (1970, 64). Other versions can be found in Lindsay (1962, 231), Bachrach (1969, 74, 95, 98), and Holmes (1988, 235).

Dahl formulates his version of the all-affected principle as follows: 'Everyone who is affected by the decisions of a government should have the right to participate in that government' (1970, 64), where by government he means the government of any association; not just that of the state. This principle is based on Dahl's 'criterion of personal choice' (8) which is quite similar to the principle of equal liberty. However, Dahl argues that personal choice has to compete with two other criteria or values—competence and economy—that can be used to judge the legitimacy of a decision-making process. But competence and economy need not necessarily be seen as competing values. That a certain minimum level of competence can qualify the right to participate in some situations is presupposed by the value attached to personal choice itself. For example, in situations that are life-threatening, competent decisions are a necessary condition for the future exercise of personal choice. And it is situations of this sort, such as performing surgery or piloting a ship, to which Dahl typically appeals (30). But here the conflict that confronts an incompetent is better described as one between present personal choice and the possibility of future personal choice. If we value an autonomous life as a whole we will opt for the latter. Furthermore, it is certainly true that we will often accept a decision-making process that is less than 'ideal' because it economizes on time and energy (48). But that need not be because we value economy *per se*, but rather because we would prefer to use the time to pursue other personal choices. Economy need not be viewed as a value competing with personal choice. Rather, it can be viewed as a background condition that necessitates competition between our various personal choices. If there were not a limited amount of time and resources available to us this would not be necessary.

The all-affected principle provides an answer to the most fundamental question that confronts any democratic theory. Democracy is, by definition, rule by the people. A theory of democracy must specify how the people will rule—whether by direct participation, elected representatives, referendum, or some other means. Socialist theories have typically emphasized the importance of giving people opportunities for direct participation wherever possible (Pateman, 1970). But before a democratic theory can even begin to specify how the people will rule, it must specify who the people are. The all-affected principle provides an answer to this question. Every association, whether it be a state or a shoe factory, should be controlled by a group consisting of all individuals who are affected by its decisions.

However, any attempt to operationalize the all-affected principle, or even just to give it greater specificity, runs into theoretical and practical difficulties.

For example, it is unclear whether the all-affected principle really is able to specify meaningfully which group of individuals should share control over the decisions of an association. This is because many decisions ultimately have some effect on every individual. This suggests that the all-affected principle is only workable if we can specify a degree of effect above which an individual qualifies for a share of control.

An apperantly still more intractable problem emerges wherever it is possible to exercise more than one kind of control over an association. Yet typically this is the case. For example, votes are not the only kind of control over national governments. Those with property have a separate kind of control (Lindblom, 1977, 170–88). Now if each of these sources of control is distributed in the same proportions, as recommended for example by Thomas Jefferson (Dahl, 1985, 3, 70, 103), this does not present a problem. But, leaving aside whether this is desirable, it is not always possible. Consider, for example, another source of control over a national government: the power exerted by foreign governments. It is hard to see how this could be parcelled out according to the Jeffersonian formula. But how, then, are the various kinds of control to be distributed among the various affected individuals? My attempt to find a solution to this problem will lead to the development of a second fundamental principle of democracy.

In order to find this solution, we need to recognize that there is an important distinction between two different ways in which control can be exercised over an association. On the one hand, control can be exercised directly by making decisions: that is, by choosing from the options allowed for by a set of given constraints. On the other hand, control can be exercised indirectly by setting those constraints in place.[25] In the example above, property owners and foreign powers place constraints on a national government (by, for example, refusing to invest or imposing tariffs), while the voters, or rather their representatives, make decisions within those constraints.

The distinction between these two ways in which control can be exercised over an association, corresponds to another distinction between two ways in which individuals can be affected by an association. On the one hand there are individuals who are affected in the sense that they are subject to the authority of an association. On the other hand there are individuals who are affected by an association without being subject to its authority. Typically the distinction between subjects and affected non-subjects is the same as the distinction between members and affected non-members. Now I want to suggest that direct control is the appropriate form of control for subjects and that indirect control is the appropriate form for affected non-subjects. But to see why this should be so we will have to clarify what it means for an association to have authority over an individual.

To begin with it needs to be made clear that 'authority' is being used here to refer to all effective or *de facto* authority and not just to legitimate or *de jure* authority. It also needs to be made clear that 'authority' refers to 'practical authority' as opposed to 'theoretical authority'. Practical authority is exercised by someone who is 'in authority'. Theoretical authority is exercised by someone who is 'an authority', and when it is exercised it is really a form of advice. These two forms of authority are distinct because while we are bound to comply with the decisions of a practical authority to which we are subject, we are not bound to follow the advice of a theoretical authority, although it may be foolish not to (Green, 1988, 27; Soper, 1989, 219). But while being bound to comply is a necessary characteristic of (practical) au-

[25] The terms 'direct' and 'indirect' control are drawn from Ellerman (1990, 46), who also refers to 'positive' and 'negative' control to make the same distinction.

thority,[26] it is not sufficient to define it. A promise, for example, often shares this characteristic. If I promise to help you I am bound to do so. What is distinctive about being subject to authority is that, at least partially, and often fully, I am bound, not by my own decision (as in the case of a promise), but by the decision of someone else (Green, 1988, 40).

Several people have tried to capture what is at stake here by arguing that being subject to authority involves a 'surrender of judgement' (Friedman, 1973, 129). According to this interpretation, when I enter an authority relationship as a subject I surrender my judgement over a certain range of matters to somebody else. I may, for example, surrender it to an individual such as a king or to a collective body in which I may or may not participate. However, to talk of a surrender of judgement can be misleading. It is not meant to imply that when an authority requires me to do something I must surrender my right to make a judgement about the requirement. Rather, it means that I must surrender my right to act in accordance with my judgement. How I act, not how I think, is what matters to those in authority (Raz, 1986, 39). Since my choices are the outcome of my judgements, surrendering my right to act in accordance with my judgements entails surrendering my right to act in accordance with my choices. Thus whenever I am subject to an authority, my choices are *excluded* from playing a role in the regulation of my actions, and are replaced in this role by the choices of the authority (Raz, 1986, 46; Raz, 1987, 79; Green 1988, 38, 42). This exclusion and replacement of one person's choices by another's is the defining feature of an authority relationship.[27]

We are now in a position to see why direct control is the appropriate form of control for subjects and indirect control is the appropriate form for affected non-subjects. Figure 3 may help to illustrate the argument of the next couple of paragraphs. Recall, before we begin, that the principle that my actions should be regulated by my choices is the basic regulatory principle that lies at the heart of the concept of freedom.

[26] Henceforth I will refer to 'practical authority' simply as 'authority'.
[27] It has also been suggested that an authority's choices must provide 'content-independent reasons for action' (Raz, 1986, 35–37; Green, 1988, 40–2). But this aspect of authority will not concern us here.

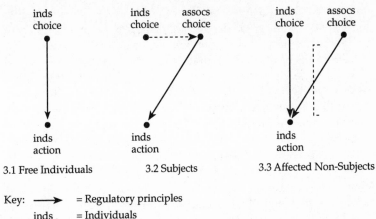

3.1 Free Individuals   3.2 Subjects   3.3 Affected Non-Subjects

Key: ⟶ = Regulatory principles
    inds   = Individuals
    assocs   = Associations

Control required to protect freedom:
⟶ = Direct control
:_____: = Indirect control

FIG. 3. *Subject and non-subject individuals*

In cases where I am subject to the authority of an association
this basic regulatory principle is replaced by another regulatory
principle. In place of my own choices those of the association
regulate my actions. Thus, so long as this alternative principle
remains in force, the only way to ensure that my freedom is
protected is to ensure that the association makes choices that are
identical to mine. Since regulation by my choice has been replaced
by regulation by the association's choice, the association's choice
must be replaced by my choice. And the only way to ensure this
is to make the association's choices myself: in other words, to
exercise direct control over its decision-making process. Of
course, according to the principle of equal liberty, I must consider
not just my own freedom but also that of all the association's other
subjects. But if the freedom that each subject gains from directly
controlling an association's decision-making process is to be compatible with an equal freedom for every other individual who is
subject to that association, then each subject's direct control can

only be partial and must be shared with every other subjected individual. In other words: all individuals who are subjected to the authority of an association should share direct control over the decisions of that association. I will call this the 'all-subjected principle'. If the range of matters over which the association has authority is the same for all subjects, then each subject is entitled to an equal share of control over the association's decision-making process.

In cases where I am not subject to the authority of an association but am nevertheless affected by it the basic regulatory principle is not replaced. It is, however, added to. The association's choices become an additional factor that must be weighed in alongside my own choices before I can act. To ensure that my freedom is protected in these circumstances, I need only constrain the association from making choices which would lead to this additional effect: in other words, I need to be able to exercise indirect control over the association. There are various forms of indirect control or constraint. The most complete form is a personal veto. Note, however, that the veto which is required is not a veto over the association's decisions *per se*, but a veto over the ability of the association's decisions to affect me.[28] Again, of course, I must share these various forms of indirect control with all the other non-subjects who are affected by the association. This may or may not involve weakening my personal indirect control.[29]

As an affected non-subject I could also protect my freedom by securing direct control over the relevant association. However, to do so would be both unnecessary and unjustified. It would be unnecessary because, as we have just seen, I only need to exercise indirect control in order to protect my freedom. And it would be unjustified because I would then be making decisions which bound others (namely the association's subjects) but which did

[28] Thus, for example, in a competitive market economy, a consumer has a veto over a firm's ability to affect him because he can take his custom elsewhere, but he does not have a veto over the firm's decisions themselves. I will return to this point in Chapter 2.

[29] Consider the example in the previous footnote. Consumers can share the indirect control that they exercise through the market without weakening their personal indirect control. Residents, on the other hand, exercising indirect control through the regulatory powers of a local government, will weaken their personal indirect control by sharing these powers with others.

not bind me and which I did not have to obey. Therefore non-subjects should be limited to exercising indirect control, reserving direct control for subjects.

The idea that it is only the subjects or members of an association who should exercise direct control over its decision-making process is explicitly endorsed by Dahl (1979, 99, 125). Other versions can be found in Walzer (1983, 292), Norman (1987, 91–99), and Gould (1988, 85, 144). But it is important to make clear that unlike some of these latter authors I am not suggesting that non-subjects should have no control, only that the appropriate control for non-subjects to exercise is of a different sort. Unless it is possible to establish that non-subjects are only negligibly affected by an association, it would be morally arbitrary from the point of view of the principle of equal liberty to deny non-subjects any control over its decision-making process.

The most familiar example of an application of the all-subjected principle is the democratic state. Since each member of the state is subject to its authority, each member shares direct control over it. Furthermore, since each member is subject to the state's authority over the same range of matters, each has an equal share of direct control over it: an equally valuable vote. Even if in practice there are numerous difficulties, this is the fundamental rationale underpinning the democratic state. Its members are simultaneously authority-bearing subjects and direct-control-exercising citizens. Non-subjects (or 'foreign nationals'), however, are not citizens, even though they may be affected by the decisions and activities of the state. This does not mean that they have no control over the state—they may, for example, impose tariff barriers against the state's produce—but their control is indirect.

At this point I want briefly to consider two potential difficulties with my position. First, some people argue that any form of authority is incompatible with individual autonomy and hence with the principle of equal liberty (Wolff, 1976, 18).[30] But we have seen: (a) that in order to be free individuals must be able to act on their choices; (b) that because of their social nature individuals will sometimes only be able to act on their choices in association with others; and (c) that in order to act in association with others an individual will have to accept that the association has auth-

---

[30] For a good discussion of the possible responses to Wolff's argument see Graham (1982).

ority to make decisions about a certain range of matters. Therefore, far from being incompatible with authority, freedom sometimes requires it. However, we have also seen that in these
circumstances the exercise of authority is only legitimate if control over it is shared among those who are subjected to it: that is,
if the authority is what we normally call 'democratic'. Democracy,
then, is the form in which freedom is exercised where the exercise
of freedom requires association. Thus there are two forms of
individual freedom: 'personal freedom', which is the form that
individual freedom takes when an individual can act on his or her
choices without association, and 'democratic freedom', which is
the form that individual freedom takes when an individual cannot act on his or her choices without association.[31]

A second difficulty seems to arise because there are certain
kinds of personal liberty that we want to protect even when the
exercise of democratic authority would otherwise be required.
These kinds of personal liberty are usually called civil rights. The
possibility of a conflict between democracy and civil rights
suggests that the conflict between authority and autonomy remains, albeit in a more limited form.[32] This apparent conflict is the
starting-point for an important strand of liberalism that focuses
on Tocqueville's concern with 'majority tyranny' (1990).[33] In fact,
however, civil rights are not in conflict with democracy. On the
contrary, democracy presupposes them (Dahl, 1985, 24–30). For if
individuals are to control shares of an association's authority,
then they must first be able to make their own choices to feed into
the association's decision-making process. But this is only possible if these individuals are able to consider and promote alternatives, and this requires the protection of typical civil rights such as

[31] Cole (1920a, 181) makes the same distinction 'between the liberty of personal
freedom and the liberty of free and self-governing association'. So does
Macpherson (1973, 109) when he distinguishes PL1 (positive liberty one), which 'is
individual self-direction or . . . the ability to live in accordance with one's own
conscious purposes, to act and decide for oneself rather than to be acted on and
decided for by others', from PL3, which 'is the democratic concept of liberty as
a share in the controlling authority'. (PL2 is the distorted form of positive liberty with which, according to Macpherson, Berlin conflates all forms of positive
liberty.)
[32] Civil rights can be viewed as limiting either the outcome of a democratic
procedure or the imputs into such a procedure. Here I have in mind the first of
these, although it is not important to the argument.
[33] See, for example, Hayek (1960, 104).

freedom of speech, freedom of publication, and freedom of association. Thus the 'limits' which civil rights place on democratic decision-making are equivalent to the preconditions for making democratic decisions in the first place.

There are, of course, other personal freedoms which we often seek to protect and to which we give the status of civil rights. Some authors who would agree with my argument so far see these as a separate category of 'private' (Plamenatz, 1973, 200) or 'non-democratic' (Jones, 1983, 161) rights: that is, a category of rights that is not integral to the democratic process. But it can be argued that typical candidates for this second category, such as the freedom to practise your own religion and the freedom to use your own language (Dahl, 1970, 16), can often be viewed as derivatives of civil rights which are integral to the democratic process. Religious rights can be seen as part of a general right to be allowed to develop your own system of beliefs and values, since it is on the basis of these that you make your own choices. Language rights can be seen as part of the right to be allowed to collect information and participate in public debate, since language is the medium through which these take place.

But even if personal freedom and democratic freedom are conceptually complementary, there may still be a problem in practice about determining exactly where the boundary should lie between the two, and when it has been illegitimately crossed. Who should make these decisions? Since the government will frequently be party to the dispute it does not seem to be a promising candidate. John Ely suggests that instead this role should be performed by the courts. Indeed, he argues that, under Chief Justice Warren, just such a role was performed by the United States Supreme Court (Ely, 1980, 73).[34]

Now before I conclude this chapter I want to return to my initial promise and justify the claim that the principle of equal liberty provides the basis for a 'constitutive morality' of socialism.

According to Ronald Dworkin:

Any satisfactory description of the constitutive morality of socialism[35] must meet the following catalogue of conditions: (1) It must state pos-

[34] See also Holmes (1988, 197 ff.).

[35] Here, as elsewhere in the following quote, I have substituted 'socialism' or 'socialist' for 'liberalism' or 'liberal'. Although he is principally concerned with its application to liberalism, Dworkin intends his definition to apply to all constitu-

itions that it makes sense to suppose might be constitutive of political programmes for people in our culture. . . . (2) It must be sufficiently well tied to the last clear socialist settlement . . . so that it can be seen to be constitutive for that entire scheme, so that the remaining positions in that scheme can be seen, that is, to be derivative given that constitutive morality.[36] (3) It must state constitutive principles in sufficient detail so as to discriminate a socialist political morality from other competing political moralities. . . . (4) Once these requirements of authenticity, completeness, and distinction are satisfied, then a more comprehensive and frugal statement of constitutive principles meeting these requirements is to be preferred to a less comprehensive and frugal scheme. (1986, 186–7)

I think it can be shown that the principle of equal liberty fulfils each of these conditions. Of course I cannot really establish this for condition four.[37] I can only say that I know of no contending socialist constitutive moralities that are more comprehensive and frugal. A morality based solely on equality, rather than equality of liberty, might appear to be more frugal, but in order to be equally comprehensive it would have to specify, as I have done, the kind of equality that is valued. In the end the onus is on a competitor to establish a breach of this condition. The fulfilment of the remaining three conditions is more straightforward. Condition one is fulfilled because the principle of equal liberty is rooted in the fundamental Enlightenment concepts of freedom and equality which dominate the political understanding of people in our culture. Condition two is fulfilled because the welfare state programme—which was the last clear socialist settlement—can be derived from the conditions in the principle of equal liberty that are concerned with the 'availability of means'. Education, health, and housing are all fundamental means without which freedom

tive political moralities. For more detail about this definition see Dworkin (1986, 184 n. 1).

[36] Dworkin distinguishes between 'constitutive [moral] positions that are valued for their own sake, and derivative positions that are valued as strategies, as means of achieving constitutive positions' (1986, 184). 'Distinct socialist settlements are formed when, for one reason or another, those moved by that constitutive morality settle on a particular scheme of derivative positions as appropriate to complete a practical socialist political theory, and others for their own reasons become allies in promoting that scheme. Such settlements break up, and socialism is accordingly fragmented, when these derivative positions are discovered to be ineffective, or when economic and social circumstances change so as to make them ineffective, or when the allies necessary to make an effective political force are no longer drawn to the scheme' (186).

[37] And nor can Dworkin in his treatment of liberalism (1986, 187).

of choice and freedom of action could not be exercised.[38] Finally, condition three is fulfilled because the comprehensive interpretation of freedom on which the principle of equal liberty is based distinguishes it from traditional liberal positions which focus on negative liberty alone. The fact that there is not a clear distinction between the constitutive morality of socialism and some radical liberalisms may seem to be a problem but is not. There have always been two ways of viewing the relationship between socialism and liberalism. According to the first, socialism is based on the same basic values as liberalism but it interprets and applies them more fully. According to the second, socialism is based on different values to liberalism or perhaps it is not based on values at all. In this work socialism falls squarely in the first camp. But it remains distinct from liberalism in the sense that while socialism may be seen as a kind of liberalism (a radical liberalism, for example), not all liberalisms can be seen as a kind of socialism.

However, irrespective of whether they are distinctively socialist, I hope that this chapter has shown that there are good reasons for being committed to a particular interpretation of the principle of equal liberty and to (at least) a minimal interpretation of the axiom of sociality. I also hope that it has shown that there are good reasons to govern associations according to the all-affected principle and the all-subjected principle, which I take to be the fundamental principles of democracy.

[38] Furthermore, the main socialist programmatic goal or 'settlement' prior to the adoption of the welfare state programme—that is, the goal of universal suffrage and democratic government—can also be derived from the principle of equal liberty.

2

Economic Democracy

The aim of this chapter is to develop a model of economic democracy. By economic democracy I mean a system in which the basic units of economic activity, namely firms or enterprises, are governed according to the democratic principles that I have been elaborating.

My strategy will be to undertake a critique of the capitalist firm. I will try to establish whether the capitalist firm measures up to the principles that we have been discussing. In setting out a model of economic democracy I will not be proposing change for the sake of change. Where existing capitalist practices live up to democratic principles they will be incorporated into the model unchanged. But where they do not, something new will be required.

It is possible to measure firms against the democratic principles of Chapter 1 because each consists of a group of individuals who co-operate over a period of time in order to achieve a common purpose, and is thus, by definition, an association. Typically this common purpose concerns the production of certain goods or services. To say that the members of a firm share this common purpose, is not to say that they all place the same priority on it. For example, some workers may consider earning an income or developing a skill to be more important purposes. Nevertheless, perhaps because of these more important purposes, they will, for the duration of their co-operation, share a common purpose with other members of the firm. Some firms, such as those that have adopted the technique of 'management by objective' (Odiorne, 1979), will seek to set out explicitly what their common purpose is, but this is not essential for their status as associations.

Because firms are associations they ought to be governed, like all other associations, in accordance with the all-affected principle. In a capitalist economy there are at least six groups of individuals who are affected by the activities of a firm. In the language of the business schools these groups are the firm's 'stakeholders'. They include the following:

1. employees or workers
2. consumers
3. shareholders or capitalists
4. suppliers of raw materials and producer goods
5. banks and other financial institutions, and
6. local residents.[1]

According to the all-affected principle, each of these stakeholders should exercise some control over the firm.

Now, as we noted in the last chapter, there are two distinct ways in which individuals can exercise control over an association. They can exercise control directly, by participating in its decision-making process, or they can exercise control indirectly, by setting constraints on the decisions that can emerge. Those who are subject to the association's authority should exercise control directly. Those who are not subject to its authority should exercise control indirectly.

In fact, under capitalism, indirect control is available to each of the stakeholders. Indirect control over firms falls into two subcategories: 'government regulation' (Dahl, 1970, 121) and 'exit control' (Hirschman, 1970, 4). Exit is a particularly desirable form of indirect control because it allows each individual to simultaneously exercise the maximum possible indirect control by completely blocking the effect which a firm's decisions would otherwise have on them. However, exit is only effective if (a) there is a competitive market and (b) the costs of exit are low. Wherever either of these conditions does not pertain, stakeholders must supplement or replace exit control with government regulation. For most stakeholders a mixture of both is needed, even for those stakeholders for whom exit control is paradigmatically advantageous.

Consider the case of consumers. In a competitive market economy exit is a particularly appropriate way for consumers to exercise control over a firm because it enables all those and only those consumers who are affected to exercise control, and because it enables these consumers to better satisfy their choices (i.e. their

---

[1] In fact this group includes some not-so-local residents. Consider, for example, the effect of British-generated acid rain on the forests of Northern Europe.

'demand') both in the short term, by getting a better deal else-where, and in the long term, by forcing improvements on way-ward firms. The mechanism is simple enough. If the quality of a firm's product deteriorates or if its price rises then customers will cease to buy that firm's product (that is, they will 'exit' from their relationship with that firm) and will instead buy what they want from a competitor. Falling revenue will alert the firm's manage-ment to customer dissatisfaction and force the firm to make alterations if it wants to stay in business.[2] In this way, exit control allows the consumer to constrain a wayward firm.

There are times, however, when exit control alone is not enough for consumers and must be supplemented by, or even predicated on, government regulation. For example, government regulation is needed where there is monopoly control over a product, especially where the product is a staple, since in these cases exit control becomes ineffectual. Government regulation is also needed wherever consumer safety is an issue, since exit control would have to rely on people actually being injured in order to come into effect. Moreover, some injuries may disable a customer so seriously that it even becomes impossible for that customer to exercise exit control.[3] In this sense the operation of exit control is predicated on government regulation of safety.

Nevertheless, it remains the case that consumer control over firms should predominantly be exercised by exit. The experience of attempts to rely predominantly on government regulations to exercise control on behalf of consumers reinforces this conclusion. In traditional Soviet-style economies these attempts seriously weakened the position of consumers *vis-à-vis* firms (Nove, 1983, 71) and led to chronic shortages of consumer goods (Kornai, 1986a, 9). Thus, as in a capitalist economy, in a socialist economy based on economic democracy, consumer control would pre-

---

[2] Note that where quality deteriorates but price remains constant there will be an immediate effect on revenue, but where price rises and quality remains constant the price rise can shield a certain number of exits (Hirschman, 1970, 23).

[3] Strictly speaking, exit control does not have to rely on experience after the fact. If all consumers had access to all the detailed technical information needed to make an assessment about the safety of each of the products that they may buy, then unsafe goods could be avoided before the fact. But even if all the information were available nobody could be expected to have the expertise required to make an adequate assessment in every case. This raises a general problem about the importance of government regulation when consumer knowledge is lacking (Hirschman, 1981, 219–20).

dominantly be exercised by exit. And this implies that the economy must be a market economy, at least to the extent of having a competitive market in consumer goods.

Various combinations of exit control and government regulation are available to each of the other stakeholders. Exit control can play a prominent role wherever a competitive market can be established between the stakeholder and the firm. Thus labour markets, stock markets, financial markets, and markets for suppliers of raw materials and producer goods all facilitate exit control.[4] Only in the case of 'local' residents is a prominent role for exit ruled out because of the inability of markets to deal with externalities such as pollution. But in that case government regulation can play an important role.

The basic point to note is that capitalism *does* provide adequate mechanisms of *indirect* control to each stakeholder. Thus in a socialist economy based on economic democracy, indirect control would look much the same as in a capitalist economy. No doubt some fine-tuning would be needed, but the basic mechanisms through which stakeholders gain indirect control would be the same. There would, however, be one important difference. Since (under the principle of equal freedom) incomes would presumably be more equally distributed in order to make the means to act on one's choices more equally available, the distribution of exit control (amongst, for example, consumers) would also be more equal since the more income an individual has the more influential an exit by that individual can be.

It is only when we begin to consider who should have direct control over a firm that the fundamental difference between economic democracy and capitalism becomes clear. Following Hirschman (1970, 19) I will sometimes refer to direct control as 'voice' control. This serves to highlight the distinction between the non-market, 'political' character of direct control and the market-based, 'economic' character of exit control.[5] To see the

[4] There are specialist literatures on each of these markets. On bankers see Jensen and Meckling (1976) and on suppliers see Williamson's (1985) chapters on vertical integration. I will return to the labour market and the stock market shortly.

[5] Note however that I am using 'voice' more narrowly than Hirschman does. According to Hirschman (1970, 30): 'Voice is . . . defined as any attempt at all to change rather than escape from the objectionable state of affairs [in a firm or other organization], whether through individual or collective petition to the management directly in charge, through appeal to a higher authority with an intention of

difference between capitalism and economic democracy we need only focus on the position of the traditional industrial antagonists: capital (the shareholders) and labour (the employees). For under capitalism, direct 'voice' control is exercised by capital. But, I will argue, in an economic democracy, it must by exercised by labour.

It is possible to make this argument on the grounds that capital is intrinsically more mobile than labour. Some reasons for thinking that capital is more mobile are discussed in Chapter 5. Mobility is relevant because it is a necessary condition for the effective use of exit control (Mueller, 1979, 125). If exit control were the only form of control available, then capital's effective control would be greater than labour's because of its greater intrinsic mobility. Thus an argument can be made that labour should be given greater direct voice control in order to compensate for its inability to effectively exercise full exit control. This, however, is not the argument that I want to pursue here. Rather, I will argue that direct voice control should be exercised by labour because the employees who sell this labour are the only human individuals subject to the authority of the firm.

In capitalist societies labour is defined by its role in the employment contract. Indeed, it is arguable that the employment contract is capitalism's most characteristic feature (Offe, 1985b, 52). According to the standard neoclassical interpretation, the employers and employees who are party to an employment contract are simply buying and selling a commodity like any other. The employee sells a certain amount of his or her labour to the employer in exchange for a wage. But labour is not a commodity like any other. It is a 'fictitious' commodity (Polanyi, 1957, 72). When a genuine commodity (such as a piece of machinery) is exchanged it is transferred from the seller to the buyer along with the exclusive right to decide what to do with it.[6] But when labour is exchanged it remains physically attached to its seller. For there is no separate or detachable entity 'labour' which the labourer can

forcing a change in management, or through various types of actions and protests, including those that are meant to mobilize public opinion.' In contrast I am using voice control to refer to that subset of these attempts where an individual or group of individuals actually makes the firm's decisions.

[6] Of course this exclusive right must be exercised within the terms of the contract of sale. For example, a buyer of uranium may be prohibited by the contract of sale from using the uranium to produce weapons.

hand over to an employing firm. 'Labour is only another name for a human activity which goes with life itself' (Polanyi, 1957, 72). Thus a firm can only gain its exclusive right to decide what it will do with the labour it buys if it gains an exclusive right to decide what the labourers themselves will do. But a firm can only gain an exclusive right to decide what the labourers will do if its decisions about what they should do exclude and replace those of the labourers. But the exclusion and replacement of choice is the defining feature of an authority relationship. Thus, when labourers sell their labour to a firm, they themselves become subject to the authority of that firm.

Moreover, the firm will have a powerful incentive to actually exercise this authority over its workers.[7] This is because there is a gap between what the firm acquires under the contract of employment and what it wants from that contract. The gap exists because the 'commodity' that the labourer sells is not labour itself, but what Marx calls 'labour power' or 'the capacity for labour' (Marx, 1976, 270). The firm buys this capacity for a certain period of time. In doing so it only acquires the potential for labour (labour power) as opposed to its actual performance (labour). Clearly this potential labour is of no use to the employer unless it is turned into actually performed labour. But the actual labour that can be acquired from a given amount of labour power is variable and remains unspecified in the employment contract. This variability leads to a conflict of interest between workers and capitalists. However much work the workers are prepared to do, the capitalists who own the firm will want them to do more. Since the cost of the labour has already been set, the more labour they can get the labourer to perform, the more profit they stand to gain. Thus, if the firm is to maximize its profits, it may be imperative for it to exercise authority over the labour power that it has bought.[8]

It seems, then, that the employment of labour involves the worker not just in the initial exchange relationship, but also in a subsequent authority relationship with the firm. According to

---

[7] Authority can exist as a potential which is distinct from its actual exercise. Having authority means that if you command you will be obeyed. Exercising authority means that you do in fact command.

[8] There are useful discussions of these issues in Edwards (1986, 280), Offe (1985b, 57), and Bowles (1986, 334).

Marx the first relationship is 'a very Eden of the innate rights of man' (1976, 280), but, once inside 'the hidden abode of production' (279), the second relationship takes over. Here 'the capitalist formulates his autocratic power over his workers like a private legislator . . . unaccompanied by either that division of responsibility otherwise so much approved of by the bourgeoisie, or the still more approved representative system' (549–50).[9]

It is this latter authority relationship which is the focus of my critique of the capitalist economy. For although it is the workers who are subject to the authority of the firm, it is, under a capitalist regime, the capitalists (i.e. the shareholders) who have direct 'voice' control over the firm. Thus, in a socialist economy based on economic democracy, direct 'voice' control over a firm must be transferred to those who work in that firm. Note that this does not imply either that labour has no control under capitalism, or that capital has no control under economic democracy. On the contrary, both continue to exercise indirect 'exit' control under both systems. In brief, then, capitalism is a system where capital can exercise both exit and voice control while labour can exercise only exit, whereas economic democracy is a system where labour can exercise both exit and voice control while capital can exercise only exit. I will call this the basic model of economic democracy.

The basic model of economic democracy does not object *per se* to the separate existence of capitalists (who are owners) and

---

[9] See also the distinction that Marx identifies in the *Grundrisse*. 'If we consider the exchange between capital and labour, then, we find that it splits into two processes which are not only formally but also qualitatively different . . . : (1) the worker sells his commodity [labour power] . . . which has . . . as a commodity . . . a price. . . . (2) The capitalist obtains labour itself . . . he obtains the productive force that maintains and multiplies capital. . . . The separation of these two processes is so obvious that they can take place at different times and need by no means coincide. The first can be and usually, to a certain extent, is completed before the second even begins. . . . In the exchange between capital and labour the first act is an exchange and falls entirely within ordinary circulation; the second is a process qualitatively different from exchange, and only by misuse could it have been called any kind of exchange at all' (Marx, 1973, 274–5). Later, in *Capital*, Marx describes in characteristic style what happens as capital and labour move from the sphere of exchange relationships to the sphere of authority relationships. Once inside the factory gates, 'a certain change takes place, or so it appears, in the physiognomy of our *dramatis personae*. He who was previously the money owner now strides out in front as the capitalist; the possessor of labour-power follows as his worker. The one smirks self-importantly and is intent on business; the other is timid and holds back, like someone who has brought his hide to market and now has nothing else to expect but—a tanning' (1976, 280).

workers (who are employees). Rather, it objects to the relationship between the two, and, in particular, to the fact that those who are employed become subject to the authority of those who own. This means that, unlike in some other models of economic democracy, worker ownership is not a necessary characteristic of the basic model. While it may be possible in certain circumstances to use worker ownership as a vehicle to achieve worker self-government, it is the system of government and not the system of ownership that defines an economic democracy.

I now want to consider three fundamental objections to the basic model of economic democracy. According to the *first*, the employees are not subject to the authority of the firm. According to the *second*, it is the shareholders who are subject. And according to the *third*, the firm need not have any subjects at all.

Recall that a person who is subject to authority is bound to comply with the decisions of that authority in the sense that their choices are excluded and replaced by those of the authority. The first objection argues that workers are not bound in this way because they can leave the firm whenever they want to.[10] There are a number of ways to answer this objection.

For one thing, it is usually not true that workers can leave a firm whenever they want to. Employment contracts typically specify a period of 'notice' (usually some number of weeks) which must be served before an employee can leave. This means that, at least for that period, employees certainly are bound to obey their employers. Under these conditions, hiring a worker is a bit like renting a house: neither the worker nor the landlord can regain authority over what they have rented out until a certain time has elapsed.

But even if we set aside the question of notice—perhaps because it is a requirement that is rarely enforced by employ-

---

[10] Alchian and Demsetz (1986, 111–12) provide a good example of this objection: 'It is common to see the firm characterized by the power to settle issues by fiat, by authority, or by disciplinary action superior to that available in a conventional market. This is a delusion. . . . To speak of managing, directing, or assigning workers to various tasks is a deceptive way of noting that the employer continually is involved in renegotiation of contracts on terms that must be acceptable to both parties. Telling an employee to type this letter rather than to file that document is like telling my grocer to sell me this brand of tuna rather than that brand of bread. I have no contract to continue to purchase from the grocer and neither the employer nor the employee is bound by any contractual obligations to continue their relationship.'

ers[11]—it is still possible to argue that workers are bound to obey the firm which employs them. Dahl suggests we compare the relationship between a worker and his firm with the relationship between a citizen and his municipality or even with the relationship between a citizen and his state. It may be true that a worker who does not want to obey a management directive can leave a firm. But, similarly, a citizen who does not want to obey an ordinance can leave her municipality and (in many countries) a citizen who does not want to obey the laws of her state can leave that state. However, in all three cases, despite the fact that membership appears to be voluntary, the cost of leaving is so high that it is for all practical purposes compulsory (Dahl, 1985, 114–15).

Both of the responses we have considered so far share an assumption with the objection that they are answering. They assume that being bound involves an unconditional compulsion: to be bound to do something is to be compelled to do it 'no matter what'. But it is also possible to answer the objection by rejecting this assumption. Indeed, I think that this is the lesson that should be drawn from the example of municipal and state authority. If, as Dahl suggests, it is only because of the high cost of departure that citizens are bound to obey municipal or state laws, then a great many citizens are not bound at all. In some countries large groups of people move between municipalities at little or no cost, and the same is true for smaller groups of people who move between states.[12] But we still think of these people as being subject to the authority of a municipality or a state and as being bound to obey their laws. Indeed, the authority of a state over its citizens is the paradigmatic example of authority. If states do not have authority it is hard to imagine who does.

This suggests that rather than denying the authority of the state we should reconsider what it means to say that a subject is 'bound'. Rather than defining someone as bound if they are unconditionally compelled to obey an association, we should define someone as bound if they are compelled to obey an association *so*

---

[11] Although clearly some employers do go to great lengths to enforce relatively long-term contracts. Consider the case of football players who want to quit early to sign up with another club.
[12] In Europe after 1992 this may well become the norm rather than the exception.

long as they are a member of it. This means that questions about the nature of authority relations within an association can be posed independently of questions about whether membership of that association is compulsory or voluntary. This is as it should be. Clearly it is important to distinguish subjects who cannot exit (such as serfs) from subjects who can exit (such as workers). But it is equally important to distinguish between the different kinds of authority to which those who can exit are subject. A dictatorial and a democratic state do not become identical simply because the members of each are able to exit. The fundamental problem with the first objection is that it depends on a definition of bound-ness which reduces questions about authority to questions about exit rights. In summary then, even if workers can leave a firm, they are still subject to its authority while they work for it. For the duration of their employment they are bound to comply with certain decisions of the firm and it is this which justifies their claim to direct control.[13]

According to the second objection to the basic model of econ-omic democracy, shareholders are subject to the authority of the firm and hence should share direct control over it.[14] The trouble with this objection is that it confuses an exclusive right to decide what to do with certain commodities with authority over persons. Certainly a firm has an exclusive right to decide what to do with the capital which capitalists invest in it. But this does not mean that the capitalists themselves are subject to the firm's authority. For unlike labour, capital is not a fictitious commodity because it can be exchanged without remaining attached to the capitalist who sells or rents it. Consider the different ways in which the owners of capital and the owners of labour are affected by con-tracts to let third parties use their respective 'commodities'. While I am using your capital you can do something else, but while I am using your labour power you cannot. Since capital can be sep-arated from the capitalist, the firm's authority does not extend to the capitalist. The firm can issue orders about how its capital will

[13] It is interesting to note that in the English common law tradition the existence of an authority relationship has long been considered the single most important, if not the only, defining feature of the relationship between employer and em-ployee or between master and servant. See Rideout and Dyson (1983, 4–6) and Batt (cited in Coase, 1986, 84–5).
[14] Proponents of this objection may or may not accept that workers are also subject to the firm's authority.

be utilized but it cannot tell the capitalists themselves what to do. Who has ever heard a company manager yelling at the shareholders to 'invest harder'? And since the shareholders are not subject to the authority of the firm they should not have direct control over it.

In this respect it is useful to compare the position of shareholders with that of banks and other financial institutions. Both provide the firm with the same commodity (capital); and both gain a return for undertaking this risk (dividends in the case of equity, and interest in the case of debt). But nobody thinks of banks as subject to the authority of the firms to which they lend, and, at least in the Anglo-Saxon world, nobody suggests that it is wrong that under capitalism banks do not exercise direct control over these firms.[15] Why, then, should shareholders be thought of as subjects entitled to exercise direct control?

To deny that shareholders are subject to the authority of the firm in which they invest is not to deny that they are affected by the decisions of that firm[16] and hence should exercise control over it. But, under the basic model of economic democracy, shareholders *do* exercise control over the firms in which they invest: they exercise indirect control through their power to 'exit'. As with the analogous control exercised by banks, this 'exit' control depends on the existence of a market: a capital market in the case of banks and a stock market in the case of shareholders. And it is clear from the experience of capitalist societies that the control which these markets give both to banks and to shareholders can be very substantial.

Indeed, even though shareholders in capitalist societies nominally have direct control over their firms, it is arguable that, for

[15] It is true that banks in the Anglo-Saxon world are called upon to exercise direct control in certain abnormal circumstances. For example, they may be called in as liquidators charged with winding up a firm which has collapsed. But they do not exercise direct control over a normally operating firm (Dahl, 1985, 79).

[16] In some cases they may even be affected to a greater extent than the firm's workers. Consider a pensioner who invests all his retirement income in a firm which collapses. At a time of low unemployment the firm's workers may easily find another suitable job, but, with the loss of his 'nest egg', the pensioner's retirement plans will be ruined. However, cases like this should be rare since capitalists—even small capitalists—can spread their risk more easily than workers. Whereas the capitalist can invest in a large number of firms, the worker can only work for one or maybe two firms (Meade, 1988, 214; Horvat, 1982, 447). The pensioner made the mistake of putting 'all his eggs in one basket'.

some time, indirect control exercised through their power to 'exit' has been by far the most important source of control available to them.[17] This argument is closely related to Berle and Means' (1932) thesis that in the modern corporation ownership and (direct) control have become separated. The shareholders still own the firm, but (direct) control has passed into the hands of a managerial elite. As a result it has become a 'Wall Street rule' that 'if you do not like the management you should sell your stock' (Hirschman, 1970, 46).

According to the third objection to the basic model of economic democracy there need not be any subjects at all. The fact that capitalism makes workers subject to the authority of a firm does not mean that socialism must do likewise. On the contrary, according to this objection, it is possible to organize work in such a way that no individual is subject to an authority relationship. This can be done, it is suggested, by making every worker into an independent contractor. Now we know from our experience of capitalism that it is possible for independent contractors to perform certain kinds of work. But is it possible to universalize this form of co-ordination, thereby eliminating authority relations from the economy and establishing a kind of 'contract-socialism' (Pateman, 1988, 152)? Recent work by 'transaction cost' economists suggests that the answer is 'no'.

The most influential work on transaction costs has been done by Oliver Williamson. Building on the seminal work of Ronald Coase (1986) and others, Williamson argues that to eliminate authority relations from the organization of work would be prohibitively costly. Williamson (1985, 229) compares various modes of organizing a typical manufacturing task—Adam Smith's oft-discussed example of the pin manufacturers—and finds that all modes which rely solely on contracts are decidedly less efficient than modes that rely on an authority relation.

The question of costs arises because we live in a 'changing world' which requires individuals and their transactions to constantly adjust to new circumstances.[18] Transactions that are solely

---

[17] Again this has been especially pronounced in the Anglo-Saxon world.

[18] 'The economic problem of society is mainly one of rapid adaptation to changes in the particular circumstances of time and place' (Hayek, 1986, 69). Typical adaptations include those required by changing consumer preferences and new technologies.

contractual can meet this requirement in one of two ways. Either the contract must include terms which enable the relevant adjustments to be made, or the contract must be renegotiated; in effect, that is, a new contract must be made (Williamson *et al.*, 1986, 141–2). The first option requires a contingent claims contract. The second option requires sequential spot contracting.

Williamson explains his findings about the inefficiency of contract-only modes of work organization by appealing to two reasonable-sounding 'behavioural assumptions' about human individuals. He calls the first 'bounded rationality' and the second 'opportunism'.

Bounded rationality is an assumption about the cognitive competence of individuals (Williamson, 1985, 45; Simon, 1983, 19). According to this assumption, individuals have only a limited ability to predict the consequences of their actions. In part, at least, this is because individuals have limited access to information and limited capacity to process it (Arrow, 1974, 37, 39).[19] Because of these limits, cognitive competence is a scarce resource, and hence like any other scarce resource, the more of it we have to use in order to achieve a goal, the more expensive the achievement of that goal becomes. This means that drawing up a contingent claims contract will be expensive. A fully-specified contingent claims contract is a contract that sets out the obligations of each party in every possible contingency. The more contingencies and their concomitant obligations we attempt to specify, the more cognitive competence we will have to use and the more costly the contract will become.

Opportunism is an assumption about the motivation of individuals who engage in transactions (Williamson, 1985, 47). It is a strong version of the assumption that individuals are self-interest seeking. Opportunist individuals are prepared to seek their self-interest with guile, and Williamson assumes that at least some individuals are prepared to act in this way. Typical examples of opportunism include providing false or misleading information to those with whom one is entering into a contract, and violating the terms of a contract after one has entered into it whenever it is convenient to do so. Opportunism takes on its greatest significance in a context of 'asset specificity'. Asset specificity refers to

---

[19] See also McPherson (1983, 356) and Williamson (1985, 46).

the fact that the value of certain assets is specific to a particular transaction. For example, if I agree to build a plant for you on a particular site, then the more it would cost to relocate the plant, the more its value will be specific to our particular transaction (Williamson, 1985, 95). Labour also often manifests asset-specificity resulting, for example, from task-specific training.[20] In each case the result is a 'lock-in effect' (53). Once such an asset has been invested, one or both of the parties to the investment contract will have a monopoly power, which, assuming opportunism, they can exploit to their own advantage each time that the contract is renegotiated. This means that sequential spot contracting will be expensive. Pure sequential spot contracting involves a series of one-off task-specific deals such as those between a customer and his or her grocer (Williamson *et al.*, 1986, 144). The more frequently renegotiations take place, the more scope there will be for utilizing the power of asset-specific investments and the more costly the contracting process will become (Williamson, 1985, 78).

Thus it is clear that, if we accept Williamson's two behavioural assumptions, any attempt to co-ordinate the relationship between firms and labourers solely by contracts would be extremely costly. Bounded rationality makes contingent claims contracts costly, and opportunism does the same for sequential spot contracting. Authority relations, on the other hand, can reduce these costs. By establishing a long-term relationship the expenses associated with renegotiations are curtailed, but at the same time the need for expensive contingency planning is avoided. Thus there is no way of efficiently organizing some forms of work without subjecting individuals to an authority relationship (Arrow, 1974, 69). In the real world of the advanced capitalist countries this will be enough to ensure that these forms of work continue to be organized in such a way that workers are subject to the authority of their firm.

Nevertheless, a proponent of the objection that we are considering may continue to argue that while it would certainly be very

---

[20] Indeed, even in unskilled jobs there is usually a certain amount of on-the-job learning as well as efficiencies that result from personal relations with co-workers. This means that simply by working for a particular firm your labour will come to manifest some degree of asset-specificity. Williamson refers to this as the 'fundamental transformation' (1985, 61).

costly to eliminate economic subjects it is still *possible*.[21] However, I think that Williamson's argument can be used to show that even this is not so. Remember that since the organization of work will have to adapt over time, contract-only co-ordination must take one of two forms: contingent claims contracting or sequential spot contracting (Williamson *et al.*, 1986, 141–2).

A contingent claims contract is a fully-specified contract that sets out the obligations of each party in every possible contingency. We have already seen how Williamson argues that such contracts can be very expensive because of bounded rationality. In fact, however, he can and does make the stronger claim that, for any reasonably complex transaction, bounded rationality makes a fully-specified contingent claims contract impossible. There are just too many possible alternatives and it is not possible to estimate the consequences of each (Williamson *et al.*, 1986, 142–3). Furthermore, unlike in, say, chess, there is no way of even specifying all the alternatives. A fully-specified contingent claims contract is impossible because of uncertainty about the future.

Sequential spot contracting avoids this problem by adapting to the future only when it is reached. No attempt is made to foreshadow future changes within the framework of any one contract (as in contingent claims contracting). Rather, the contract itself is continually renegotiated to meet these changes as they arise. But this procedure can also fall prey to uncertainty: not in the future, but in the present. Consider a complex, rapidly changing production process that requires each of a large number of workers to simultaneously perform different but interrelated functions. Given the bounds of human rationality there is no way that all the individuals whose actions must be co-ordinated can renegotiate their contracts either quickly enough or often enough without overloading their cognitive competence. The problems posed by bounded rationality will be further exacerbated in such a situation by the interdependence of the various renegotiations. Each contractor will need to consider each of the possible deals which the other contractors may reach before being able to make

---

[21] Perhaps the objector might argue that, in the name of freedom, we should eliminate subjection whatever the cost. I am not convinced that this is right, however, since, as I noted in Chapter 1, efficiency (or 'economy') is itself linked to freedom because a less efficient system may restrict us from pursuing choices which we could otherwise pursue.

his or her own deals. This seems to lead back to another kind of contingent claims contracting. In this case the contingent claims contract would have to specify all the various contracts that the contractor is prepared to enter into as a function of each of the other possible contracts which may be agreed between third parties.[22]

So, at least for certain forms of work, it is simply not possible for contract-only co-ordination to displace authority relations between a firm and its workers.

Note, moreover, that the claim that contract-only co-ordination is impossible depends solely on the assumption of bounded rationality.[23] So it is not susceptible to criticism of the assumption that individuals are opportunists. The possibility of doing away with opportunism in particular and self-interest in general is a recurring theme in socialist literature. There is a tendency on the part of some socialist writers to assume that the genuine absence of opportunism that is sometimes found in revolutionary situations can be built into a post-revolutionary society as a permanent feature.[24] This seems highly unlikely to come about. But the point is that, even if it did, the need for authority would persist due to bounded rationality alone. It is of course possible to suggest that bounded rationality is also an avoidable feature of human nature. But in light of the 'tremendous weight' of empirical evidence to the contrary this is hardly a tenable position (Simon, 1983, 22).

So each of the three objections to the basic model of economic democracy fails. According to the first objection employees are not subject to the authority of their firm. This objection fails because it mistakenly conflates questions about authority with questions about exit rights. According to the second objection capitalists are subject to the authority of their firm. This objection fails because it mistakenly conflates exclusive rights over capital

[22] On top of all of this there are likely to be multiple 'co-ordination problems' in the specific game theoretic sense of the term (Schelling, 1960, 89). But these would exist no matter how rational the contractors were.

[23] Williamson (1985, 48) thinks that without opportunism, a general clause contract could take the place of contingent claims contracting. However, this seems to ignore problems of interpretation (Harel, 1989, 15, 16), and these can exist even between non-opportunists.

[24] In her essay 'The Revolutionary Tradition and Its Lost Treasure', Hannah Arendt (1963) also seems to build her hope on this sort of possibility.

with authority over capitalists. Finally, according to the third objection the firm need not have any subjects at all. But this objection also fails because it makes unrealistic assumptions that ignore human bounded rationality and opportunism.

I now want to compare my argument for the basic model of economic democracy with other arguments that criticize the unfreedom of labour under capitalism. This is important, since my critique is based on a concept of democracy that is itself dependent on the value of freedom, so naturally it cannot ignore other critiques that are rooted in a commitment to the same value. My argument has relied on a critique of capitalism which emphasizes one specific form of labour unfreedom. In particular I have focused on the absence of what was called in Chapter 1 'democratic freedom'; that is, the direct control which those who are subject to an authority should have over it. But there are a number of other dimensions to the freedom or unfreedom of labour.

For example, we can look not only at who has direct control over the authority of a firm but also at the scope of that authority. In considering the third objection to the basic model we have already ruled out the suggestion that all firms could dispense with authority altogether. But the fact that a firm requires authority of a certain scope does not mean that it can exercise any amount of authority over its workers without infringing their freedom. I do not here want to try to determine what the scope of a firm's authority should be.[25] But, whatever the appropriate scope is, a firm which exercises authority beyond that scope is infringing on the freedom of its employees. And the greater the scope of its extra authority the less free are its workers. I have not focused on this 'scope of authority' dimension because it does not seem to me to be a major cause of labour unfreedom in advanced capitalist societies. There are of course still 'scope of authority' problems in these societies,[26] but they pale into insignificance beside comparable problems in orthodox communist societies (where your employer could determine whether or not you got a passport) and many Third World countries (where employers

[25] In part, at least, this is because the appropriate scope will vary with a firm's technological requirements.
[26] For example, there is still sometimes contention about the control of hairstyles and dress.

often retain a quasi-feudal authority which can extend to the right to marry and have children).[27] Furthermore these problems are not instrinsic to capitalism. Capitalist societies are not dependent on infringing workers' freedom in this way.

So there are two dimensions of labour unfreedom that involve authority: one is concerned with the question of who has direct control over the authority, and the other is concerned with the scope of that authority. But these are not the only dimensions. In fact there is a second type of argument about labour unfreedom which is not concerned with authority at all, but rather with exchange. Recall that labour is characterized by the employment contract, and that the employment contract involves two relationships: an initial exchange relationship, and only subsequently an authority relationship. Whereas the authority relationship exists within a firm, the exchange relationship exists at the 'edges' of a firm: that is, at the point of entry or exit. According to this second type of argument, workers are unfree because they are forced to sell their labour power. The argument can be made at two different levels. At one level it can be argued that workers are not free to enter or exit a particular firm. At another level it can be argued that workers are not free to enter or exit a particular economic class. Each of these levels can be represented as a dimension of labour freedom or unfreedom. The first is concerned with firm entry and exit. The second is concerned with class entry and exit. Figure 4, below, lists all four of the dimensions of labour unfreedom that I have been discussing.

Let me begin with the first of these dimensions: that is, firm entry and exit. There is no doubt that there are ways of organizing work that make labour unfree in this respect—consider, for example, slavery or penal forced labour. There is also no doubt that capitalism has, now as well as in the past, brought about a degree of labour unfreedom along this dimension. Legally, in a capitalist society, workers can sell their labour to any firm they choose. The 'absence of constraint' condition for freedom is fulfilled. This is why Marx describes the exchange of labour under capitalism as 'a very Eden of the innate rights of man' (1976, 280). But in practice

---

[27] On marriage, examples can be found on large agricultural estates in the Philippines and Latin America. On childbirth, examples (aimed at birth control) can be found in India—the Indian State Railways ran a model scheme—and in China.

things may be different. For the 'availability of means' condition may not be fulfilled. Hence the ironic tone of Marx's comment. During times of high unemployment many workers will not be able to leave the firm which currently employs them for fear of being put out of work altogether. And even in times of full employment many workers may not have the skills to enter the firm of their choice. But, Marx's predictions notwithstanding, problems like these are not intrinsic to capitalism. The post-war experience shows that it is possible for capitalist societies to maintain full or near-full employment,[28] thus dealing with the first problem. Similarly, it is perfectly possible for capitalist societies to provide workers with adequate education and training,[29] thus dealing with the second problem. So while it is certainly very important that correct employment and training policies are pursued, it remains true that, given these, workers in a capitalist society need not experience serious unfreedom along the 'firm entry and exit' dimension.

It is the second exchange-based dimension of labour unfreedom that seems to be more troublesome for capitalism. The claim here is that while workers may be free to enter and exit individual firms, they are not free to enter or exit particular economic classes. Specifically it is claimed that workers are trapped in the working class with no option but to sell their labour to a capitalist employer.

Marx makes this claim at a number of points. For example, comparing the situation of capitalist workers with that of slaves and serfs he argues that, 'The worker leaves the capitalist to whom he hires himself whenever he likes. . . . But the worker, whose sole source of livelihood is the sale of his labour power, cannot leave the whole class of purchasers, that is, the capitalist class, without renouncing his existence. He belongs not to this or that capitalist but to the capitalist class' (Hunt, 1984, 96).

In the realm of freedom-based critiques, a critique which is based on this second 'class entry and exit' dimension seems to be the main alternative to the critique based on the 'direct control' dimension that I have been emphasizing. My 'direct control' based critique leads to a policy which emphasizes the develop-

---

[28] Evidence for this is presented in Chapter 7.
[29] See Chapter 8.

ment of economic democracy. But an alternative critique may lead to alternative policy prescriptions. If the 'class entry and exit' based critique should lead to a different policy emphasis, then it is at least possible that the movement to economic democracy may have to be put on hold while other more pressing developments are given priority. The question then is whether this alternative critique does in fact give rise to an alternative policy emphasis. There are two reasons for doubting that it does.

First, it is unclear that there *is* a separate critique based on the class entry and exit dimension of labour freedom. It is not true that workers under capitalism are never able to move into another class. Marx himself occasionally notes that some workers can become self-employed and that others can even become capitalists (Elster, 1985, 208–16), although the significance of these exit options is open to various interpretations (Cohen, 1988). Arguably, then, the problem is not that workers cannot exit from their class. Rather, the problem is the nature of the authority to which members of their class are subjected. But this takes us straight back to the 'direct control' based critique.

Second, even if there is a separate class entry and exit critique, a policy which emphasizes the development of economic democracy seems to provide an appropriate response. For the establishment of an economic democracy adds to the options which are already available under capitalism, the option of becoming a member of a new class of self-governing workers. Under economic democracy you can still become self-employed. You can still become a capitalist or shareholder. You can even remain in the position of a worker under capitalism by not participating or by electing the capitalists as your managers. But in addition you can become a self-governing worker.[30] Moreover it is difficult to envisage an alternative system that would be superior to economic democracy in providing freedom along the class entry and exit dimension given, as we have seen in dealing with the third objection to the basic model of economic democracy, that many

[30] Some like Nozick (1974, 255–6) say that this option is already open under capitalism. But it is only available in the form of worker-owned co-operatives, and a number of major obstacles stand in the way of workers seeking to establish such co-operatives (Cohen, 1988, 276–7; Miller, 1981). In addition, even if Nozick were right, this would only serve to establish that there is no separate class entry and exit critique of labour freedom which could be used to challenge the priority I have given to the development of economic democracy.

workers are necessarily subject to the authority of their firms in a complex industrial economy.

So if there is a class entry and exit dimension to labour unfreedom under capitalism as well as a direct control dimension, it does not undermine my policy prescription that the development of economic democracy should be the centre-piece of a contemporary socialist programme. For economic democracy would eliminate unfreedom along both the direct control and the class entry and exit dimensions.

Let me summarize my discussion of the various dimensions of labour freedom and unfreedom in diagrammatic form (see Figure 4). Using these four dimensions we can characterize and compare different ways of organizing work. The diagram shows the ideal-typical situation of labour in three different social systems: socialism, capitalism, and slavery. The position of capitalist and socialist workers along each dimension has been justified in the course of this chapter. The position of slaves is by definition maximally unfree: 'All forms of labour on behalf of another,

		LESS FREE	MORE FREE
AUTHORITY RELATIONS	Direct Control	Slave Cap. worker ——→	Soc. worker
	Scope	Slave	Cap. worker Soc. worker
EXCHANGE RELATIONS	Firm Entry and Exit	Slave	Cap. worker Soc. worker
	Class Entry and Exit	Slave Cap. worker ——→	Soc. worker

Key: Slave = The ideal-typical position of a slave
Cap. worker = The ideal-typical position of a worker in a capitalist society
Soc. worker = The ideal-typical position of a worker in a socialist society
——————→ = The transformation from capitalism to socialism

FIG. 4. *The dimensions of labour freedom*

whether "free" or "unfree", place the man who labours in the power of another; what separates the slave from the rest . . . is the totality of his powerlessness in principle' (Finley, 1968, 307).

The diagram makes it easy to see why some socialists have been tempted to label capitalism as a form of slavery: so-called 'wage-slavery' or 'wagery' (Cole, 1972, 83). Although capitalism is not the same as slavery it does share some of its ideal-typical characteristics. In particular it shares a high degree of unfreedom along the 'direct control' dimension, and it may also share a degree of unfreedom along the 'class entry and exit' dimension. Of course not all historical examples of either capitalism or slavery are exact replicas of their respective ideal types. Indeed, there have been examples where the unfreedom of capitalist workers along the 'firm entry and exit' and 'scope' dimensions has approached that of ideal-typical slaves,[31] and other examples where the freedom of slaves along these dimensions has approached that of ideal-typical capitalist workers.[32] But it is a category mistake to compare ideal-typical examples of one system with real historical examples of another. If we restrict ourselves to ideal-typical cases (or even just to historically typical cases) then it is clear that capitalism lies along a multidimensional continuum somewhere between slavery and socialism.

[31] This typically occurs during times of mass unemployment and recession, when there is little or no real chance of changing jobs and consequently very little chance to impose sanctions against employers who attempt to exceed the legitimate scope of their authority.

[32] A comprehensive comparative study by Orlando Patterson (1982) cites examples not only of free entry into slavery, but also of more or less free exit from it. 'In Russia between the seventeenth and nineteenth centuries self-sale as a result of poverty was the most important reason for enslavement among the mass of domestic slaves' (130). In the Middle East as well as parts of Africa and Asia 'the ability to change masters was surprisingly widespread because of a peculiar Islamic custom that permitted it. . . . the most common version was for the disgruntled slave to go to the compound of the master he wished to have buy him and cut a piece of flesh from the ear of that master's camel or horse. The owner of the slave was then required to compensate for the damage by handing over the slave to the offended master' (202). Patterson also shows that in over fifty per cent of all known slave societies, there were some legal restraints on the scope of a master's authority over his slave (198). In general, studies both of American slavery and Russian serfdom suggest that from the seventeenth century onwards there was a continuum of unfree and semifree forms of labour which merged into so-called 'free', archetypally proletarian forms (Jordan, 1969, 48; Kolchin, 1987, 32, 37, 41; Mintz, 1978, 88–9, 96).

So capitalist labour is not slave labour, but nor, as is so often claimed, is it 'free labour'. The socialist model that I have been defending would maintain labour freedom along the two dimensions where it already exists under capitalism and extend it to the two dimensions—'class entry and exit' and 'direct control'—where it does not. Only by introducing a system of economic democracy can genuine labour freedom be achieved along all four dimensions.

3

Feasibility

I hope I have shown that a major change to what I have called the basic model of economic democracy is desirable. I now want to show that such a change is feasible.

Alec Nove's *The Economics of Feasible Socialism* has helped to focus attention squarely on the feasibility of socialist proposals. At the beginning of his book, Nove sets out a definition of feasibility. 'I should like', he says, 'to include in my definition of "feasible socialism" the notion that *it should be conceivable within the lifespan of one generation*—say, in the next fifty years; conceivable that is without making extreme, utopian, or far-fetched assumptions' (Nove, 1983, 11).[1] By the end of the book it is clear that this is not merely to be included in his definition; it is his definition. 'Let me recapitulate;', begins the last chapter, 'by possible or feasible I mean a state of affairs which could exist in some major part of the developed world within the lifetime of a child already conceived, without our having to make implausible or far-fetched assumptions about society, human beings, and the economy' (Nove, 1983, 197).

In essence Nove is offering a temporal definition of feasibility. If a socialist project cannot be brought to fruition within a certain period of time—fifty years—it is unfeasible. But while time may be involved in our assessments of feasibility,[2] it does not play the central role which Nove ascribes to it. In fact feasibility is a much more variegated concept than Nove allows. If we do not distinguish between the various types of feasibility we are in danger of conflating some quite different issues.

In its primary sense, to talk about feasibility is to talk about the feasibility of some sort of goal. I propose to distinguish three types of goal-feasibility. The differences come out most clearly when we look at how a goal can be criticized for lack of feasibility.

---

[1] Italics in original.   [2] As we will see below.

A goal can be said to be not feasible if:

1. *It cannot be achieved under any circumstances.* This is the type of feasibility which Nove has in mind when he criticizes Marx's vision of communism. This, he claims, could not be achieved under any circumstances because it assumes the possibility of abundance and of a 'New Socialist Man'. Whatever the circumstances we must assume a continuation of scarcity and hence conflict over resource allocation, and a population of human beings which are 'recognizable, similar to those that now exist' (Nove, 1983, 62). Note, however, that to establish that a goal is not feasible in this first sense does not necessarily doom it to irrelevance. Such a goal might still be an important regulative ideal: that is, it might be a criterion for judging the present and something towards which to strive. Nove complains that to give this role to such a goal would be 'to place oneself for ever in the posture of a righteous (lefteous) oppositionist to any regime calling itself socialist' (Nove, 1983, 15). This complaint would only be fair if a regime were being criticized on the basis of a goal towards which no movement at all were possible. But typically when such criticisms are made it is possible to move towards the goal even though the goal itself may be unattainable. For example, people frequently criticize various forms of social inequality, not to demand an unattainable total equality, but to point to the possibility of a more equal society than we have at present.

2. *It cannot be achieved under present circumstances.* Athenian democracy is not feasible in this sense. For while there were circumstances—those of Greece in the fifth century BC—under which it could be achieved, this is no longer possible due to the size and complexity of modern industrial countries (Dahl and Tuft, 1973). It is this second type of feasibility which Frederick Engels had in mind when he criticized the 'utopian socialists' in *Socialism: Utopian and Scientific* (1975, 50–62). Engels did not think that Owen, Fourier, and Saint-Simon had hit on an idea whose time would never come. He did not accuse them of type 1 unfeasibility. Rather, he criticized them for thinking that socialism could be achieved there and then. On the contrary, Engels claimed that socialism would only be feasible once society had developed in certain ways. In particular, widespread industrialization could not be circumvented. Only after the coming of in-

dustrial capitalism would there be a class with an interest in bringing about socialism and the power to successfully pursue their interest.

3. *Once it is achieved, it does not work.* The first two senses of goal-feasibility deal with the possibility of a transition to a new state of affairs. The third sense deals with what happens once this state of affairs has been attained. Brus (1985) reserves the term 'feasibility' for the first two senses of feasibility, and distinguishes the third sense by using the term 'viability'. Brus correctly points out that Nove's principal concern is with viability in this sense. Nove wants to show that a Soviet-style socialist economy does not work, and to elaborate the structure of a socialist economy that would. But what does it mean to say that an economy does or does not work? After all, the Soviet Union was a going concern for some 70 years. But surely the simple fact of a system's continued existence is not enough. Thus, according to Brus, 'What is at stake is the viability of socialism, where the term "viability" refers to something more than its capacity to survive' (1985, 48). He goes on to say that to be viable a system must be able to provide solutions to the 'challenges [of the] contemporary world', though there are no longer any unique solutions. But what counts as a challenge is itself controversial. This illustrates the general point that once we move beyond the minimal issue of whether a system can survive,[3] there is no value-neutral way of specifying its viability. Whether or not a socialist system 'works' depends on what our goals are. Suppose economic democracy makes production less efficient. Does this mean that it does not work or is it simply that we are prepared to sacrifice a certain degree of efficiency because we value other goals? Either way, however, efficiency in one of its forms is an important factor in measuring type 3 feasibility.[4]

In the chapters that follow I will not be considering whether economic democracy is feasible in this third sense. This is not because type 3 feasibility is unimportant. Far from it. If economic democracy were to be markedly less efficient than capitalism, then serious questions would indeed arise about whether or not it ought to be pursued. As it is, however, the evidence both for and

---

[3] Rawls (1972, 504, 580) uses 'feasibility' to refer to type 3 feasibility in this minimal sense.
[4] Although how efficiency is measured is itself controversial (McPherson, 1983).

against the superior efficiency of economic democracy is ambiguous and inconclusive.

Consider, for example, the theoretical debate about the importance of supervision.[5] On the one hand, according to Alchian and Demsetz, and Williamson, capitalism has superior efficiency because by linking the receipt of profits to the task of supervision it can better tackle opportunism. On the other hand, according to Marglin, Bowles, and Putterman economic democracy would both reduce the incidence of opportunism by fostering greater commitment and reduce the cost of that supervision which is still required by giving that task to the workers themselves. The empirical evidence, such as it is, is also inconclusive. Firms governed by their workers seem to perform at least as well as (Abell, 1983, 89), and maybe even slightly better than (Elster and Moene, 1989, 29–31), conventional capitalist firms.

Another influential debate takes as its starting-point the theory of labour-managed market economies developed by Ward (1967) and Vanek (1970; 1971). This theory assumes that each worker's sole objective will be to maximize his or her own income (Ward, 1967, 186; Vanek, 1971, 13), and on this basis it predicts that labour-managed firms will make 'perverse' or inefficient employment and investment decisions. However, Vanek (1970, 171) also argues that this income maximization assumption is totally unrealistic, and that labour-managed firms have not one but a multiplicity of objectives. Empirical tests carried out in the former Yugoslavia support this argument (Prasnikar and Svejnar, 1989).

So neither on theoretical nor on empirical grounds can a firm case be made for the claim that, in terms of efficiency, economic democracy is inferior to capitalism. Indeed arguably the opposite is true. For this reason I think that it is legitimate to set to one side the question of whether economic democracy is a type 3 feasible goal. The task that I want to undertake here is a different one. I want to consider whether economic democracy is a goal which can be achieved under present circumstances. I want, that is, to focus on whether economic democracy is a feasible goal in the second sense outlined above. Obviously if the type 2 feasibility of a goal can be established then the type 1 feasibility of that

---

[5] Relevant articles by the authors mentioned in this paragraph can be found in an excellent anthology edited by Louis Putterman (1986). There is also a useful summary of the debate in McPherson (1983) and in Putterman (1990).

goal follows automatically. If the goal can be achieved under present circumstances then there are certainly *some* circumstances under which it can be achieved. Henceforth, then, I will be concerned solely with type 2 feasibility and, unless otherwise stated, when I speak of 'feasibility' I will be speaking solely of 'type 2 feasibility'.

Type 2 feasibility is a relationship between a goal and an actor (or a coalition of actors). When we ask whether a goal is feasible we are asking whether it is feasible for this or that actor (or coalition). A goal is feasible for an actor if it is possible for the actor to achieve the goal under present circumstances. Note, however, that a goal is feasible for an actor regardless of whether the actor wants to achieve the goal. For example, suppose that an army could easily take a fort but chooses to bypass it. The fact that the army does not want to take the fort does not affect our assessment of whether or not it was feasible for the army to do so. An actor's preferences are irrelevant in determining whether or not a goal is feasible for that actor. In asking about feasibility we are asking whether an actor (or a coalition of actors) could achieve a goal *if it wanted to*. Here the actor (or rather the coalition of actors) with which I will be concerned is the labour movement. Thus, in raising the question of feasibility, I am asking whether, if the labour movement wanted to achieve economic democracy, it could do so.

So feasibility is not about whether a certain goal has been adopted by the labour movement. It is about whether, if adopted, that goal can be achieved. There is, however, an important connection between the feasibility of a goal and whether or not it is adopted. Goals, especially radical goals, are often opposed, even by those who would otherwise support them, because it is believed that they cannot be achieved. Thus, demonstrating the feasibility of a policy can be seen as clearing the way for its adoption. 'It may well be that the impossible at a given moment can become possible, only by being stated at a time when it is impossible' (Kolakowski, 1968, 90–1).

Whether or not an actor can achieve a goal depends on whether or not there is a feasible strategy for achieving it. I will sometimes refer to the question of whether there is a feasible strategy for achieving a goal as the question of its 'strategic feasibility'. A strategy is a series of steps that an actor proposes to take which lead from one set of circumstances to another. A feasible strategy is a strategy composed of feasible steps. A step is feasible for an actor if it is possible for the actor to take that step given the pre-existing circumstances. The first step of a strategy is feasible if it is possible for the actor to take that step given the circumstances that exist at present. Each subsequent step is feasible if it is possible for the actor to take that step given the circumstances that would exist following the attainment of the previous step.

Moreover, just as the actor's preferences are irrelevant in determining whether or not a goal is feasible, so, too, they are irrelevant in determining whether or not a step is feasible. However, just because of this, there is a difference between the feasibility of a goal, and the feasibility of a strategy for achieving it. The difference rests on the fact that the desire to achieve a goal does not entail the desire to pursue the steps that are needed to achieve it. In considering the feasibility of a goal we can only assume that the actor wants to achieve the goal. In considering the feasibility of a strategy we can also assume that the actor wants to achieve each of the steps that make up that strategy.

In what follows I will be principally concerned with this latter, strategic feasibility. In particular, I will argue that there is a feasible strategy for achieving economic democracy. I will not argue that this strategy is the only, or even the best, feasible strategy. Rather, my main concern is to deal with the sceptics who believe that economic democracy is not a strategically feasible goal at all. To refute these sceptics I need only to show that there is at least one feasible strategy for achieving this goal.

Note that time does not enter into my definition of strategic feasibility. To attain a goal may take 50 years or 100 years. What is important is not how long it takes to achieve the goal, but that there are a series of steps starting with present circumstances which lead to its achievement. Of course it is true that our judgement about the possibility of a step may become more and more uncertain with each successive step. So it may be difficult to judge the strategic feasibility of a goal which could only be achieved far into the future. To this extent, but only to this extent, time may indeed be involved in the assessment of feasibility.

Now the circumstances that exist at present can be defined by specifying the actor's strength, the strength and preferences of other relevant actors, and the political and economic environment (or terrain) in which all these actors interact.[6] Each of these factors will be addressed in the chapters that follow.

In the next chapter, Chapter 4, I will specify which are the relevant actors in an advanced capitalist country and set out the various ways in which they can organize both themselves and relations between themselves to form different industrial relations systems. In Chapter 5 I will argue that one such system— corporatism—maximizes the strength of organized labour and has other important advantages. In Chapter 6 I will set out how these advantages provide the labour movement with the basis for a feasible strategy for achieving economic democracy, given the preferences of other relevant actors. In Chapter 7 I will examine how this strategy would work in a stagflationary environment like that which prevailed from the mid 1970s to the early 1980s. And in Chapter 8 I will examine how it would work in an environment of structural adjustment like that which prevailed from the mid 1980s to the early 1990s.

So is economic democracy a strategically feasible goal for the labour movement? In order to make this question more manageable I will limit my discussion to those advanced capitalist countries which have politically significant labour movements. I will consider a country to have a 'politically significant' labour movement if its post-war history suggests that it has the potential to elect a pro-labour government. A pro-labour government will paradigmatically, but not always,[7] be a government dominated by a labour or social democratic party. In effect, then, this will limit my discussion to the countries of Western Europe and Australasia. It may well be that the strategy that I will propose, or at least aspects of it, will prove to be feasible in other countries, such as those of newly democratic Central and Eastern Europe (Archer, 1989). But I will not try to defend any such claims here.

---

[6] Recall that the preferences of the actor for whom the feasibility of a goal is being assessed are not relevant to that assessment.

[7] See Chapter 6.

4

Industrial Relations

In this chapter I want to lay the groundwork for the argument which will follow. First I will specify social actors which are relevant to the goal of achieving economic democracy. Then I will consider the various ways in which these actors can organize both themselves and relations between themselves.

I want to claim that there are three actors or sets of actors which are relevant: the capitalists (or 'capital'), the workers (or 'labour'), and the government. Economic democracy as it was defined in Chapter 2 is a system of governing firms in which direct control over them is redistributed. To achieve economic democracy this control must pass out of the hands of the capitalists and into the hands of their workers. Thus an actor is 'relevant' to the goal of achieving economic democracy if it can affect the distribution of direct control between capitalists and workers.

The employment relationship which characterizes a capitalist economy defines two class actors. In one class are the capitalist employers who own firms and exercise direct control over them either by themselves or through those they delegate to manage. In the other class are the workers whom these firms employ. These class actors are collectives which are themselves composed of individual human actors who may be organized into a more or less cohesive unit.

Class is an abstraction which divides people in such a way as to emphasize their relationship to employment and ownership. People can also be divided into groups that emphasize other things that they hold in common, such as sex, race, nationality, and income. The significance of analysing contemporary capitalism in specifically class terms is often disputed and I do not want to make a general defence of this practice. However, I do want to claim that class analysis remains important for those interested in economic democracy. The significance of an analysis based on one group rather than another depends on what problem we are tackling and what goal we are seeking to achieve. Class analysis remains significant for those interested in economic democracy for the simple reason that it divides the world into those who will be invested with direct control and those who will be divested of direct control should this goal be achieved.

The capitalists and the workers are both relevant actors because both can affect the distribution of direct control over firms. Capitalists have the power to resist the redistribution of direct control because they currently exercise all or most of this control, and because firms are dependent on their ongoing investment. Workers have the power to promote the redistribution of direct control because they can organize themselves into unions which can impose sanctions that hinder or stop production.

Governments can also affect the distribution of direct control over firms. Ownership of firms and relations between employers and employees are regulated by a complex web of laws and incentives which legalize and promote certain distributions of power. Governments can change these laws and incentives in order to legalize and promote different distributions of power. They can then move to enforce these laws. Even when they choose not to use their legislative power, governments can use their ability to set the political agenda in order to affect the balance of power between the class actors. They can do this by making appeals, suggesting courses of action, and by giving rhetorical support to one class or the other. For example, governments often label union actions as irresponsible or call on employers to resist wage demands. Moreover, governments are charged with managing the economy, and the economic policies they choose to pursue can have a major effect on the relative strength of capital and labour. For example, a government which fosters full employment will also be strengthening the position of labour. Finally, since governments are themselves major employers they can use their own employment practices to set an example for other employers and to establish new norms. Thus the government is also a relevant actor.

Thus far I have argued that the capitalists, the workers, and the government are relevant actors because they can affect the distribution of direct control over firms. But it is also true, certainly in the case of the capitalists and the workers, that they would be affected by that distribution, and hence have an interest in it. But the fact that an actor has an interest in the distribution of direct control does not, in itself, make the actor strategically relevant. History is littered with weak actors who have a strong interest in a change, without having the ability to effect it—either to promote or resist it—themselves. For Marx it was a unique feature of capitalism that it produced a subordinate class of workers who not only had an interest in changing society, but the power to do so as well.

But amongst those with the power to effect a change, surely it is only those with an interest in that change who will be motivated to use their power. Thus should we not say that the relevant actors are those who have both the power to effect a change and an interest in using it? The trouble is that there are many groups which do not have an immediate interest in a change—that is, the change, in itself, would not affect them—but who may nevertheless be prepared to use their power to bring about or resist that change. For example, an interest group may be prepared to engage in log-rolling. In other words it may be prepared to use its power to bring about a change in which it does not have a direct interest, in exchange for another group's support in bringing about a different change in which it does have a direct interest. Thus we must be on the look-out for actors who have no immediate interest in economic democracy but nevertheless have the power to effect such a change.

Might not household consumers be a case in point? Household consumers have no immediate material interest in either helping or hindering workers from gaining direct control over their firms. So long as they continue to be able to exercise their influence through a market in consumer goods they will be unaffected by economic democracy. In fact, however, household consumers are not a relevant actor. This is not because of their lack of immediate interest in economic democracy, but rather because they have very little power to affect the distribution of direct control in the first place. Through the market they can affect what those who have direct control produce. But that is a different power.

There are a number of reasons for this lack of power.[1] The most

[1] These reasons do not apply to corporate consumers who sometimes can influence who has direct control over a firm from which they buy. However, these corporate consumers themselves are subject to the direct control of capitalists who are unlikely to jeopardize their own position by promoting the cause of direct control for workers even if these workers are in another firm.

important reasons are centred around the fact that in the advanced capitalist countries the relationship between household consumers and the products they buy is fragmented in a way that the relationship between workers and the products they make is not.[2] A worker makes the same product or group of products, many times, in the same place, whereas a consumer buys many products, often only a few times, in many different places. Workers are brought together to produce the same products in the same place and hence they are able to organize and thereby exercise power over the way production is organized. On the other hand, each product that a consumer buys is only one of many different products he or she will buy, each of which is available in a number of different places. What is more, unless the product is a staple, he or she may only need to buy the same product a few more times, if ever.[3]

Since household consumers do not gather around any one product or place of work it is difficult for them to organize themselves in order to influence the way production is organized. Buying takes place quickly and at widely different places and times. It would be extremely difficult for you to find out who else was purchasing a particular product. And even if you could all get together, it would be unclear to whom you should make your demands since there are usually a number of enterprises making any one product. This was very different in Soviet-style economies, where governments provided just such a focus for organized demands in virtue of their monopolistic price setting role. The existence of a flourishing market for consumer commodities allows household consumers to exercise influence by way of 'exit' rather than 'voice'. But while exit influence can affect what is produced it is unlikely to affect how it is produced.

It might be argued that consumers could use their exit influence to impose a boycott on undemocratic firms. In the United States, for example, boycotts of anti-union firms have at times been pursued in the form of 'union label' campaigns. But these campaigns presuppose the existence of significant numbers of unionized

---

[2] I mean 'products' to be conceived broadly to include all the goods and services.

[3] Enterprises which retail staple goods like food are one of the few kinds of enterprises where consumers can have some effect over the distribution of direct control. Almost all consumer co-operatives are enterprises of this kind.

firms from which those participating in the boycott can buy the goods that they need. At a certain stage along the road to economic democracy, a boycott of some particularly intransigent firms may well have a role to play. But before such a boycott could be effective there would already have to be a significant number of democratic firms. Consumers cannot boycott all firms at once.

We are left, then, with a list of three relevant actors. Now relations both within and between these actors can be organized in different ways, and, in what follows, I want to consider each of these intra- and inter-actor relations in turn. I then want to show that these organizational relations define a multi-dimensional matrix which enables us to specify all the familiar industrial relations systems.

Let me begin by looking at the organization of class relations. First I will consider the organization of relations within classes and then I will consider the organization of relations between classes.

Organization within classes revolves around the level of centralization. A highly organized class combines three attributes. These are illustrated diagrammatically in Figure 5.

The first attribute is the concentration of power. Concentration of power refers to the extent to which a peak council or confederation is able to control the activities of its affiliates. In the case of organized labour, concentration of power usually depends on factors such as whether the peak council participates in collective bargaining; controls the distribution of strike funds; possesses the right to veto negotiated settlements; collects dues from members; and maintains a large staff.[4] However, it should be noted that concentration of power can exist in 'proxy' form even when none of the above factors are present. A union movement in which one strong union acts as a pacesetter—establishing conditions which then flow on to the other unions—may be effectively the same as one in which there is a high degree of concentration of power. This kind of proxy concentration of power exists in Germany, for example, because of the pacesetting role of the metal workers union and in spite of the fact that industrial unions in that country

---

[4] Compare with Schmitter (1981, 294), who calls this attribute 'organizational centralization', and Cameron (1984, 164–5), who calls it 'confederation power in collective bargaining'.

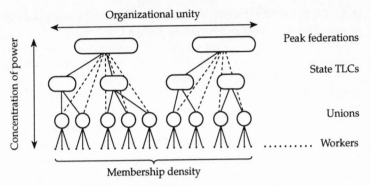

Key: ⎓ Both denote membership

Note: In a number of countries, including Australia (which will be discussed in greater detail in Chapter 9), unions are members of both peak federations and state or regional trades and labour councils (TLCs).

FIG. 5. *Union centralization*

formally have a large degree of autonomy (Lehmbruch, 1979, 309; Streeck, 1984a, 10).

The second attribute of a highly organized class is organizational unity. Organizational unity refers to the unity or fragmentation of the class at the peak council or confederation level. In the case of organized labour organizational unity refers to the extent to which unions are themselves organized into peak councils. This usually depends on the number of confederations, whether there are separate confederations for blue and white collar workers, and the number of unions: organizational unity is stronger if there are a small number of large industrial unions.[5]

The third attribute of a highly organized class is high membership density. Membership density refers to the extent to which a class has succeeded in drawing its members into its organizations. In the case of organized labour it is a measure of the percentage of the total workforce that is unionized (Cameron, 1984, 164–5).

So centralization is a function of three attributes: concentration of power, organizational unity, and membership density. How-

---

[5] Again, compare with Schmitter (1981, 294), who refers to this attribute as 'associational monopoly', and Cameron (1984, 164–5), from whom I draw the label 'organizational unity'.

ever, to refer to the extent of class organization as 'centralization' is slightly misleading. For one thing, it could be thought to refer to the concentration of power alone, rather than to all three of the attributes discussed above. The term could also be misleading because it may seem to imply that a highly organized class is one which stifles rank and file activity. But as we will see in the next chapter this is not necessarily so. In fact, there is some evidence that the most effective organization of labour actually requires an active rank and file (Lehmbruch, 1984, 69). This suggests that it may be better to discuss the extent of internal class organization in terms of 'articulation' (Crouch, 1992, 170; 1993, 54–5) or 'co-ordination' between peak councils and the rank and file. Nevertheless I will stick to the term 'centralization'. This is partly because it is consistent with common usage and partly to emphasize that a highly organized class is one which aggregates the widest possible number of its members into a single class organization or 'centre' which is then able to mediate all the various local and sectional interests within that class. The essential feature of a highly organized class is that it is able to establish and pursue class-wide goals.

Now let me turn to the organization of relations between classes. Organization between classes revolves around the level of inter-class co-operation. The level of class co-operation depends on the degree of conflict or consensus that exists between the two class actors. Co-operation can only begin if there is a shared goal about which to co-operate. Consensus is the mutual recognition of such a shared goal. If there is not a shared goal, then there must at least be consensus about a preferred combination of goals. In the terms of rational choice theory this means that co-operation can only begin if there is mutual recognition that the classes are playing a non-zero-sum game.

Co-operation is also fostered if there is mutual trust between the classes that neither is surreptitiously trying to make non-co-operative gains at the other's expense. If a class suspects that it is being 'suckered' in this way it may cease to co-operate whether or not there are shared goals.

There is a range of bipartite arrangements which tend to foster consensus and trust. In reality these are often incorporated into tripartite forums in which the two class actors are joined by government representatives. Joint consultative bodies, negotiating forums, and works councils all involve different levels of commitment to class co-operation. But all foster it. By encouraging an exchange of information they enable shared goals (or shared combinations of goals) to be identified, and hence foster consensus. By ensuring that the classes will have to meet and do business again they encourage them to act in good faith, and hence foster trust.

Finally, let me turn to the third relevant actor: the government. Again we face the same two questions about how both intra- and inter-actor relations are organized. First there is the question of how relations within government are organized. Second there is the question of how relations are organized between the government and the two class actors.

Governments cannot change their internal organization at will. They inherit a complex state apparatus which carries in to the present the outcomes of past political struggles and a long tradition of political organization. This history manifests itself in two attributes of state organization which are analogous to two of the three attributes of class organization that were discussed above.[6]

The first attribute revolves around the distribution of authority between the various levels of government. This is essentially a question of the extent to which a state is organized along federalist lines. At stake here is how government powers are distributed between central, state (or provincial), and local levels of government, and to what extent they are concentrated in one centre. Federalism is to the organization of the state what the concentration of power is to the organization of labour. Both concern the extent to which decision-making power lies in their respective centres.

The second attribute revolves around whether the state is prepared to share public space.[7] At stake here is whether the state is organized to monopolize public authority, or whether, and if so to what extent, it is organized to allow associations in civil society to act like 'private governments' and exercise political authority alongside it. Since the core of political authority is authority over universal issues which concern the citizenry as a whole, the crucial test for a state is whether it is prepared to coexist with associations like churches and labour movements which claim to speak with authority about such universal issues. Monopolization of

---

[6] See Figure 5 above.
[7] I have taken the concept of 'public space' from Crouch (1986) and will discuss his particular use of this concept in greater detail in Chapter 9.

political space is to the organization of the state what organizational unity is to the organization of labour. Both concern how many organizational centres there are: one concerns any organizational centre of a people, the other concerns organizational centres of workers.

The third attribute of labour organization is the membership density of unions. There is no analogous attribute of state organization for the simple reason that the membership density of the state is always 100 per cent because membership is compulsory.

The organizations of relations between government and the class actors revolves around the level of public involvement. Public involvement has a dual character which is a function of the fact that relations between government and class actors can be organized in two ways, depending on whether the state is organized to share or monopolize political space.[8] The state can see itself either as one among many associations or as an association which stands over and above all others. Typically there is a bit of both.

To the extent that the state stands over and above all other associations, a government can unilaterally act to establish and enforce a particular relationship between a class actor and itself. By asserting its claim to all-encompassing political authority, the government can legislate to regulate a class actor. It can do this by regulating industrial relations in general (e.g., by instituting compulsory arbitration), or by directly regulating both the membership and internal organization of a class actor (e.g., by enforcing a particular method of electing union leaders). This is one form of public involvement. Public involvement here implies the involvement of public bodies (government) in class affairs. By asserting its right to legislate, the government is implicitly recognizing that the class's actions are affecting the public interest. Since the government claims a monopoly over the right to affect the public interest it must either prohibit the class from affecting the public interest,[9] or else clearly delimit an area of the public interest and delegate the class a right to affect it.

---

[8] My discussion of the dual character of public involvement draws in part on Offe (1981, 136–41).

[9] For example, the French Le Chapelier laws in 1791 and the British Combination Acts until 1824 were extreme attempts to do this by legislating class actors out of existence altogether.

To the extent that the state is one among many associations, a government can only establish a relationship with a class actor on the basis of voluntary negotiations. Respecting the autonomy of the other actor, the government must win its agreement by offering concessions. The 'social contracts' which have sometimes been drawn up between Labour governments and trade unions are the best example of this sort of relationship. This requires public involvement of a different sort. Public involvement here implies the involvement of class actors in public affairs. To win agreement a government can offer influence over the formulation and implementation of public policy. To some extent the government is offering this simply by negotiating with a class actor. But the government can also give more formal influence to a class actor by giving it the right to be represented on certain decision-making bodies. It may also give the class actor resources to enable it to exercise this influence. These resources may be financial (e.g., to employ an expert economist), but they may also be ideological (e.g., public backing to legitimize union involvement in an area of government from which they have been traditionally excluded). In return the government usually wants the class actor to comply with the policies which it has helped to formulate. It may also want to affect the internal organization of the class to ensure that it is more centralized, more representative, or whatever.

Parties provide a channel for public involvement. Many parties formulate their policies under the direct influence of class actors. The formal control which unions exercise over the British Labour party is one of the best known examples. But this sort of influence is exercised in other parties as well. The British Conservative party, for example, selects its parliamentary candidates using a panel on which places are reserved for industrialists. Since the policies of a ruling party form the basis of a government's policy, class involvement in parties has a similar effect to the kind of public involvement in which class actors are given direct influence over public policy formulation.

Figure 6 summarizes the discussion so far. Having identified three actors which are relevant to the goal of economic democracy, I have been trying to give an organizational characterization of the different ways in which relations both within and between these actors can be organized. These relations define a total of six dimensions. Three concern the degree of centralization of each

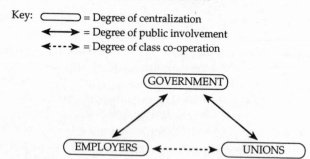

FIG. 6. *The six dimensions of an industrial relations system*

actor. The fourth concerns the degree of class co-operation. And
the fifth and sixth concern the degree of public involvement in
relations between the government and the two class actors, where
public involvement concerns both class involvement in public
affairs and public (i.e. government) involvement in class affairs.

There have been a number of attempts to quantify these dimensions. However, while numerical indicators can serve a useful
function, it is important to be aware of their limitations. Consider
labour centralization: the dimension which has been the most
frequent subject of attempted quantification. We have seen that
the centralization of labour is a function of three attributes: concentration of power, organizational unity, and membership density. With the exception of membership density these attributes
are themselves a function of a number of other factors. Concentration of power is a function of whether a peak council participates in collective bargaining, controls the distribution of strike
funds, possesses the right to veto negotiated settlements, collects
dues from members, and maintains a large staff. Organizational
unity is a function of the number of peak councils, whether there
are different peak councils for blue and white collar workers, and
the number of unions. Schmitter (1981, 294) and Cameron (1984,
164) have both attempted to quantify these attributes by attaching
numerical values to each of these factors and aggregating them to
provide a composite score.[10]

Cameron then goes one step further and combines all three
attributes to provide a single numerical indicator for labour

---

[10] Each uses a slightly different list of factors, and whereas Schmitter attaches
values from 0 to 3 to each factor, Cameron attaches values from 0.0 to 1.0.

centralization. According to Cameron (1984, 166) labour centraliz-ation = (concentration of power + organizational unity) × mem-bership density. There are a number of serious problems with numerical indicators of this sort. For a start there is no agreement about the list of factors and attributes that should be included. More importantly, even if there were an agreed list of factors and attributes, there is no way to decide how to combine them or what weight to give to each. Why multiply membership density by the other two attributes rather than add them? Why attach the same weight to veto rights as to the control of strike funds? Cameron does not attempt to justify his particular combination or weight-ing. His choices are arbitrary, or, at best, intuitive.

Some political economists have suggested that the quantifi-cation of labour centralization and the other dimensions that we have been discussing is being held back only because of the complexity and variability of the phenomena and because of the difficulties of data collection and measurement. Gerhard Lehmbruch, for example, believes that 'neither obstacle is in-superable' (1982, 2), although he himself attempts no more than a qualitative distinction between strong, medium, and weak cases (1982, 16–23). My discussion suggests that this optimism may be misplaced. The problems of combining and weighting various factors and attributes point to the fact that there are intrinsic limitations to the possibility of quantification.

These limitations do not undermine the value of the six-dimen-sional analysis illustrated in Figure 6. This analysis remains use-ful because it provides us with concepts—centralization, class co-operation, and public involvement—which enable us to sys-tematically categorize different industrial relations systems. Let me illustrate this by showing how these concepts enable us to define the industrial relations systems which are often thought of as being at opposite extremes: corporatism and *laissez-faire*.

Since there is much confusion about just what 'corporatism' refers to I must first clarify how I will be using this term. There are two quite different ideas of corporatism present in contemporary usage.[11]

According to the older of the two, corporatism is an alternative type of social order: something in the same genus as capitalism

---

[11] This point has been made by a number of writers. See, for example, Cawson (1986, 22) and Cox (1988, 26).

and socialism. However, unlike capitalism or socialism it is an organic social order based on functionally distinct associations. This idea has roots in Hegel and draws much of its inspiration from the guild structure of the medieval *standestaats*. Durkheim was an exponent of corporatism in this sense, and many English-speaking scholars were introduced to similar ideas through translations of Gierke's *Political Theories of the Middle Age*. The idea of corporatism as an organic social order was especially influential among Catholic social theorists, particularly after it was officially authorized in Leo XIII's 1891 papal encyclical *Rerum Novarum*. It also influenced a number of nationalist theorists and through them entered the ideologies of fascist regimes, especially those of Catholic southern Europe.[12]

More recently, corporatism has been used to refer to a particular form of industrial relations system. According to this idea, corporatism is one of a number of possible industrial relations systems that can exist within a capitalist social order. It is corporatism in this sense that has been at the centre of a renewed debate about the concept that began in the 1970s. Lehmbruch (1979), Crouch (1979; 1982), and Panitch (1986) are good examples of contemporary corporatist theorists who unambiguously use corporatism in this way.

But while all contemporary corporatist theorists have focused on industrial relations issues, not all have restricted their use of 'corporatism' to this domain. In particular, Streeck and Schmitter (1985), two prominent participants in the contemporary debate, have returned to the older idea of corporatism to develop a theory of a corporative–associative social order. And Claus Offe (1981), another prominent participant, also uses corporatism to refer both to an industrial relations system and to an alternative social order. Because of this confusion I want to make it clear that I will be using corporatism solely to refer to an industrial relations system.

It is my contention that, as an industrial relations system, corporatism is defined by high levels of centralization along with high levels of class co-operation and public involvement. Each of

---

[12] For the history of Catholic and nationalist corporatist thought see Peter Williamson (1985, 19–81) and Otto Newman (1981, 3–39). Williamson (1985, 83–133) also discusses the attempts to implement corporatism in fascist Italy and Portugal.

the better known definitions of corporatism deals with one or more of these dimensions. Schmitter (1981, 294) equates corporatism with centralization. Maier (1984, 40) emphasizes class co-operation. Offe (1981, 136) defines it as public involvement, as does Maier (1981, 56) in an earlier essay. Regini (1984, 124) combines public involvement and centralization. And Crouch (1979, 187) refers to centralization and consensus, which he relates to both class co-operation and public involvement. But only Lehmbruch (1979, 5; 1984, 61) recognizes that corporatism is in fact a 'pluridimensional concept' which combines them all. Surveying the different conceptualizations of corporatist industrial relations systems that have emerged, Lehmbruch identifies three 'analytically distinct developments' which he aggregates into his 'pluridimensional concept'.[13] Lehmbruch's three analytically distinct developments are virtually identical with my concepts of centralization, class co-operation, and public involvement.

There is much less confusion about what constitutes a *laissez-faire* system, although argument rages about the extent to which it ever existed in a pure form. A *laissez-faire* system has two basic preconditions. The first is an unbesmirched boundary between the political functions of the state and the economic functions of civil society. The second is a system of individual contracts on which all social relations within civil society are based (with the possible exception of the family). By definition, therefore, industrial relations are conducted solely between individual employers and employees. Hence there can be no class centralization and, in particular, there can be no organization of labour.

This in turn leads to low conflict or high class co-operation. This is not because individual workers have no grievances, but rather because there are no channels (or organizations) through which

---

[13] 'three analytically distinct developments have been labelled as "corporatism":

1 the development and strengthening of centralized interest organizations—or "peak" associations—which possess a representational monopoly;

2 the granting to these associations of privileged access to government, and the growth of—more or less institutionalized—linkages between public administration and such interest organizations;

3 the "social partnership" of organized labour and business aimed at regulating conflicts between these groups, in co-ordination with government policy (usually in the form of "tripartism")' (Lehmbruch, 1984, 61).

A similar idea is also enunciated earlier in Lehmbruch (1979, 2–6).

they can be pursued without great risk to the workers themselves. To agree to work for an employer is to agree to co-operate. To be non-co-operative is to break the agreement and risk losing your job. The only safe way to express grievances is to combine with other workers to spread the risk.[14]

With respect to public involvement, the implications of *laissez-faire* would seem to be straightforward. A clear distinction between state and civil society should lead to no public involvement. In fact the opposite is true. For, paradoxically, the *laissez-faire* state must continually intervene in civil society to maintain the system's two basic preconditions. Class (or at least worker) organization undermines both. Combinations of workers can make demands on the state and thus undermine the distinction between the state and civil society (where economic actors are supposed to belong). And they most certainly undermine the sanctity of individual contracts in the labour market. Thus the state must continually intervene in the 'class' affairs of the labour market to stamp out any attempts to organize labour. As a result public involvement (which is here exclusively government involvement in the affairs of labour) is very high.

So *laissez-faire* is characterized by no class centralization, high class co-operation, and high public involvement (although exclusively of one kind).

Of course corporatism and *laissez-faire* are not the only ways to combine the six dimensions. While there are purely organizational reasons why certain values on one dimension require certain values on another,[15] this in itself does not limit the number

[14] This slightly overstates the case since it is possible to express grievances by reducing productivity through a kind of private 'work to rule' or 'go slow' which managements typically put down to 'motivation' and 'morale' problems. Something similar to this seems to have been widespread in the former Soviet Union. But it also plays a role in the advanced capitalist world. For example, in Britain, where union organization was seriously weakened in the course of the 1980s, an authoritative survey has found that managers now think that 'morale' is the most important industrial relations problem in their firm (Millward *et al.*, 1992, 363). However, there are severe limits to the extent that grievances can be expressed in this way. Any overt display of worker dissatisfaction can be immediately disciplined. Moreover in Britain, unlike in the former Soviet Union, high unemployment produces a countervailing 'fear factor' which serves to 'motivate' workers (Metcalf, 1989, 20).

[15] For example, we have just seen this in the case of a *laissez-faire* system where zero centralization requires high public involvement to keep associational growth in check.

of possible combinations to two. Consider pluralist free collective bargaining for example. This system dominated British industrial relations for the first 20 years of the post-war period (Crouch, 1979, 19–65, 180–3). Free collective bargaining is named for its two defining features.

It is 'free' in the sense that it is free from state interference in the bargaining process. Of course it is not totally free since all states claim some responsibility for regulating industrial relations (if only to register organizations). Nevertheless, compared with other industrial relations systems, there is negligible public involvement.

It is 'collective' in the sense that workers band together in order to express their grievances more safely. The bigger the collective the safer it becomes. However, if the collective gets too big—national, say—it will begin to notice the public effects of its actions, which will in turn lead to pressures for greater public involvement (Crouch, 1990, 114). But then the system would be moving away from pluralist free collective bargaining and towards corporatism. Thus there will tend to be a number of medium sized collectives which operate at a medium level of centralization. It is in this sense that it is a 'pluralist' system.

But just because there are only medium sized collectives class conflict will be more likely, both because these collectives will be unable to opt for co-operative strategies for fear of bearing the costs of the conflictual strategies of others while foregoing the possible benefits (Olson, 1982), and because they will not be able to make use of as wide a range of trade-offs as their more centralized counterparts. Thus in pluralist, free collective bargaining systems class conflict will be high and class co-operation low. Empirical evidence supports this conclusion. Countries like Britain, Ireland, the United States, Canada, and Australia as well as France and Italy, where there has been a strong tradition of free collective bargaining, have all tended to have high levels of strike activity (Cameron, 1984, 153).

In summary, then, pluralist free collective bargaining combines marginal public involvement, medium levels of centralization, and low class co-operation.

There are, of course, many other alternative industrial relations systems. For example, closely related to corporatism and *laissez-faire* are neo-corporatism and neo-liberalism. Neo-corporatism is a form of corporatism in which union involvement in public affairs is a significant component of the high level of public involvement which all forms of corporatism share. Neo-liberalism is the outcome desired by those who aspire to a *laissez-faire* system but realize that under present circumstances it would be impossible to totally prohibit class organization. However, I will not go on listing different industrial relations systems here. For in the next chapter I plan to focus exclusively on corporatism.

5

Potentials and Dangers
of Corporatism

In this chapter I want to examine the potentials and dangers of corporatism. I will argue that while corporatism poses some serious dangers, it also offers the prospect of making some headway towards economic democracy.

Many socialists have been highly suspicious of if not outrightly hostile to corporatism. They have viewed corporatist institutions as an attempt by politicians and union leaders—often acting in the short-term interests of a labour or social democratic government—to weaken or restrain the power of organized labour to pursue its own interests. There is no doubt that this has often been the case. Therefore, although I will argue that a corporatist strategy offers a chance to achieve greater economic democracy, it is important to look carefully at the dangers which such a strategy can generate. Only by systematically setting out the dangers that could befall a corporatist strategy can we hope to avoid them when elaborating the strategy itself.

The dangers of a corporatist system flow directly from its organizational structure.

Class co-operation leads to the danger of *class collaboration*. This is the danger most frequently cited against corporatism. For class co-operation to proceed a consensus must be formed on some of the matters that are of mutual interest to unions and employers. The fear is that this will invariably lead unions to abandon radical aspirations and consent to the maintenance of capitalism. This fear is endorsed by certain corporatist theorists. Gerhard Lehmbruch (1979, 167), for example, argues that corporatist policies 'have largely served the function of integrating organized labour into the economic status quo'. And Leo Panitch (1986, 151), who has made some of the most widely discussed socialist criticisms of the dangers of corporatism, concludes that 'corporatism within liberal democracies has become a powerful vehicle for reinforcing class dominance'.

But it is not inevitable that consensus will only be reached on the employers' terms. After all, the unions are also able to set their terms for co-operation, and the agreement that is reached will depend to a large extent on the balance of class power. It may even be the case that the consensus reached favours the unions. So it is not co-operation *per se* which is the danger, rather it is the terms on which co-operation takes place. Class collaboration would pose no danger if it were the capitalist class which was doing the collaborating, and it were labour which was dictating the terms of the consensus. But while class co-operation is possible on these terms in principle, the history of corporatist experiments may suggest that it is impossible in practice. In fact, however, this is not the case. A number of studies, notably of the Scandinavian countries, have shown that ongoing class co-operation *is* compatible with a gradual shift in the balance of class power which favours labour.[1]

Public involvement is associated with two dangers. The first concerns excessive government involvement in union affairs, or *incorporation*. The second concerns excessive employer involvement in government affairs, or *capitalist domination of the state*.

Incorporation leads to suppression of union autonomy and the subordination of union goals to those of the government. Extreme levels of incorporation are the defining features of fascist corporatism. The similar but variously named distinction between state and societal corporatism (Schmitter, 1979a, 20), authoritarian and liberal corporatism (Lehmbruch, 1979, 54), and pure and bargained corporatism (Crouch, 1979, 188)[2] are all designed to emphasize the fact that fascist-style incorporation is anathema in the advanced capitalist countries. Nevertheless, it is widely held that some level of incorporation is a feature of contemporary corporatism. Schmitter, for example, argues that 'the decay of pluralism and its gradual displacement by societal corporatism can be traced primarily to the imperative necessity for a stable, bourgeois-dominated regime . . . to associate or incorporate sub-

---

[1] The most influential of these is Walter Korpi's *The Democratic Class Struggle* (1983, 4 and *passim*). See also Korpi (1978, 68–70, 317–26) as well as Esping-Andersen (1985) and Stephens (1979).

[2] Offe (1981, 140) makes a related distinction based on 'restraint' and 'delegation' as the two sides of corporatism which respectively restrict or expand union autonomy.

ordinate classes and status groups more closely within the political process' (1979a, 24).

Some level of incorporation exists wherever the government's
relationship to the unions allows it to dominate. In this sense it is
a similar danger to class collaboration. Both involve the subordination of organized labour to the goals of one of the other
industrial relations actors. But, similarly also, incorporation is not
an inevitable result of public involvement. For remember that
public involvement is a two-sided relationship which also allows
for union influence over the government. And the balance of
power in the union–government relationship need not always be
in the government's favour. Indeed, under certain conditions it
can enhance the power of both.

But typically, in order to legitimize union involvement in
public affairs, governments feel that they need to foster the involvement of capitalist employers as well. And this leads to the
danger of capitalist domination of the state. Given the government's need to make the market operate effectively, employers
already have a huge indirect influence over government policy
(Lindblom, 1977, 172). Public involvement threatens to give them
a further directly political channel of influence on top of this. But,
again, remember that public involvement is a two-way relationship which also allows government involvement in the affairs
of employers. And it is possible for the balance of power in
employer–government public involvement to favour the government. This is often something that unions value highly.

An exclusive focus on the two dangers of public involvement
ignores its two advantages: union involvement in the affairs of
the government and government involvement in the affairs of
employers. By combining these advantages, the unions can link
state power more securely to their goals. They can also establish a
tripartite arrangement which will greatly strengthen their ability
to set the terms on which they will co-operate with employers,
thereby helping to avoid the danger of class collaboration. Union–
government public involvement opens up the possibility for a
'social contract' between the two which government–employer
public involvement could then be used to enforce. The emergence
of Australian corporatism in 1983 is a good example of this. First
the unions reached an 'Accord' with the Labor Party which soon
after formed the government. The government then held an

'economic summit' with unions and employer representatives at which the terms for class co-operation were settled. According to one of the employer representatives 'it was like playing singles tennis against a championship doubles combination'.[3]

Finally, there is the danger that centralization will lead to *oligarchy* and in particular to oligarchic union leadership. Oligarchy is not only a danger because of centralization. It can also arise as a result of class co-operation and public involvement. That is, to use a more general term, it can arise as a result of 'interest intermediation' (Schmitter, 1979b; 1982).

The *pelegos* phenomenon might be a good name for this latter danger. Pelegos is a Brazilian word for sheepskin saddle blankets. In the 1950s, Brazilians gave this name to their union leaders who were seen to be performing an analogous role: sitting above the workers and underneath their masters with the effect of merely cushioning the former from the weight of the latter (Sabel, 1981, 223). It matters little whether the rider is the capitalists or the government. The point is that the union leaders take on an identity and interests separate from their members.

The Brazilian pelegos are a particularly graphic product of a more general danger that arises whenever there is interest intermediation. Intermediation creates the possibility of oligarchy because it enables union leaders to have a dual relationship with their members: they represent their members, but they can also discipline them.[4] Herein lies the danger. The possibility of doing deals with the employers or the government provides the opportunity for union leaders to play off their members and their bargaining partners to their own advantage. Moreover, as a result of frequent interaction, union leaders may come to feel that they

---

[3] See Chapter 9.

[4] Interest intermediation 'encompasses both the means through which interests are transferred from, aggregated over, and articulated for members to collective decision-making bodies, public or private (representation), and the ways in which interests are taught to be transmitted to, and imposed on members by associations (social control)' (Schmitter, 1981, 295). According to Crouch (1983, 452) a mixture of representation and discipline is 'the crucial character ... at the heart of corporatism'. Indeed Crouch (1983; 1985) has attempted to capture all industrial relations systems on a one-dimensional continuum going from purely representative to purely disciplinary representation. However, this is only one of at least three attempts by Crouch to classify industrial relations systems. His earliest work (1977) provides a multidimensional classification and he also develops a two-dimensional approach (1979).

share more with government and employer élites than with their members.

In the worst case it can result in leaders agreeing to discipline their members in exchange for increased privileges for themselves: a personal say in government policy, for example, or perhaps a more material benefit like a new holiday house. Through deals like these union leaders can build up enormous personal power and wealth which allows them to move well beyond an undignified pelegos status.[5] But what they continue to share with the pelegos is a separation of their identity and interests from those of their members. Undignified or not, these union leaders begin to take on some of the attributes of an oligarchy.

But my primary concern here is the suggestion that centralization itself may contribute to the danger of oligarchy. The emergence of this danger may be a function of the possibility of doing deals, but leaders would only be able to make use of this possibility if the structure of unions allowed it in the first place. The suggestion is that centralization does just that. Large centralized organizations, so the argument goes, limit the effective control which members can exercise over their leaders and hence open the way for these leaders to discipline their own members.

But does centralization really have this effect?

The first thing to note is that oligarchy is a potential problem for most organizations, whether or not they are unions and whether or not they are centralized. It is a product of the fact that all but the smallest organizations require some sort of officialdom simply in order to operate. Amongst union organizations, oligarchy has manifested itself both in countries like Austria where unions are highly centralized (Guger, 1992), and in countries like the United States where unions are highly decentralized (Lipset, 1983, 388).

Nevertheless, it may still be the case that large centralized union organizations are more likely to be oligarchic than smaller decentralized ones (the size of an organization being a function of two of the three factors that go to make up centralization: membership density and organizational unity). But—and this is my second point—it is far from clear that this is so. There is, of

---

[5] Prior to his arrest for murder and gun-running in 1989 the Mexican oil workers' leader, Joaquin Hernandez Galicia, was a good example of this.

course, a long-standing tradition of thought running through Rousseau and Montesquieu which argues that members can only participate effectively in a small organization (be it a state or a union). But Dahl and Tufte (1973, 108) have pointed out that this is not the only effect of size on membership effectiveness. For while participation becomes harder, dissent becomes easier, and these two trends could well cancel each other out.[6] It is true that an oligarch in a centralized organization is more likely to be dangerous than an oligarch in a decentralized organization, but this does not mean that oligarchy is more likely to develop in one rather than the other. It is not the size of centralized unions, but, rather, the concentration of power within them that leads to the danger of oligarchy.

One way to respond to this is to point out that it is not clear that maximum concentration of power is optimal for unions. According to Lehmbruch (1984, 69), 'the optimum structure is, apparently, not rigid hierarchical centralization but rather one which provides for some limited autonomy for lower organizational levels while giving sufficient authority to the peak association to co-ordinate their activities effectively'.[7] Underlying these observations is an argument that the power of central union leaders depends not only on material resources (like strike funds) that are strengthened by size, but also on motivational resources (especially their members' willingness to act) that are strengthened by local autonomy.[8] However, for a charismatic oligarch this may not be true. Of course if maximal concentration of power is not optimal, then neither is maximal centralization, since concentration of power is one of its constituents.

[6] A large centralized organization also has other benefits. It increases the aspects of your environment over which you can have an effect. Dahl and Tufte call this factor 'system capacity'. By belonging to a centralized union federation, for example, you can hope to influence not just wages, but taxes and unemployment as well. 'Common sense tugs in opposite directions. One moment it seems to say: be effective—make your association small. The next it says: be effective—make your association as large as need be' (Dahl, 1970, 98–103).

[7] A similar conclusion was drawn by an Australian trade union study tour of Western Europe which was seeking to understand the basis for the success of 'strategic unionism' in Sweden and Norway (ACTU/TDC, 1987, 175–8).

[8] Compare with Offe and Wiesenthal (1985, 186–7), who argue that there is a trade-off between these two sorts of resources such that beyond a certain point it becomes suboptimal to increase the size of a union. However, this argument ignores the possibility of a federal union structure which allows a high level of centralization to coexist with local autonomy. Compare with Olson (1982, 24).

But even if all the elements of centralization, including concentration of power, are maximized, a union can still protect itself against the danger of oligarchy. Indeed, whether or not a labour organization is centralized at all, the best protection against oligarchy is the same: strong internal union democracy. This is compatible with maximal concentration of power because while all authority to act may rest with the centre, the decision-making process that dictates how the centre will act may be very decentralized (allowing maximum imput from the rank and file).

This is a matter that deserves far more attention than it gets from writers on corporatism. Joel D. Wolfe and Walter Korpi are two exceptions.

Wolfe (1985, 421) thinks that union democracy, and especially any form of participatory democracy, is incompatible with corporatism, but only because he assumes that corporatism necessarily involves disciplining union members to accept deals which are not in their interests. Indeed in a later article (1988) he argues that unions are particularly well equipped to maintain leadership accountability and avoid oligarchy because the collective interests that they represent are formed outside the unions (in the workplace), and hence beyond the manipulation of leaders.[9]

Korpi's position is closer to mine. He argues that internal union democracy is a function of constitutional rights that specify 'legitimate participants in and forms for decision-making' (1978, 207). And he concludes that although Swedish unions are highly centralized (in all respects including concentration of power) they remain internally democratic (208). However, while it is possible, as I have done, to draw a distinction between concentration of power as a locus of action and the decision-making process which dictates how that power will be exercised, Korpi warns that in practice effective rank and file involvement in decision-making may require some local autonomy to act as well.

So the dangers inherent in a corporatist system are serious, but they are not inevitable. Indeed, as I have tried to show, the same characteristics which give rise to these dangers offer the possibility of important advantages. And it is because of these advantages that corporatism offers the prospect of achieving greater economic democracy. Corporatism has three key advantages:

[9] Compare with Pizzorno (1981) and Sartori (1969), who emphasize the role which leaders can play in shaping the interests of an interest group.

1. it maximizes workers' strength,
2. it enables them to use this strength to obtain the widest variety of goods, and
3. it enables these goods to be distributed to the working class as a whole.

These advantages are a product both of centralization and of the various trade-offs and exchanges that class co-operation and public involvement make possible.

Workers' strength is fundamentally dependent on the internal organization of their class. In this respect, labour stands in stark contrast to capital. For when individual workers meet individual capitalists on the labour market there is a large power imbalance that favours the capitalist. This imbalance in the labour market is in part due to the historically specific conditions under which it arose (and which continue to mark the way it operates), and in part due to intrinsic features of its two main parties.

Three historically specific characteristics of emerging capitalism helped to establish this power imbalance. The first established the need for a labour market. The second and third dictated the market strength of its parties. First, the capitalists or owners of spare capital (i.e. capital that was not needed for day-to-day living) gained control of the most important means of production (Polanyi, 1957, 74–5). This meant that workers had to enter an employment contract with a capitalist in order simply to engage in the production process and make a living. Second, there were relatively few capitalists.[10] This decreased competition on the demand side of the labour market. Third, there were a great many workers. This increased competition on the supply side of the labour market. Supply-side competition took two forms: (*a*) competition between those within the employed workforce, and (*b*) competition between those in the employed and those in the unemployed workforce. This competition virtually guaranteed that individual workers would be price-takers on the labour market.[11]

---

[10] This is especially clear when viewed in a regional context. As late as 1918 Tawney (1964, 104) was reminding his readers that in England 'there are still many towns which are almost dependent on less than half a dozen great firms'.

[11] 'Huge reserves of unskilled labour existed in the agricultural sector of the economy and this made any union strategy based on manipulation of labour supply impractical. In effect, economic circumstances had created a situation in

The intrinsic features which helped to establish a power imbalance on the labour market come about because units of capital can be added together in a way that units of labour cannot. Capital can be easily 'merged' and brought under a unified command structure. And, as joint stock companies show, even if the capital is owned by many different people, the structure of control can be unified. Labour cannot be merged in this way. For labour is always attached to a particular labourer, and, since labourers cannot merge themselves, they cannot merge their labour. Means of production are also mergeable, though not to the same extent as capital. This is because, to some extent, control of machines and primary resources is dependent on control over labour. The machines themselves will not complain, but those who work them might. The possibility of merging many units of both capital and the means of production under a unified command structure gives capital a significant power advantage over labour (Offe and Wiesenthal, 1985, 178; Korpi, 1978, 22–3).[12] This is because the more resources you control the more powerful you are, and mergeable resources are easier to control than unmergeable ones.

Since workers cannot merge, the best they can do to compensate for this advantage is to organize themselves into an association. Association provides workers with a way of gaining some of the benefits of a unified command structure. Furthermore, by organizing themselves into an association workers can also tackle their historically given position of market weakness. For association enables workers to restrict the supply of their labour and hence undermine one of the two forms of supply-side competition which so weakened their market position: competition within the employed workforce. Note, however, that this does not necessarily undermine the other form of supply-side competition: competition between those in the employed and those in the unemployed workforce. Nevertheless, organization has the dual

which the mass of unskilled labour glutted the market and made even the maintenance of a "living wage" extremely difficult. This was the situation that typified the latter half of the nineteenth century in Britain and, to a lesser extent, the 1920s in the United States of America' (Mulvey, 1978, 8). A similar situation arose in countries that industrialized later. In Italy, for example, major population movements from the peasant south to the industrial north took place as late as the 1950s (Piore and Sabel, 1984, 155).

[12] Korpi talks about concentration and mobilization, whereas Offe and Wiesenthal talk about mergeability and unified command structures.

benefit of simultaneously dealing with some of the main historical and intrinsic power advantages of capital. Hence its fundamental importance.

Mergeability is not the only intrinsic feature of the labour market parties that gives capital an advantage. Range of applicability and ease of transformation are two features which are also relevant (Korpi, 1978, 23; 1983, 16). Whereas labour, and especially traditional forms of skilled labour, has a limited range of use and is costly to retrain, capital can be deployed for a great variety of purposes and can be quickly transformed for one use rather than another. To compensate for these advantages labour would have to acquire widely applicable skills and have easy access to retraining facilities. Until recently this has been difficult if not impossible for the great majority of workers.[13] But, as we will see in Chapter 8, a growing trend towards labour flexibility is changing this. Here, however, I simply want to note that even if these two factors themselves could not be compensated for, it is still theoretically possible for labour to counterbalance capital's power advantage through organization alone. This is because if labour organizations can restrict the supply of labour *to a sufficient extent*, they can accumulate more power than they need merely to counterbalance capital's historically given market advantages, and thus they themselves can emerge in a position of market strength. This surplus strength can then be used to counterbalance capital's remaining intrinsic advantages.[14]

So workers' strength is fundamentally dependent on organization. But organization is a difficult business, and it is especially difficult for workers. This is because collective action is dependent on the formation of a collective identity. There are two reasons for this.

The first has been discussed by Offe and Wiesenthal. Because labour is 'attached' to its worker-owner it brings with it a broad range of interests—wages, job satisfaction, health and safety, lei-

---

[13] There has always been a small élite of multi-skilled workers.

[14] Presumably this was behind Engels's remark that unions 'imply the recognition of the fact that the supremacy of the bourgeoisie is based wholly upon the competition of the workers among themselves, i.e. upon their want of cohesion. . . . If the competition of workers among themselves is destroyed, if all determine not to be further exploited by the bourgeoisie, the rule of property is at an end' (Korpi, 1978, 23).

sure and employment security are all uncontroversial examples—
which cannot all automatically be aggregated under a single
given interest calculus.[15] Moreover, labour suffers from interest
ambiguity since it is both in conflict with capital growth over the
share of production, and dependent on capital growth for employment security (Offe and Wiesenthal, 1985, 176, 180, 190).[16] But
without a single interest calculus there is no basis for workers to
settle on an optimal strategy and hence no basis for collective
action. Only the formation of a collective identity can overcome
this problem by providing a collective interest to which all can
ascribe.[17]

Second, collective identity is important as a way of overcoming
Olsonian (1965; 1982) problems of collective action. Since the outcome of collective action is a public good (i.e. a good available to
all workers), and since the participation of any one worker will
impose a cost on that worker without, by itself, having any appre-
ciable effect on the outcome, it may be individually rational for
each worker to desist from participating in collective action even
though each will be worse off as a result. This is the so-called 'free
rider' problem. The formation of a collective identity can undermine the free rider problem by fostering a sense of solidarity
which places a value on participation which outweighs its costs.[18]

This second reason why workers' collective action is dependent
on the formation of a collective identity should not be confused
with the first. The second 'Olsonian' reason is about how to avoid
suboptimal outcomes which would result from individually

[15] Ross (1948) made a similar point in his debate with Dunlop (1950) about the
nature of trade union behaviour and objectives. For a summary see Mulvey (1978,
17–19).

[16] See also Traxler (1990, 44, 46).

[17] See also Pizzorno (1978, 293; 1981, 252–3), Offe (1981, 147), and Regini (1984,
142).

[18] The problem that Olson identifies depends on the assumption that rational
individuals will only consider their private material interests (Olson, 1982, 19–20).
The value of public goods cannot be an incentive to undertake collective action.
An empirical study of rebellious behaviour in New York and Hamburg by
Edward N. Muller and Karl-Dieter Opp (1986) concluded that this assumption is
not valid. 'Considerations of what is collectively rational can override the individually rational logic of the private interest theory' (Muller and Opp, 1986, 485).
The Olsonian problem would also be less significant if workers saw themselves
primarily as members of federated local plant-level organizations (Crouch, 1982,
65–7; Olson, 1982, 25).

rational behaviour. The first 'interest calculus' reason is about how to establish what count as optimal outcomes in the first place.

But these difficulties are not insuperable, and if they become very well organized the associated workers may even gain a power advantage over the capitalists (or rather the units of merged capital) that employ them. To do this the workers do not need to be stronger in absolute terms. They only have to be strong enough to be able to impose sanctions which would make the cost of struggle prohibitive for the employers.[19] To counteract this the firms themselves will be forced to organize in order to supplement their now inadequate historical and intrinsic power advantages. But now a different logic begins to take over.

Initially capitalist employers will find that it is easier for them to form associations than it was for labour. The capitalists have a clear and, in Anglo-Saxon countries, a legally reinforced aim of maximizing profits. This provides them with a single interest calculus and admits of no interest ambiguity. What is more, since there are many fewer capitalists than there are people working for them, employers' associations have fewer potential members to organize than unions (especially if it is only the employers in large unionized firms who organize). And the smaller the group the less important is Olson's free rider problem, because in small groups a single abstention is no longer marginal and may in itself jeopardize the outcome (Offe and Wiesenthal, 1985, 182; Pizzorno, 1981, 251; Traxler, 1990, 50). Both these factors—the presence of a clear interest calculus and the lesser importance of the free rider problem—mean that capitalist employers are likely to be able to form an association without engaging in the difficult task of forming a new collective identity.[20]

But although capitalist employers will find it easier to form an association, the kind of collective action that their association will be able to undertake will be limited. The very factor that made membership recruitment easy—the lack of dependence on the formation of a collective identity—will serve to limit membership

[19] In fact they only have to credibly threaten to impose such sanctions even if they are actually not strong enough to do so. See Chapter 6.
[20] Elster (1985, 363) comes to a similar conclusion when he suggests that 'capitalist collective action rests on selfish rationality in iterated games, whereas working class collective action rests on externalities in the utility function'.

loyalty (Traxler, 1990, 49). Member capitalists will only be prepared to back collective action by their organization so long as it
serves their individual self-interest in the profitability of their
firms. Thus employer associations will rarely be able to retain the
level of membership loyalty which is required for high-cost acts
of collective solidarity, and will usually restrict their activities to
information gathering, lobbying, and the like.

We can now see that labour associations and employer associations face very different problems. For labour, membership recruitment poses the greatest difficulties since it is dependent on
the formation of a collective identity. But having confronted this
task at the point of recruitment, labour associations can retain a
high level of membership loyalty, even in high-cost struggles, by
appealing to this collective identity. Workers will also be less
prone to judge success or failure according to short-term criteria
because their actions are based on a collective identity which
imbues them with a greater sense of legitimacy. For capital, on the
other hand, it is not recruitment but membership loyalty that
poses the greatest difficulties. As a result, association only enables
it to accrue limited additional power.

Suppose, however, that this limited additional power is not
enough to check the pretensions of organized labour. In this case
the capitalists have no choice but to try to strengthen their capacity to take collective action by attempting to forge a collective
identity. But this will be a much harder task for capital than it was
for labour. The formation of a collective identity is dependent on
an ideology or set of values that fosters cohesion within the collective.[21] Ideological resources which foster a sense of class cohesion
are not readily available for the capitalist class. Just because they
have long-standing historical and intrinsic power advantages,
members of the capitalist class have been able to pursue their
individual material interests, and have never had to develop the
kind of class-based ideological resources which have been an
essential feature of the labour movement (Pizzorno, 1981, 253).
Indeed, if there is an ideology with which the capitalist class is
associated it is one which glorifies 'non-ideological' individual
material interests as the main source of legitimate social action.

---

[21] 'Ideology reinforces the solidarity of those who belong to [an] organization
by generating the feeling that all of them share certain goals towards which
durable collective action can be oriented' (Pizzorno, 1981, 253).

More generally, since all such 'bourgeois ideologies' eschew class-based values, they are not very helpful for forming the required class-based collective identity.[22] In short, precisely because capital has so long been dominant, firms will find it difficult to generate a collective identity which would enable their associations to renew their power advantage over a highly organized labour force.

What the preceding discussion shows is that it is not just organization, but very high levels of organization, which is of fundamental importance if labour is seeking a power advantage over capital. Let me try to summarize the discussion. In their much discussed article, Offe and Wiesenthal (1985) identified two logics of collective action. But in a sense there are three. Capital is already organized, or 'merged', when it confronts individual workers on the labour market (logic one). Therefore, to have any chance of overcoming the power advantage which capital gains from mergeability, and in order to improve its market position by restricting its supply, labour must associate or organize (logic two). However, if labour can achieve high levels of organization the advantage begins to flow the other way. Capital, or rather units of merged capital, will then also be forced to associate but will have difficulty in gaining the same power advantage from association that labour did (logic three). The more organized labour becomes, the more capital will have to rely on associative forms of power and the more it will be subject to this difficulty. At very high levels of organization it is labour that has the power advantage. Hence the advantage of very high levels of organization. And hence the advantage of corporatism. For centralization is one of the defining features of corporatism and represents the maximum possible level of organization. Whereas a decentralized industrial relations system like neo-liberalism favours capital by restraining logic two's ability to challenge logic one, a centralized system like corporatism can favour labour by pitting an unrestrained logic two against logic three.

---

[22] It is possible that a kind of 'negative class consciousness' (Hilton, 1973, 130) could emerge if the capitalists thought of the workers as a class and noticed that the workers were treating them (the capitalists) as a class. But this kind of class identity does not involve class-based values which could then be appealed to in order to generate solidarity.

Centralization is not the only characteristic of corporatism that strengthens the position of labour. When centralization is combined with public involvement and class co-operation, a system of generalized political exchange (Pizzorno, 1978; Marin, 1990b) or societal bargaining (Korpi, 1983, 20) can be established.[23] This mechanism allows unions to further strengthen their position by combining their industrial power with the political power of the government. The possibility of this sort of coalition between the unions and the government is especially important when the government is controlled by labour and social democratic parties which have long-standing historical and institutional ties with the union movement. In these cases a coalition between the unions and government is effectively a coalition between the industrial and political wings of the labour movement. There are also some, less frequent, cases where a coalition between labour and capital has been used to force changes on a government.[24]

Generalized societal bargaining is also important for another reason. It gives corporatism its second advantage by enabling workers to use their strength to obtain the widest variety of goods. A system of generalized societal bargaining enables complex three-way trade-offs between organized labour, employers, and the government. These trade-offs enable unions to use the leverage which they gain from their industrial strength to achieve goals over which they have no direct leverage. Low unemployment, tax cuts, increased welfare spending, new investment, and, last but not least, greater economic democracy are all typical examples of these goals.[25]

---

[23] I prefer Korpi's term 'societal bargaining' because 'political exchange' might seem to refer only to the public involvement. See also Marin (1990b), Regini (1984, 128 ff.), and Lehmbruch (1984, 67).

[24] The legalization of black trade unions in South Africa following the Wiehan and Riekert Commissions in 1979 owed something to such a coalition. Examples can also be found in the advanced capitalist countries. In Germany, for example, both unions and employers associations strongly opposed aspects of a 1989 amendment to the Works Constitution Act (Jacobi *et al.*, 1992, 240–1; Archer, 1992, 156).

[25] Of course economic democracy does involve some issues, such as the organization of work, over which unions do have direct industrial influence. But it also involves matters outside the industrial arena. Above all, it involves company law through which government sets a basic constitution or dispensation for control of the firm.

Many of these will feed back into the first advantage and further increase workers' strength. Low unemployment is a good example of this. Minimizing unemployment is not only good in itself. It also greatly increases labour's market strength by increasing the demand for labour.[26] Again, societal bargaining enables workers to achieve goals like low unemployment because it is characterized by both high levels of union–government public involvement and high levels of centralization. Public involvement enables unions to exchange something over which they have some direct control (such as wage demands or industrial disruption) for control over something which would otherwise be outside their sphere of influence (macro-economic policy). Centralization enables unions to engage in this sort of bargaining at a national level.[27]

What distinguishes the danger-stressing pessimists among corporatist theorists from the potential-stressing optimists is the recognition that trade-offs like these can be in the interest of the workers. Whereas the pessimists tend to see corporatism as a system that arose in the interests of the state or capital or probably both, the optimists emphasize that unions can enter into corporatist arrangements as part of a rational strategy for achieving workers' goals (Regini, 1984, 127).

The paradigm corporatist trade-off is an incomes policy (Lehmbruch, 1979, 152). Incomes policies typically lie at the heart of corporatist deals because, of all the issues which are of mutual concern to the government, business, and the unions, wage rates are one of the few over which unions have a great deal of direct influence (Panitch, 1986, 147).[28] Wages are the principal reward which workers receive for entering the labour market, and influencing this reward is widely viewed as the primary *raison d'être* of unionization,[29] and thus is the goal to which most union organiz-

[26] Korpi (1983, 4) and Sabel (1981, 220) both emphasize this as one of the most important features of corporatism.

[27] There is a wide variety of evidence from cross-country comparisons which suggests that the maintenance of low levels of unemployment is a characteristic feature of corporatist systems (Cameron, 1984; Bruno and Sachs, 1985; Rowthorn and Glyn, 1990). See Chapter 7.

[28] Indeed, in one influential economic model of trade union behaviour—the so-called 'monopoly model' (Oswald, 1985, 166)—unions are assumed to be able to set the wage rate unilaterally.

[29] See, for example, the Hancock Committee (1985).

ation is geared. But it is important to note that incomes are not the only issue over which unions have a major influence. Working practices and conditions also fall into this category, and, as we will see in subsequent chapters, they are also important bargaining chips in certain circumstances.

Corporatist incomes policy trade-offs take many forms.[30] Where a labour or social democratic government is in power they often involve a deal in which unions agree to restrain their wage demands in return for tax cuts or increased transfer payments (like social security benefits and pensions). This allows improvements in the 'industrial wage' to be traded off for improvements in the 'social wage'. It is easy to see why it may be rational for unions to agree to this sort of deal. The logic of the deal is straightforward: they seek to maximize their members' income. In the chapters which follow I will argue that the same sort of trade-off can proceed for non-income benefits, and that, in particular, greater income can be traded off for greater control.

Finally, the third advantage of corporatism is that it enables unions to distribute their gains amongst the working class as a whole. This is crucial because a strategy for achieving economic democracy is useless if it only achieves economic democracy for a select few. The arguments that justify economic democracy for one group of workers justify it for all workers. If everybody cannot share the freedom of economic democracy then we have merely reproduced a different sort of 'class' society.[31] But this is just where a less centralized system of industrial relations is likely to lead. In a less centralized system, whatever strength labour manages to acquire will be tied to particular groups of workers. Unable to co-ordinate either their demands or their actions with other groups of workers, the only rational strategy will be to formulate and pursue goals in their own sectional interest. If the industrially strong make gains they will not flow on to the industrially weak.[32] Corporatism, on the other hand, because it involves

[30] For a comprehensive list of these forms see Boston (1983, 77–8), and for a good European-wide comparative discussion of them see Flanagan *et al.* (1983, 660–85).

[31] Much of the writing about an emerging dualism in the labour market is concerned precisely with new divisions of this sort (Goldthorpe, 1984b).

[32] The case of the United States illustrates this well. Unskilled auto workers earn almost three times as much as unskilled textile workers (Rowthorn, 1992).

a centralized union movement, forces workers to mediate their different sectional interests and allows the power of industrially strong sections of the work-force to be used to the advantage of the industrially weak. In this sense corporatism is a class policy.[33]

[33] It is notable that corporatism has often been strongest in those countries where social democratic parties have a past which is heavily influenced by Marxism and its class-based ideology (Goldthorpe, 1984b, 327).

6

The Corporatist Trade-off Strategy

In the last chapter I tried to show that corporatism has three key advantages over alternative industrial relations systems. In this chapter I will try to show that these advantages provide the basis for a feasible strategy for achieving economic democracy. In particular I will appeal to corporatism's first and second advantages.

Corporatism's first advantage is that it maximizes workers' strength. This advantage gives labour a major influence over a number of critical industrial relations issues. In this and subsequent chapters I will be especially concerned with two such issues: the level of wage increases and the modernization of production. Wage increases are fairly self-explanatory. However, the modernization of production may involve one or more of a variety of issues. Production requires both workers and their tools, and so its modernization may involve (1) the modernization of the workforce itself (which typically leads to issues about training and skills), (2) the modernization of the tools (which typically leads to issues about new technology), or (3) the modernization of the relationship either between the workers themselves or between the workers and their tools (which typically leads to issues about the organization of work). For reasons that will become clear I will sometimes refer to the level of wage increases and the rate of modernization of production as 'exchangeable goods'.

Corporatism's second advantage is that it enables workers to use their strength to obtain a wider variety of goods than in other industrial relations systems. This advantage gives labour the opportunity to acquire some of the direct control which it needs in order to move towards greater economic democracy. In particular it gives labour the opportunity to trade-off exchangeable goods like wage increases for greater control.

In a pure capitalist firm all direct control is vested in the hands of the capitalists (or shareholders). However, this direct control can be disaggregated in two different ways.

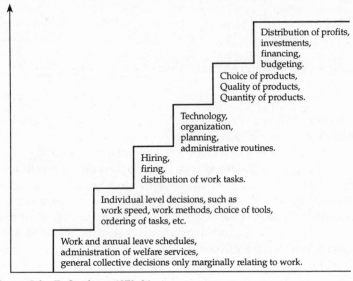

Distribution of profits, investments, financing, budgeting.

Choice of products, Quality of products, Quantity of products.

Technology, organization, planning, administrative routines.

Hiring, firing, distribution of work tasks.

Individual level decisions, such as work speed, work methods, choice of tools, ordering of tasks, etc.

Work and annual leave schedules, administration of welfare services, general collective decisions only marginally relating to work.

Source: John D. Stephens, 1979, 24.

FIG. 7. *Stephens's levels of controls*

Firstly, direct control can be disaggregated into a bundle of separable control rights. Each control right entitles the holder to make certain decisions about the operations of a firm. There have been several attempts to list and order the various control rights (or decision-making rights) which exist in a typical capitalist firm. Here I will rely on the list drawn up by John D. Stephens (1979, 24), which is reproduced in Figure 7. The steps in Figure 7 can be thought of as various levels of control. Higher levels of control are more important than lower levels in the sense that they carry greater consequences for the future of the firm (Stephens, 1979, 23).

Secondly, each level of control can itself be disaggregated. Direct control over any given level does not have to be an all or nothing matter. There is also a spectrum of intermediate degrees of control which enable it to be shared. In particular, each level of control can itself be disaggregated according to the degree of control which workers exercise over the decisions made at that level. Moving from lesser to greater degrees of control, the spectrum of control which workers can exercise over a decision includes: the right to notification about the decision, the right to information about the decision, the right to consultation about the decision, the right to minority representation on the body which makes the decision, the right to negotiate the decision, the right to veto the decision, the right to parity representation on the body which makes the decision, and the right to majority representation on the body that makes the decision.[1]

In summary, direct control over a firm can be disaggregated according to the level of control at which it is exercised and according to the degree of control exercised at that level. Thus workers may increase their direct control at a firm in one or both of two ways. On the one hand, they may gain some control over a level over which they previously had no control. For example, in West Germany the pace-setting metalworkers union gained some control over technological change in agreements with employers in Nord Württemberg–Nord Baden in 1973 and again in 1978 (Gourevitch *et al.*, 1984, 137, 168; Streeck, 1981, 149–50). On the other hand, workers may increase the degree of control over a level over which they previously did have some control. For example, in Sweden the position of union safety stewards was strengthened in 1973 to give them a temporary veto over any decision they thought unsafe (Gourevitch *et al.*, 1984, 260).

Sometimes an attempt is made to increase workers' control at every level of control simultaneously. Some of the most important economic democracy initiatives in the 1970s and 1980s were of this kind. These initiatives can be divided into two categories. One set of initiatives challenges the idea that ownership of a firm gives capitalists the right to exercise direct control (or, at least, to appoint those who do). In Sweden the 1976 co-determination law gave unions the right to negotiate the outcome of decision-making at all levels. In West Germany the 1976 co-determination law almost, but not quite, achieved parity representation for workers on supervisory boards. And in Britain the 1977 Bullock Inquiry unsuccessfully recommended a form of minority representation for workers on company boards. Another set of initiatives accepts the idea that ownership of a firm gives capitalists the right to exercise direct control, and instead seeks to acquire these rights by making the workers themselves into owners. By

[1] Cf. Poole (1975, 25–6) and DEIR (1986, 61–5).

far the most important, as well as the most ambitious, example of this was the Swedish Meidner plan, which went through a number of permutations before being legislated into existence in a much watered down form in 1983.

The fact that direct control over a firm can be disaggregated into various incremental increases is important because this makes it possible to envisage a gradual step-by-step transition to economic democracy. Past experience suggests that the achievement of economic democracy would not be a feasible goal if a dramatic one-step transition were the only available strategy. Such a one-step strategy would only be feasible if workers could suddenly accumulate enormous power resources. On the few occasions where this has happened—for example in parts of Central Europe following the First World War—these power resources have proved impossible to maintain. The workers' power was more a function of rapid changes in the external environment than of their own internal organizational strength. A gradual transition allows workers to slowly build up and consolidate their own organizational strength. It requires only that each step results in a partial or incremental increase in the amount of direct control exercised by workers.

The idea that incremental reforms within the capitalist system can gradually bring about a revolutionary change in the system itself has a long pedigree in the history of socialist thought. The possibility of 'revolution through reform' was an especially distinctive idea of Austro-Marxism (Bottomore and Goode, 1978, 39).[2] But it also gained a prominent place in England through the writings of G. D. H. Cole (1972, 91, 106, 148–9) and in Sweden through the work of Hjalmar Branting, Ernst Wigforss, and others (Esping-Andersen, 1985, 21–2; Tilton, 1990, 29, 43, 60).

I will argue that a gradual transition is possible, and that, as a result, economic democracy is a strategically feasible goal for the labour movement. In particular I will argue that:

1. a trade-off in which workers exchange an 'exchangeable good' (such as increased income) for an incremental increase

---

[2] See, for example, Otto Bauer's concept of the 'slow revolution': 'We must construct socialist society gradually, by planned organized activity, proceeding step by step towards a clearly conceived goal . . . the social revolution must be the outcome of the bold, but well-considered activity of many years' (Bauer, 1978, 150).

in control is feasible in a corporatist industrial relations system, and

2. a series of these trade-offs in which workers accumulate greater and greater control until they finally achieve full economic democracy is feasible in a corporatist industrial relations system.

These propositions are concerned with what I will call the 'corporatist trade-off strategy'. This strategy is made up of a number of steps all of which share a similar structure and rationale. I will call these steps 'control trade-offs'. Proposition 1 is concerned with the feasibility of these constituent steps taken individually. Proposition 2 is concerned with the feasibility of repeating these steps in order to compound their affect. Taken together these propositions are designed to show more precisely how the advantages of corporatism that were mentioned above provide the basis for a feasible strategy for achieving economic democracy. If both are true then economic democracy is indeed a strategically feasible goal for the labour movement.

Recall, however, that I am not arguing that the corporatist trade-off strategy is the only or the best feasible strategy for achieving economic democracy—only that it is one of them. It may be that there are other equally feasible strategies. There have certainly been occasions when it has been possible to take steps that increase workers' control without undertaking a corporatist trade-off.[3] Why, then, am I proposing this particular, and apparently convoluted, route to economic democracy?

There are two facts that point to the salience of the corporatist trade-off strategy. Recall that both the strength and the preferences of relevant actors have a bearing on the feasibility of a goal. The first fact concerns labour's strength. The second fact concerns capital's preferences. The first fact is that labour's strength varies with respect to its goals. Some goals are easier for labour to achieve than others. In particular there are some goals, like higher wages and better working conditions, that labour finds it easier to

---

[3] For example, the introduction of supervisory boards in the Netherlands in 1973 was a response to rank and file strike action which involved no specific trade-off on the part of the work-force (Flanagan *et al.*, 1983, 146). The same is true of the Italian 'Workers' Statute' of 1970 which greatly increased union control of the workplace (Lange *et al.*, 1982, 126). However, it could be argued that these gains were implicitly conditional on the restoration of order (Pizzorno, 1978). See p. 117 n. 17 below.

achieve than increased direct control.[4] This explains why labour may seek a trade-off. If labour's strength did not vary with its goals in this way there would be no reason for labour to seek a trade-off at all since it could just as easily seek increased control directly. The second fact is that capital prefers some of its goals more than others, and hence prefers to make some concessions more than others. This explains why capital may agree to a trade-off. For, under certain conditions, a trade-off may allow capital to protect a high priority goal by sacrificing a goal of lower priority.

However, as I have said, my main concern is not to demonstrate that the corporatist trade-off strategy is the only, or the best, feasible strategy. Rather, my main concern is to deal with the sceptics who believe that economic democracy is not a strategically feasible goal at all. To refute these sceptics I need only show that there is at least one feasible strategy for achieving it. And one way to do this is to substantiate both of the propositions listed above. Let me deal with each in turn.

Proposition 1 is concerned with the feasibility, *within a corporatist industrial relations system*, of a single constituent trade-off in which workers trade an exchangeable good (such as increased wages) for increased control. To begin with I will simply assume that the industrial relations actors are constrained to remain within a corporatist system. But this assumption is unrealistic. I have to be able to deal with the possibility that the capitalists or one of the other actors may respond to the corporatist trade-off strategy by trying to opt out of the corporatist 'game' altogether and instead play a 'meta-game' which seeks to change the industrial relations system itself. In order to guard against this possibility I will also have to establish that the maintenance of a corporatist industrial relations system itself is feasible. Thus, in order to establish that a single control trade-off really *is* feasible, I will first assume that labour, capital, and the government are constrained to operate within a corporatist system, and then later consider under what conditions that assumption itself is feasible.

---

[4] In part, at least, this is a product of the earliest struggles of the labour movement which were fought to win recognition of the union as a bargaining partner in matters of wages and basic working conditions. This led to the institutionalization of labour organizations which were most adept at winning gains in these areas.

So until further notice I will assume that the industrial relations actors are constrained to operate within a corporatist system. Given this, under what conditions is a single control trade-off feasible? Such a trade-off can take place if and only if labour, capital, and the government each individually agree to it. It is clear that both labour and capital must agree since the trade-off can only take place if each parts with some of its goods. But at first sight it is not so clear why the government must also agree, since it does not seem to be affected either as a donor or as a recipient of goods. But this appearance is misleading, since the trade-off is almost certain to require action on the part of the government. For example, any significant transfer of control will typically require legislative changes. Furthermore, even if no positive action on its part is required, the government's tacit agreement will still be necessary, since it has the power to impose sanctions which could obstruct an agreement between the two class actors. If labour, capital, and government agree to a trade-off then it can take place, since, as we saw in Chapter 4, they are the only 'relevant' actors.

So, under what conditions will each of these actors agree to a trade-off? In order to answer this question I will assume that, at least for the duration of any bargaining process, all three actors are rational actors. Let me briefly try to justify this assumption.

The assumption that labour, capital, and the government are rational actors can in fact be broken down into three separate assumptions which lie at the foundations of rational choice theory. First, I must assume that labour, capital, and the government can be treated as three unified integrated actors, just as if they were three individuals (the unity assumption). Second, I must assume that each of these actors has preferences (or interests) and is consistent about the weight it attaches to each of its preferences and the order in which it would prefer them to be met (the ordered preferences assumption). Third, I must assume that each actor is seeking to minimize costs and maximize benefits in its own self-interest (the self-interest maximization assumption).

There are many well known criticisms of these rationality assumptions. The unity assumption ignores the fact that each of the actors is composed of a multitude of strategically independent agents. As a result, each of them (especially the voluntary associations that constitute the class actors) has to solve its own internal collective action problem (Olson, 1982, 17–35). The ordered preferences assumption refers to a weighted ordering of preferences. That is, it assumes that it must be possible to attach cardinal, and not just ordinal, values to each preference. But why should we assume that the widely differing preferences of each actor are susceptible to such an evaluation (Harsanyi, 1977, 40–1; Elster, 1989, 61)? The self-interest maximization assumption has been criticized by Amartya Sen (1982, 84–106). He argues that moral and ideological commitment can lead people to rationally choose to act in ways that are contrary to their self-interest (94). In the case of individual actors this often occurs because of a sense of commitment to a community or a class (100, 106). But a similar sense of commitment can emerge in the case of class actors, especially during times of war or economic crisis.[5]

Because of criticisms like these, rational choice theory is a singularly inappropriate tool for analysing many kinds of social phenomena. Nevertheless, the particular phenomenon of class conflict in a corporatist system fits the assumptions of rational choice theory reasonably well. By definition, in a corporatist system, relations within each of the actors are highly centralized, and so the unity assumption is not unreasonable. The closer a corporatist actor is to its ideal type, the more reasonable it will be to make this assumption. The ordered preferences assumption is also reasonable. I have already discussed how the development of a class organization depends on the development of an interest calculus that specifies what counts as collective interests and the priority to be placed on each. Profitability provides this calculus for capital. Labour must follow the initially more difficult, but ultimately more rewarding, task of developing a collective identity. In fact it may well be more reasonable to apply the ordered preferences assumption to actors that are organizations than to

---

[5] The classic example is the sense of national commitment that led the European working class to sacrifice its avowed self-interest at the outbreak of the First World War. 'We shall not forsake our own fatherland in its hour of danger', the German Social Democratic Party Chairman, Hugo Hasse, told the Reichstag (Miller and Potthof, 1986, 55). More recently, looking at the labour movement's response to economic crises in the 1970s, Flanagan *et al.* (1983, 662) argued that 'currency and balance-of-payments crises could sometimes serve as the economic equivalent of war'.

actors who are individuals. The process of aggregating its members' interests forces an organization to go through a process of preference formation in which the weight and priority of its various collective interests must be set out before its preferences can be 'revealed'. In democratic organizations this will be especially explicit. Lastly, what about the self-interest maximization assumption? As I will use it here, 'self-interest' is not restricted to selfish or material objectives. An actor's interests will be treated as a function of all of its values and objectives, both selfish and unselfish, material and non-material (Harsanyi, 1977, 13; Olson, 1982, 19–20). In this way Sen's criticisms of the self-interest maximization assumption can be avoided.

We are now in a position to return to the substantive question: under what conditions will each of the industrial relations actors agree to a control trade-off? By assuming that they are rational we can assume that each will seek to maximize its gains. Each will know how to maximize its gains because each has a 'preference ordering' (or, in Offe's language, an 'interest calculus') which enables it to place each of its goals (or interests) in order of priority. Thus, any attempt to establish a comprehensive set of conditions under which each actor would agree to a trade-off would require a comprehensive knowledge of each actor's preference ordering or interest calculus. Of course comprehensive knowledge of this kind is simply not available, and, even if it were, we could not make any general statements about it, since it would probably differ from country to country.

Fortunately, however, I do not need to establish a comprehensive set of conditions. To establish that a trade-off is feasible I only need to establish that there is at least *one* set of conditions that are jointly sufficient to ensure the agreement of all three actors, and that this set of conditions is fulfilled. In what follows I will try to specify a set of conditions that are jointly sufficient to ensure the agreement of labour, capital, and the government. In Chapters 7 and 8 I will try to show that, in the economic environment that has prevailed in recent years, these conditions have in fact been fulfilled.

Setting out these conditions proves to be simpler than it seems. In order to specify them, let me consider the situation of each of the actors in turn. I will start with labour.

There is certainly evidence that workers desire greater control over their firms than they currently have.[6] In Britain, for example, this is borne out by surveys of both workers and their representatives.[7] According to one survey, 89 per cent of workers' representatives favour 'industrial democracy', and 78 per cent believe that much more is needed (Ursell, 1983, 332–3). International comparisons confirm this (IDE, 1981, 186–92). And historical research suggests that a desire for greater control has long been present among the workers of the advanced capitalist countries. In general, following the initial struggles for union recognition, there have been at least two periods when interest in control issues has been especially strong in the advanced capitalist countries: one from the late 1910s into the 1920s,[8] and another from the late 1960s into the 1970s.[9] Although outside our immediate area of concern, it is also worth noting that there have also been periods when control issues have aroused intense interest in both the United States and Eastern Europe. In the United States there were repeated waves of 'control strikes' in the first half of the twentieth century (Montgomery, 1979, 97–101). In Eastern Europe workers' self-government was a key goal of the revolutionary movements in Hungary in 1956 (Kis *et al.*, 1987), in Czechoslovakia in 1968 (Fisera, 1978), and in Poland in 1981 (Dabrowski, 1989; Morawski, 1987).[10]

----

[6] What follows is merely an attempt to make this claim plausible. It is not meant to provide a comprehensive analysis of the evidence.

[7] For a summary of research see Brannen (1983, 73–8). For specific findings from surveys conducted at the time of the public debate about the Bullock Inquiry on Industrial Democracy see Knight (1979), especially Tables 40D–48D (146–50), Cressey *et al.* (1981), Ursell (1983), and Hanson and Rathkey (1984). For a more recent study see Poole and Jenkins (1990, 52–3). Some studies purport to show a lack of interest in 'control' *per se*, but even these studies show that workers aspire to significantly greater 'influence' (Gallie, 1978, 120–48).

[8] For a good account of the upsurge of interest in control issues in Britain written at the time, see Goodrich (1975), especially the chapter entitled 'The Demand for Control'. On France see Ridley (1970); on Italy, Gramsci (1977); on Germany, Pannekeok (1950) and Gerber (1988).

[9] It is arguable that the period during and immediately following the end of the Second World War should also be included. For example, during the war British unions participated in Joint Production Committees (Schuller, 1985, 43), and immediately following the end of the war West German unions made a strong push for co-determination (Gourevitch *et al.*, 1984, 95–8).

[10] In 1968 Czechoslovaks were asked whether 'the establishing of workers councils would be beneficial to all large corporations'. 53% thought it would, 10% thought it would not, 4% held 'another viewpoint', and 33% did not know or

Of course the fact that workers want more control does not necessarily mean that they would give up an exchangeable good like a wage increase in order to get it. Whether or not they would depends on their preference ordering, and it is commonly claimed that, although workers want greater control, material interests and, in particular, wage increases are a higher priority. In Chapters 7 and 8 I will try to deal with this sort of claim by showing that, even if the workers' *only* preference is to maximize their material well-being, it can still be rational for them to trade off increased wages for greater control.

In fact, however, as we saw in Chapter 3, labour's actual preference orderings are not relevant to the task at hand. This is because, for the purpose of establishing the feasibility of a goal (in this case, a trade-off), we can simply assume labour's agreement. Recall that in asking whether a goal is feasible, I am asking whether that goal is feasible *for the labour movement*. That is, I am asking whether that goal could be achieved, if the labour movement wanted to achieve it. I am not asking whether the labour movement wants the trade-off. I am assuming that it does; and asking whether, given this, it is a goal that could be achieved.

The labour movement is a coalition. It typically consists of two wings—an industrial and a political wing—which have the capacity to determine and co-ordinate the preferences of two of the three relevant actors. The industrial wing actually constitutes one of these actors: namely, the unions. The political wing usually takes the form of a pro-labour party: paradigmatically a social democratic or labour party.[11] Thus by assuming that the labour movement wants a trade-off I am assuming that both the unions and the labour party want one. Clearly, then, for the purposes of establishing its feasibility, I can assume that the unions would agree to a trade-off.

But what about the government? As with the unions, I can assume that the labour party would agree to a trade-off. But the agreement of the labour party alone is obviously not enough. To

would not answer (Piekalkiewicz, 1972, 281). In 1981 Poles were asked whether they favoured the 'full self-management of enterprises'. 78.7% said that they did (Ziolkowski, 1988, 152).

[11] Although it may also take the form of a pro-labour faction in a non-labour party. The post-war Christian Democratic parties of West Germany and Italy provide important examples of this.

ensure the government's agreement the labour party must form the government.[12] What conditions must a labour party fulfil in order to form a government? Since the end of the Second World War the advanced capitalist countries have all been governed by parliamentary democracies in which a party's tenure in government depends on its electoral success. Obviously there is no one uncontroversial theory about what parties must do in order to achieve this success. Here I will draw mainly on one group of theories that has been summarized and defended by Geoffrey Garrett (1986).

According to these theories the main parties of the left and right have a core constituency of partisan supporters. The parties maintain the support of their core constituency by attempting to redistribute wealth and other goods in their favour. In the case of pro-labour parties this core constituency consists principally of manual workers and their adult dependents (Przeworski and Sprague, 1986, 167–79). But the manual working class has never formed more than a minority of the electorate (31–40). Thus the electoral fortune of pro-labour parties depends on the choice made by unaffiliated 'swinging' voters.

But surely, at least for the purposes of establishing the feasibility of a trade-off, Przeworski and Sprague's definition of labour's core constituency is too narrow. Since I am assuming that the labour movement—the organized workers' movement—supports a trade-off, am I not implicitly assuming that the organized workers (both manual and non-manual) who make up that movement also support a trade-off, and hence would support a party committed to achieving it? Furthermore, in a corporatist—and hence highly centralized—industrial relations system would these workers not constitute a majority of the electorate? I think not. While it may be better to think of labour's core constituency as consisting of union members who are committed to a trade-off,

---

[12] This is not to deny the possibility that a non-labour government may agree to a trade-off. The Italian Christian Democratic government between 1977 and 1979 is frequently cited as an example (Lange *et al.*, 1982, 157–73; Regini, 1987, 198–200; Bull, 1988, 90–4), although it is important to note that at that time the Christian Democrats were dependent on the parliamentary support of the Communists. While not in the government itself, 'there is little doubt that . . . [the Communist Party] was a daily participant in the major decisions of the national government, especially those concerned with the management of the political economy' (Lange *et al.*, 1982, 161).

I do not thereby have to assume that all union members are so committed. By assuming that the labour movement supports a trade-off I am only implicitly assuming that a *majority* of union members are committed to it. Even in a country as highly union-ized as Sweden,[13] more than 84 per cent of unionists would have to be committed before they could form an electoral majority.[14] This seems unlikely. Even amongst blue collar (or manual) union-ists this percentage of support has never been forthcoming, and amongst white collar unionists half of this percentage is the norm (Esping-Andersen, 1985, 122; Przeworski and Sprague, 1986, 176). Furthermore, public sector workers would not stand to benefit in the same way from economic democracy and hence may be less sympathetic. Even in Sweden, which has only a small national-ized sector, private sector unionists alone cannot form a majority.

So whichever way labour's core constituency is defined, a pro-labour party can only form a government if it has the support of swinging voters. Now there is a good deal of evidence to suggest that swinging voters give their support to the party which they think will best manage the national economy (Butler and Stokes, 1974, 388–402; Kinder and Kiewiet, 1981; Lewis-Beck and Eulau, 1985; Feldman, 1985; Garrett, 1986). If this is true, then electoral success depends on maintaining the support of core voters by pursuing redistributive policies, while simultaneously winning the support of swinging voters by demonstrating a capacity for successfully managing the national economy. In order to get elected or re-elected a pro-labour party has to fulfil both of these requirements.

At times this has favoured the pro-labour parties. At other times it has favoured their opponents. For example, following the Great Depression in the 1930s it was possible to argue that redis-tributing income to labour served the national economic interest (Bowles and Gintis, 1986, 6). Since the mid 1970s, however, it has been more plausible to argue that redistribution of income away

[13] Where about 85% of the workforce belong to trade unions.

[14] There were 6.2 million people eligible to vote in the 1988 general election (Bergstrom, 1988, 4, 11). 86% actually voted, although a 90% participation rate has been typical in previous elections. Of these eligible voters about 2.3 million are members of LO, the blue collar union federation, and about 1.4 million are mem-bers of the two main white collar federations. (These figures are slightly inflated because they include 16- and 17-year-old union members who cannot vote.) For details see The Swedish Institute (1987).

from labour best serves the national interest (Bowles and Gintis, 1986, 7).

When can a pro-labour party that supports a trade-off fulfil both the requirements for electoral success? We can assume that the first requirement will always be fulfilled. A trade-off would redistribute control to the organized workers who form the party's core constituency. And, by assumption, control is precisely what the organized workers want. This leaves the question of national economic management. Whether a trade-off fulfils the requirements of national economic management depends on both the current economic environment and the nature of the exchangeable good. It is possible to conceive of a situation in which the trade-off alone fulfils this requirement, and consequently that, simply in virtue of its support for this trade-off, a pro-labour party could be elected to government. However, it is more realistic to think of the trade-off as standing alongside a package of policies. It would then be this package of policies that would have to fulfil the requirements of national economic management. In this case the trade-off itself would only have to satisfy a weaker requirement: it would only have to be *compatible* with the requirements of national economic management.[15] Here I will simply assume that a pro-labour party can put together a satisfactory package of policies.[16] By making this assumption I can focus attention on whether the trade-off itself is compatible with the requirements of national economic management.

The criterion for judging the requirements of national economic management will vary both over time and from country to country. It will be a function of the specific problems facing a country in a given period, and how these are interpreted by economists, by politicians, by the media, and ultimately by the voters: especially those swinging voters whose vote is based on these considerations. For example, there is evidence that in the

[15] A trade-off is compatible with the requirements of national economic management if it does not hinder (or prejudice) their fulfilment. The set of compatible trade-offs includes, as a special case, the subset of trade-offs which positively foster the fulfilment of these requirements.

[16] This clearly restricts the generality of my analysis. But it is not an unreasonable restriction. Post-war political history suggests that pro-labour parties are able to put together an electorally satisfactory package of policies (Cameron, 1984, 158–163; Castles, 1978, 9–11), although this may be becoming more difficult (Piven, 1991, 1–19). Alternatively, the discussion that follows could be thought of as considering when a trade-off is feasible for the labour movement *once in government*.

second half of the 1960s in Britain the country's balance of payments became the main criterion for judging the economic competence of political parties (Butler and Stokes, 1974, 399–402). Earlier in that decade the level of unemployment had played this role (396). In the next two chapters I will identify two criteria for judging economic competence that were applied across the advanced capitalist world: one from the mid-1970s to the early 1980s, and the other from the mid-1980s to the early 1990s. I will then consider whether a trade-off is compatible with these criteria.

I have been trying to establish what conditions need to be fulfilled in order for the government to agree to a trade-off. We have seen that for the purpose of establishing its feasibility, we can assume that a pro-labour party would support a trade-off. Thus, if that party forms the government, the government will also support trade-off. So what conditions must a pro-labour party fulfil in order to form a government? We have seen that if we assume that such a party can put together a package of policies that meet the requirements of national economic management, then only one condition remains to be fulfilled: the trade-off must be compatible with the requirements of national economic management. If this condition is fulfilled then we can assume that a pro-labour party will form a government which will join the unions in agreeing to the trade-off.[17]

That just leaves the capitalists. What further conditions must be

[17] Note, however, that this conclusion and the voting theories on which it is based are only valid during peacetime. At other times wider questions of defence and social order take precedence over questions of economic management. During these periods a trade-off must meet a different condition if it is to win the support of government: it must assist (or at least be compatible with) the government's efforts to remove threats to social order. Indeed, it is arguable that the maintenance of social order is the most basic goal of all government activity (Schott, 1984, 187; Pizzorno, 1978, 279–80). Given that class conflict is a major source of disorder, the fact that a trade-off is a potential source of class co-operation is in itself a reason for the government to endorse it. When social order is under serious threat—for example, during a time of war or revolution—the government will be especially keen to enforce class co-operation, and may actively promote a trade-off like the one that we are discussing. Something of this sort happened in a number of European countries during, and immediately after, the First World War, when various government-sponsored attempts were made to increase the influence of workers over workplace decision making. In Britain, for example, Whitley Works Committees were set up during the war in response to widespread worker militancy (Phelps Brown, 1983, 140–4). In Germany, Works Councils were set up after the war in order to try to absorb some of the energies that had fired the revolutionary workers' councils (Ryder, 1967, 237–9; Miller and Potthoff, 1986, 71–7; Moses, 1982, 291–320).

fulfilled if the capitalists are also to agree to a trade-off? We certainly cannot assume that, left to themselves, the capitalists would want a trade-off. However, we can assume, as discussed earlier, that they are rational actors. This means that the capitalists will only agree to a trade-off if they prefer an exchangeable good more than the control that they would lose. Now we clearly do not have comprehensive knowledge about the preference ordering (or the interest calculus) of the capitalist class. But we do know something about this class's preferences and interests. In particular, we know something about their 'vital interests', and, as it happens, this is sufficient for ascertaining the feasibility of a trade-off. Vital interests are literally 'vital'. They are interests which must be met for the actor's 'life' to continue. Because of this, vital interests always take precedence over all other interests. They are non-negotiable interests, or, to put it another way, they are interests for which all other interests are negotiable.

It is sometimes suggested that control itself is one of the capitalists' vital interests, and hence that a trade-off of the sort contemplated here would be impossible. I think that this view is mistaken. For while capitalists certainly place a high value on control, they place an even higher value on making a profit. 'Making a profit' does not mean 'making the maximum profit', it simply means 'not making a loss'. In this sense, 'making a profit' is a paradigm example of a vital interest. By investing capital in a firm a capitalist may be seeking to pursue a wide range of goals. But whatever these other goals, if the firm in which the capitalist has invested does not make a profit, it cannot continue to operate, and these other goals cannot be pursued.[18] Hence the capitalist has a vital interest in making a profit.

Clearly, however, profits can be threatened to varying degrees. Figure 8 shows the the maximum control which the capitalists will be prepared to trade off for any given threat to profits. At one extreme, when profits are reduced to zero (P_0), that is, when making a profit itself is threatened, then it can be rational for the capitalists to trade off their total direct control (C_t) since making a profit is a vital interest. At the other extreme, where there is no threat to profits, that is, where the capitalists' total profits (P_t) are

[18] Since there are situations in which losses can be sustained in the short term, this statement should be taken as applying to some appropriate longer period of time (as defined, perhaps, by bankruptcy laws).

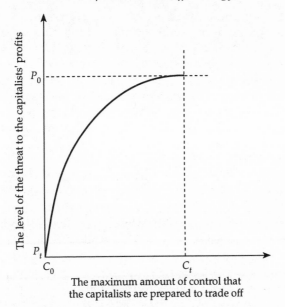

FIG. 8. *The maximum control that capitalists are prepared to trade off for any given profit-threat*

secure, then it is not rational for the capitalists to trade off any of their control (C_0), since we are assuming that left to themselves the capitalists do not want to give up any control. If we make the usual assumption of a decreasing marginal rate of substitution, then in between these two extremes, the smaller the threat to profits, the smaller the amount of control the capitalists will be prepared to trade off for any given unit of threatened profits. Hence the shape of the curve.

Thus if the workers have an exchangeable good that threatens the capitalists' profits, then it can be rational for capitalists to agree to some form of control trade-off.[19] Here, then, is one of the conditions we are looking for: the workers must have an exchangeable good that threatens the capitalists' profits.

Note, however, that this condition has been formulated 'con-

---

[19] This threat need not be explicit. A tacit understanding on the part of management that the threat exists is enough to fulfil the condition. Thus the presence of a threat, and, more generally, the exercise of workers' strength, may appear almost invisible, and for this reason indicators of industrial action such as the level of strike activity are not necessarily a good guide.

servatively' on the basis of a worst case assumption about the capitalists' desire to maintain control. The advantage of making worst case assumptions is that they lead to strong conditions which, if fulfilled, leave no room for further dispute. However, it may be that in reality the worst case assumption about capitalist preferences is too pessimistic, and hence that the resulting conditions could be weakened. There have always been a few cases (for example, amongst Quaker capitalists) where this has been so. Now, however, there are some reasons for thinking that this is so more generally.

For one thing, there is a growing body of evidence that suggests that increasing the control that workers have over their immediate working environment increases their productivity and hence can increase profitability.[20] If they accept these findings, the capitalists themselves may opt for a trade-off which increases workers' control, especially where these increases do not threaten their overall control of their firms' higher level strategic decisions.[21] The trade-offs that constitute the first few steps along the corporatist road to economic democracy are, in themselves, unlikely to threaten this overall control.

It is also worth pointing out that it is actually a very common thing for capitalists to trade off control for either a greater or even just a more secure profit. Such a trade-off is made whenever a capital owner chooses to invest through, say, banks or government bonds, or through pension and life assurance funds,[22] rather than through share ownership *per se*. The capital that is raised in this way is ultimately used to support a variety of economic activities, including those of private firms. But the capitalists whose money is being lent to or invested in these firms are happy to leave control of these firms in other people's hands. So presumably what matters to them is not control *per se*, but rather the consequences of control. This suggests that there are at least some

[20] Paul Blumberg (1968) reviews some of the earlier literature and provides some additional evidence of his own based on a reinterpretation of the so-called 'Mayo experiments'. See espcially Chapters 2, 3, 5, and 6. Blumberg's work marks the beginning of a still growing wave of similar literature, some of which I will consider in Chapter 8.

[21] Sections of the US automobile industry, for example, have already opted for this approach (Wood, 1988, 103–9).

[22] Pensions and life assurance funds own more than three-quarters of British shares (Huhne, 1990).

capitalists who would not object in principle to handing control of their firms over to their workers, so long as they felt confident that they would continue to make a healthy profit. A gradual step-by-step process of change would give the capitalists (and for that matter the workers themselves) time to develop this confidence.

In spite of these considerations I will stick with the worst case assumption about capitalist preferences in order to make my eventual conclusions as strong as possible. For this reason I will stick to the condition that the workers must have an exchangeable good that threatens the capitalists' profits if the capitalists are to agree to a control trade-off.

This condition is enough to ensure that the capitalists will agree to some sort of control trade-off. But it does not tell us how much control they will be prepared to exchange. Later, when we consider the accumulation of control, this will obviously be of crucial importance. Figure 8 specifies the maximum amount of control that the capitalists will be prepared to exchange for a given threat to profitability. However, this is not necessarily the amount of control that will be exchanged should a trade-off take place. Normally there are a number of trade-off options, each of which is preferable for both capitalists and workers to the default option of failing to reach an agreement. This situation is illustrated diagrammatically in Figure 9.

The vertical axis measures the capitalists' utility and the horizontal axis measures the workers' utility. The capitalists' utility is the sum of all goods which capitalists value (including profits and the amount of control exercised by capitalists), weighted in accordance with the cardinal values ascribed by the capitalists' preference ordering. The workers' utility is the sum of all goods which workers value (including wages and the amount of control exercised by workers), weighted in accordance with the cardinal values ascribed by the workers' preference ordering.

The disagreement point, D, represents the utility that capitalists and workers would receive if there is no agreement and the workers carry out their threat to profits. The capitalists' utility at D is reduced from their maximum potential utility by the amount of profits which they lose as a result of the workers executing their threat. The workers' utility at D is dependent both on the nature of the exchangeable good that they acquire (for example, winning

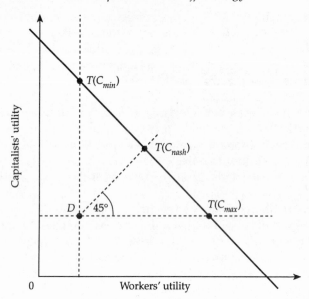

FIG. 9. *A simple bargaining game*

a wage increase may increase their utility, whereas prohibiting the introduction of new technology may not), and on the cost of executing their threat (for example, utility may be reduced if strike action has to be taken).

$T(C_{max})$ represents the maximum control trade-off to which the capitalists would agree given the profit threat embodied in the disagreement point D. For this reason it rests on the dotted horizontal axis running through D, since, in accordance with Figure 8, the capitalists are indifferent about whether they trade off that amount of control or lose the threatened profits. $T(C_{max})$ is to the right of D because we are assuming, for the purposes of establishing its feasibility, that there is some control increase which the workers would prefer to the exchangeable good.

To the left and above $T(C_{max})$ lie other trade-offs involving smaller increments of control than $T(C_{max})$. They are to the left of $T(C_{max})$ because the workers would always prefer a control trade-off involving larger increments of control to one involving smaller increments. They are above $T(C_{max})$ because $T(C_{max})$ represents the maximum in utility terms that the capitalists are prepared to trade. These trade-offs can be joined to form a line each point of which represents a possible trade-off. This is because the parties are either bargaining over divisible goods (such as money or control in the form of shares), or they are bargaining over indivisible goods (such as the introduction of safety stewards or new technology) but with the possibility of side payments (such as money or shares). For simplicity this line has been drawn straight in Figure 9, although this need not necessarily be so (Elster, 1989, 58–9). All points on this line (that is, all trade-offs) that are to the right of the dotted vertical axis through D and above the dotted horizontal axis through D are preferable for both capitalists and workers to disagreement. But while both capitalists and workers would prefer any of these trade-offs to no agreement, they come into conflict over which particular trade-off to choose. The workers want a trade-off as close as possible to $T(C_{max})$ and the capitalists want a trade-off as close as possible to $T(C_{min})$.

In these game theoretic terms, Figure 9 represents a 'mixed interest' (Harsanyi, 1977, 111) or a 'mixed motive' game (Schelling, 1960, 89). The characteristic feature of these games is that they involve both conflict and mutual dependence.[23] The interests of the class actors are in conflict over which trade-off to choose, but their interests are also mutually dependent because both would prefer any one of these trade-offs to disagreement. Mixed interest games can be divided into what are conventionally called 'co-operative' and 'non-co-operative games' (Luce and Raiffa, 1957, 89; Harsanyi, 1977, 110). Co-operative games allow the players to communicate with each other and to make joint binding commitments. They can in turn be divided into simple and general bargaining games (Harsanyi, 1977, 141). In simple bargaining games the disagreement point is fixed and cannot be changed during the game.[24] The control trade-off game represented by Figure 9 can be thought of as a simple bargaining game. Communication can be facilitated[25] and agreements en-

[23] Marin (1990b, 60) refers to these games as games of 'antagonistic co-operation'. This would be a better name for them if it were not for the fact that the notion of a 'co-operative' game has taken on the particular meaning described below.

[24] The disagreement point is also referred to as the 'threat point' (Elster, 1989, 59), the 'conflict point' (Harsanyi, 1977, 141; Schott, 1984, 138), or the '*status quo* or security point' (Weintraub, 1975, 49; Bacharach, 1976, 91).

[25] Facilitating communication between the class actors is often one of the government's main intentions in setting up tripartite bodies. The West German version of tripartite 'concerted action' which Karl Schiller set up in 1967 is a typical example (Lehmbruch, 1984, 67).

124   *The Corporatist Trade-off Strategy*

forced by the government.[26] And the disagreement point can be fixed by the workers' profit-threat.

Is there a unique solution to a simple bargaining game? Or, in terms of Figure 9, is there any one trade-off on which rational workers and capitalists could agree? The founders of game theory, John von Neumann and Oskar Morgenstern (1947), thought not. They argued that the standard rationality postulates of neo-classical economic theory[27] could predict only that rational players would choose a trade-off on the line between $T(C_{max})$ and $T(C_{min})$. Subsequently there have been a number of attempts to find a uniquely rational solution by introducing additional 'stronger' rationality postulates.

The most widely discussed 'solution' is that proposed by John Nash. Nash's solution depends on four postulates which are usually referred to as Pareto optimality, symmetry, linear invariance, and the independence of irrelevant alternatives. He proved that these postulates defined a unique solution, where the solution is given by that trade-off which maximizes the product of the additional utility that each party would receive over and above what they would receive at the disagreement point. In Figure 9 this solution would be at point $T(C_{nash})$.[28] Another solution has been proposed by John Harsanyi, who builds on the work of Frederik Zeuthen. The Zeuthen–Harsanyi solution depends on a postulate about risk aversion. If certain additional postulates are made this solution will also occur at $T(C_{nash})$.[29]

[26] For this reason industrial relations in general and wage determination in particular are usually assumed to be 'co-operative games', although phenomena like wage drift cast doubt on the enforceability of agreements, and hence on the general applicability of this assumption.

[27] Von Neumann and Morgenstern appealed to two rationality postulates: individual rationality, as specified in the rationality postulates discussed earlier, and joint rationality, or Pareto optimality, which states that players would not agree on a trade-off if there is another attainable trade-off which would make one of the players better off without making the other player worse off (Bacharach, 1976, 88; Harsanyi, 1977, 142).

[28] The significance of the 45° line rests on the symmetry postulate which in effect states that if the set of possible outcomes is symmetrical around the 45° line, with the disagreement point on that line, then the solution should also be on that line (Elster, 1989, 57).

[29] Exposition and critical discussion of the bargaining theories of Nash, Zeuthen–Harsanyi, and others can be found in wide range of sources. I have made use of the following: Bacharach (1976), Coddington (1968), Elster (1989), Harsanyi (1977), Luce and Raiffa (1957), de Menil (1971), Schott (1984), and Weintraub (1975).

The trouble with solutions like these is that the additional rationality postulates on which they rely are all controversial. Furthermore, empirical tests cast doubt on whether human beings actually make a number of the rationality postulates that Nash and others attribute to players (Rapoport and Perner, 1974, 103–14; Rapoport *et al.*, 1976, 364–94; Elster, 1989, 63).[30] For these reasons I will here adopt a different approach which does not rely on additional rationality postulates. This approach is best exemplified in the work of Thomas Schelling.

According to Schelling (1960, 22–8), the key to bargaining success is commitment. If the workers make a commitment that the only trade-off that they will accept is the maximum control trade-off, then the capitalists have effectively been placed in a situation in which the maximum control trade-off is the only option available, and they have no choice but to agree to it. In fact, to be more precise, what really matters is not whether the workers are committed, but rather whether the capitalists *believe* that the workers are committed. If the capitalists believe that the workers are committed the effect will be the same whether or not the workers actually are committed. And, if the capitalists do not believe that the workers are committed, then the workers will have no effect even if they are in fact committed. In other words, what matters is not commitment but credible commitment (Schelling, 1960, 35–43). So if the capitalists are to agree to $T(C_{max})$, the maximum control trade-off, the workers must make a credible commitment that such a trade-off is the only trade-off that they will accept. But this is still not enough to ensure the capitalists' agreement.

So far, in discussing commitment. I have only mentioned the capitalists and the workers. But of course there is a third bargaining partner: the government. Even when the workers are credibly committed, the government is in a position to let the capitalists off the hook. The government could, for example, restore profitability, in the short term at least, by offering the capitalists tax concessions or industrial subsidies. It could also undermine the

---

[30] Thus Luce and Raiffa (1957, 119–24) argue that Nash's solution should be viewed as prescribing the norms which an independent arbitrator ought to follow rather than as describing the behaviour of actual human beings. But it is precisely for their descriptive force that rational choice considerations were introduced into our discussion in the first place.

credibility of the workers' commitment by refusing to commit itself to make the legislative changes that may be required to facilitate increased control. Indeed, whenever there has been a major attempt to increase workers' control, the capitalists have typically concentrated much of their effort on weakening the commitment of the government.[31] Thus, if the capitalists are to agree to the maximum control trade-off, both the workers and the government must make a credible commitment that such a trade-off is the only trade-off that they will accept. But even this is not enough to ensure the capitalists' agreement.

There is one more problem. The capitalists can also try to become credibly committed. Indeed, this is precisely what they are trying to do when they make a 'final offer'. If the capitalists can succeed in convincing their bargaining partners that they are committed, then they, not the workers, will be able to dictate the terms of any trade-off. In reality, then, bargaining is likely to be characterized by a situation in which each bargaining partner claims to be committed to its preferred trade-off. But in a typical bargaining situation the possibility of becoming credibly committed will not be equally available to each of the bargaining partners (Schelling, 1960, 28). Thus the victors will be the ones who are best able to credibly commit themselves. This means that in order to ensure that the capitalists agree to the maximum control trade-off, both the workers and the government must make a credible commitment that such a trade-off is the only trade-off that they will accept, and their commitment must be more credible than any capitalist counter-commitment.

I now want to argue that, for the purpose of establishing the feasibility of a control trade-off, we can assume that this further commitment condition will usually be fulfilled in the advanced capitalist countries of Western Europe and Australasia. There are two reasons for assuming that both the workers and the government have the capacity to commit themselves more credibly than the capitalists.

The first reason concerns their institutional capacity. In particular it concerns the fact that their organizations are more demo-

---

[31] The Confederation of British Industry, for example, successfully lobbied the Labour government to set aside the recommendations of the Bullock Committee.

cratic (Schelling, 1960, 27–8). In democratic organizations, negotiators can be given a restricted mandate and forced to comply
with it by those whom they represent. This gives government
and (especially) union negotiators a very effective mechanism
for credibly committing themselves.[32] They can point out that
they do not have the authority to act outside their mandate, and
furthermore that they will ultimately be replaced if they do. There
is no comparable way in which shareholders can mandate top
company officials, let alone the officials of collective associations
of capitalists. Ballots and mass meetings of shareholders are not
held in the course of industrial disputes. Precisely because top
company officials (like totalitarian governments) have the power
to alter their commitments, it is much harder to convince an
opponent that they are not prepared to do so if sticking to their
commitment would leave them in a worse position than breaking
it.[33]

The second reason why workers and the government can commit themselves more credibly than the capitalists concerns their
ideological capacity. The more difficult it is for a committed party
to rationalize its way out of a commitment, the more credible that
commitment will be (Schelling, 1960, 40). Rooting a commitment
in a larger ideological commitment is one way of making it more
difficult to rationalize a way out of the commitment. It will
be especially difficult if the larger ideological commitment is an
expression of fundamental moral principles.[34] Both unions and
governing parties base their policies on larger ideological considerations. In the particular case of a control trade-off, the unions
and a pro-labour government would be basing their commitment
on fundamental moral principles of freedom and democracy.
Moreover, as we have seen, a centralized union movement such
as we would find in a corporatist system could not even exist
without a unifying collective ideology. On the other hand, we
have also seen that capitalists will find it difficult to generate a

[32] Of course I am referring here only to governments and unions in the advanced capitalist countries presently under consideration.

[33] And this is what would happen if they stuck to their position and negotiations broke down. Remember that both parties would prefer some agreement to
no agreement.

[34] Elster (1989, 279) makes a related point in his discussion of the impact of
social norms on credibility.

larger ideological commitment that goes beyond their common concern with profits.[35]

Can workers and the government make use of their institutional and ideological capacity for more credible commitment to commit themselves to a control trade-off? Yes, but only if they also have the strength to act on that commitment and the desire to be so committed. If either is missing the capitalists will have no reason to take their threats seriously.[36]

The government's ability to legislate and impose sanctions, and hence its strength, is unlikely to be disputed. The workers have the required strength so long as they have an exchangeable good that threatens the capitalists' ability to make a profit.[37] Thus the strength requirement reduces itself to a condition that has already been stipulated. Whether the government and the unions want to commit themselves depends on whether they want a control trade-off. But we have already stipulated the conditions that must be met if the unions and the government are to agree to a trade-off. For the purposes of establishing its feasibility we can simply assume that the unions want the trade-off. And we can also assume that the government will want the trade-off so long as it is compatible with the requirements of national economic management.

In other words, so long as the profit-threatening condition and the national economic management condition are met, we can

[35] Ideological capacity may also help to explain why militant ideologically motivated union officials have often been highly effective in decentralized industrial relations systems. Given their espousal of the fundamental importance of class struggle, communists and other ideologically motivated militants would find it difficult to shy away from threatened industrial action should negotiations break down. They would appear hypocritical. In fact, they may even prefer a conflict despite its costs to the workers. In comparison, a 'moderate' official could be more easily prevailed upon to back down from any commitment to industrial action on the grounds that acting on the commitment would be irrational from the point of view of improving the workers' material conditions.

[36] Of course the capitalists may not realize this. Thus, strictly speaking, these are not necessary requirements. For example, the government or the unions might rely on bluff and pretend to have strength that they do not in fact have. But this would be risky, since they would be in constant danger of being 'found out'.

[37] The 1984 British miners' strike illustrates the importance of strength. The miners' institutional and ideological capacity to credibly commit themselves was well established from their 1974 strike. But because, amongst other things, their employers had stockpiled coal, they did not have the strength to seriously threaten profits.

assume that the 'further' commitment condition will be met, and hence that the capitalists will agree to the maximum control trade-off.

Until now I have been setting out conditions for the feasibility of a single control trade-off *assuming that the industrial relations actors are constrained to operate within a corporatist system*. But as we noted earlier, it is unrealistic to make this assumption without further qualifications. In particular, these conditions will only serve to establish the feasibility of a single control trade-off if the maintenance of a corporatist industrial relations system is itself feasible for the labour movement. So under what conditions is the maintenance of a corporatist industrial relations system feasible for the labour movement?[38] To answer this question we must go through an argument similar to the one we have just completed. As before, the task will be to establish under what conditions the three industrial relations actors will each agree, this time, not to a trade-off, but to the maintenance of corporatism. As before I will deal with labour first, then with the government, and finally with the capitalists.

Writers on corporatism have suggested a large number of conditions that may be necessary for its maintenance. Almost all of these refer to the ideological beliefs and institutional form of the labour movement. For example, some writers point to the importance of German-style social democratic ideology with its Marxist-influenced past (Lehmbruch, 1984, 77; Goldthorpe, 1984b, 327), and almost all agree on the necessity of a centralized trade union structure. Now particular institutional forms, such as centralized trade union structures, are, by definition, necessary for the maintenance of corporatism. But particular ideological beliefs are not relevant to our present inquiry since, for the purpose of establishing whether the maintenance of corporatism is feasible for the labour movement, we can simply assume that the labour movement wants to maintain corporatism. Therefore we can assume that the unions will agree to maintain corporatism. Likewise, and for the same reasons as before, we can assume that a labour government will agree to maintain

---

[38] Note that I am assuming that a corporatist system already exists. Thus I am concerned only with the conditions for the maintenance of corporatism and not with the conditions for its emergence in the first place. For more on the emergence of corporatism see Chapter 9.

corporatism *so long as it is compatible with the requirements of national economic management.*

Part of the reason why so many writers on corporatism have focused on conditions that must be fulfilled by the labour movement was that it was usually assumed that it was labour and not capital that was most likely to try to break out of a corporatist system (Streeck, 1984b, 291–8). More recently, however, even those who focused almost exclusively on the pro-capitalist aspects of corporatism have acknowledged that circumstances may arise in which it is the capitalists rather than the workers who have an interest in breaking out of the system (Panitch, 1986, 7–9). Indeed, according to Panitch, it was precisely when the workers began to seek significant control trade-offs that the capitalists began to try to break out.[39] So rather than accept the costs of reaching an agreement within the rules of the corporatist 'game', the capitalists may prefer to rewrite the rules. They may opt, for example, to play instead within the rules of a neo-liberal game. But, in order to do this, they must first play a 'meta-game'. This meta-game (or game about games) will have the same basic structure as the corporatist game. But both what the parties are bargaining over and the disagreement point will differ.

In a meta-game the parties will be bargaining over which industrial relations system to adopt. In a normal industrial relations game—whatever the system—the parties are bargaining over the distribution of the resources (including income, control, and so on) that are generated by economic firms. In a meta-game the parties stop bargaining about the distribution of resources itself, and instead bargain about the system within which bargaining about the distribution of resources should take place. A great many of the disputes which took place early in the history of the labour movement were in fact meta-games. These disputes were often fought in order to force an employer to recognize a union as a legitimate bargaining partner. In effect the dispute was about whether a *laissez-faire* system or a collective bargaining system should be adopted. Likewise, the capitalists in a corporatist sys-

[39] 'As social democratic parties took up demands for industrial democracy and investment planning, it now turned out that it was capital that balked at co-operation on such revised terms' (Panitch, 1986, 7). In particular, in Sweden, 'the attempt by working class institutions to pose fundamental challenges to managerial prerogatives or private ownership as a quid pro quo for wage restraint finds capital withdrawing from the process' (Panitch, 1986, 9).

tem can enter into a dispute about whether corporatism or some other industrial relations system should be adopted.

Just because a meta-game involves bargaining over different industrial relations systems, the number of possible disagreement points is limited. Both the workers and the capitalists can either threaten the no system option—that is, they can threaten to close production down altogether—or they can threaten to act in a way that is costly to their opponent if they are forced into a system that is not of their choosing. As before, the outcome depends on which party is able to commit itself more credibly. Neither the workers nor the capitalists are likely to be able to credibly commit themselves to closing down production for long—although, depending on the attitude of the government, the capitalists may be able to move offshore.[40]

The workers are better able to credibly commit themselves to the second kind of threat. Provided, of course, that they have a profit-threatening good,[41] the workers can threaten that each time the capitalists attempt to bargain in a non-corporatist system they will automatically opt for the disagreement point in that game. For example, if there is a tight labour market, the workers can threaten a wage explosion if the capitalists insist on a neo-liberal system. In effect the workers commit themselves in the meta-game by appealing to their capacity to commit themselves in a game. And as we have seen, in any given game, the workers have a better institutional and ideological capacity to commit themselves than the capitalists.

The ability of the government to commit itself to a corporatist system is likely to be especially important. It seems clear that the government has the institutional and ideological capacity to make a very credible commitment to a threat of legal sanctions (such as fines, or even imprisonment). A threat to impose legal sanctions would be institutionally credible because of the likely electoral consequences for a government that was unable to uphold its own laws. Such a government would face a good chance of losing office. A commitment to impose legal sanctions would also be ideologically credible because the failure to stand by such a com-

[40] While acknowledging this possibility it is important to recognize that in many sectors capitalists remain dependent on the skills and training of their domestic work-force.

[41] And this is a condition which has already been stipulated.

mitment would be seen as undermining fundamental principles concerning the legitimacy of democratically elected governments and the rule of law.[42] Thus the government is likely to be the actor with the greatest capacity to credibly commit itself, and hence the government's commitment to the maintenance of a corporatist system will be critical. But this commitment will only be forthcoming if the government wants to maintain a corporatist system. And, as we have already seen, it will only want to do this if a corporatist system is compatible with the requirements of national economic management. This, then, is the only additional condition that needs to be fulfilled in order to ensure that the maintenance of a corporatist industrial relations system is feasible.

This brings me to the end of my discussion of proposition 1. Let me summarize the outcome of this discussion. I have been trying to specify a set of conditions that would be jointly sufficient to establish the feasibility of a single control trade-off in a corporatist industrial relations system. There appear to be three such conditions:[43]

1. the workers must have an exchangeable good that threatens the capitalists' profits,
2. the trade-off must be compatible with the requirements of national economic management, and
3. the corporatist industrial relations system must be compatible with the requirements of national economic management.

My main task in the next two chapters is to see whether these three conditions have been fulfilled in the economic environment that has prevailed in recent years.

Now suppose that proposition 1 proves to be true and a single control trade-off is indeed feasible. In order to show that the

---

[42] For these reasons the cost to the government of allowing one of its laws to be breached is much greater than the cost of the illegal act itself.

[43] Remember, however, that these conditions are only jointly sufficient if we assume that a pro-labour party can put together a package of policies that meet the requirements of national economic management, and hence will be able to form a government. In other words, these conditions are jointly sufficient for establishing the feasibility of a control trade-off *during a period of labour government*. They are jointly sufficient in general if we assume that, from time to time, there will be periods of pro-labour government. This assumption seems reasonable for the advanced capitalist countries in the post-war world.

corporatist trade-off strategy as a whole is feasible I must also substantiate proposition 2. According to this proposition a series of control trade-offs in which workers accumulate greater and greater control until they finally achieve full economic democracy is feasible in a corporatist industrial relations system. As before, my task will be to establish a set of conditions that are jointly sufficient to substantiate this claim. Proposition 2 can be broken down into two constituent elements. First, a *series* of control trade-offs must be feasible. And second, it must be feasible for these to enable workers to *accumulate* greater and greater control. Without the first element the second would not be possible.

Why would a trade-off be followed by another trade-off, let alone by a series of them? Since it was rational, at the time, for each actor to agree to the original trade-off, something must happen subsequently which destabilizes that original trade-off, making agreement irrational for one or more of the actors. These sorts of changes can be categorized according to whether their origin is internal or external to the industrial relations system. Internal changes can in turn be divided into intra-actor and inter-actor changes. Thus there are three sorts of changes that might destabilize any given trade-off: intra-actor internal changes, inter-actor internal changes, and external changes. I will briefly consider each of these.

First consider intra-actor internal changes. These will occur if there is a breakdown of one or more of the rationality assumptions. For example, the unity assumption might break down under the pressure of generational changes which weaken the workers' collective identity and result in greater free riding. Alternatively, the preference ordering assumption might break down, either because the collective ideology on which it depends breaks down or because of 'log-rolling' between policy coalitions (McLean, 1987, 26, 185; Mueller, 1979, 49–58). A collective ideology and the collective identity and interest calculus that depend on it can only be maintained if they are continually recreated by each successive generation. Even when this is successful, partial breakdowns are a normal part of the process.

Second, consider inter-actor internal changes. These will occur if the industrial relations actors bring about a change in the relations between themselves. These changes can also affect the balance of power between them. After a control trade-off the only inter-actor internal changes are those that result from the trade-off itself. Can a control trade-off itself change the balance of power between the industrial relations actors and hence contribute to its own instability? I will consider this possibility in more detail shortly.

Third, consider external changes. These can also affect the balance of power between the industrial relations actors. Technological innovation, changing consumer preferences, rising prices for raw materials, and wars are all typical examples of external changes. In anticipation of them most industrial relations agreements (such as wage settlements) are designed to be renegotiated every year or two.

By appealing to a combination of these reasons, almost all writers on corporatism argue that no one trade-off will be stable for long (Boston, 1983, 90; Gourevitch *et al.*, 1984, 11; Lange, 1984, 119; Lehmbruch, 1979, 303; Panitch, 1986, 151; Regini, 1984, 131; Sabel, 1981, 215). Moreover, the track record of actual trade-offs invariably supports this conclusion. So it seems reasonable to say that corporatist trade-offs (including control trade-offs) are unstable over time.[44]

But instability alone will not generate a series of control trade-offs. For this to take place the conditions for the feasibility of a single control trade-off must be repeatedly fulfilled. There are a number of economic theories that claim that cyclical behaviour is an inevitable feature of a capitalist economy. I will not discuss these here. Instead I will simply point to the fact that in the advanced capitalist countries the conditions for the feasibility of a control trade-off have indeed been repeatedly fulfilled since the Second World War. If the pattern of the past is a good guide, then we should expect the repeated fulfilment of these conditions to continue into the future.

Instability plus the repeated fulfilment of the conditions for the feasibility of a control trade-off will generate a series of control trade-offs, but it will not guarantee that workers will accumulate greater and greater control. What further conditions need to be met in order to ensure that this accumulation occurs? As we have seen, the amount of control that can be acquired in any one trade-

---

[44] This is not to say that the system of trade-offs (that is, the corporatist system)—as opposed to an individual trade-off that takes place within that system—is invariably unstable.

off is dependent on the extent to which the workers can threaten the capitalists' profits. And this in turn is dependent on the workers' strength or power. Each of the three types of change discussed above can affect workers' power. I will now consider the effect of each in turn.

Intra-actor internal power is dependent on the centralization of an actor. Since the trade-offs are taking place within a corporatist system, the workers' organizations are by definition maximally centralized. Thus there is no scope for intra-actor internal changes to increase the workers' power, and hence these changes cannot be the source of any process of accumulation.[45]

There is, however, a danger which may arise as a result of intra-actor internal changes: the workers may find themselves caught in a 'revolutionary dilemma'. On the one hand, workers' organizations must be highly centralized in order to have the strength to bring about economic democracy. On the other hand, economic democracy requires the control which is won in this way to be distributed among firm-based workers' organizations. But these two requirements seem to be in tension with each other. If firm-based organizations are established before the transition to economic democracy is complete, they might weaken the class-wide loyalties and hence the strength of the workers, thereby undermining the process of accumulation.[46] But if, instead, control gains accrue to the union peak council, national union leaders might find it difficult to hand over control to firm-based organizations even after the accumulation process had been completed, thereby undermining the ultimate goal.[47] The vehicle for achieving economic democracy might undermine the goal itself. That is

[45] This conclusion only holds for the ideal-typical case of corporatism. In reality there will always be some scope for further centralization even in a highly centralized system. However, in such systems this will not be the major source of potential greater power.

[46] There is no doubt that this has been one of the main hopes of capitalist advocates of partial increases in workers' control, and one of the main fears of unionists who have resisted such increases.

[47] Not only would authority over firms not be exercised by the workers who were subject to that authority, but the market co-ordination of relations between firms would also be undermined. The danger to market co-ordination was one of the main themes of those who opposed Rudolf Meidner's original scheme for union-controlled wage earner funds in Sweden (Esping-Andersen, 1985, 299; Pontusson, 1987, 20). For Meidner's response to some of these concerns see (1978, 109–13).

the dilemma. Analogous dilemmas have accompanied most revolutionary attempts to introduce political democracy since the French Revolution. Hence the name the 'revolutionary dilemma'.

A solution to this dilemma would exist if there were an important ongoing role for national union officials even after the introduction of economic democracy, thereby ensuring that their support for economic democracy did not put them out of a job. Shop stewards would not face this problem because they would have an ongoing role in the firm-based organizations. I can imagine two types of ongoing role for national union officials. A strong case can be made for both, quite independently of the need to solve the dilemma that we are discussing.

One possibility is that unions could become guarantors of the new democratic economic constitution. They could develop a quasi-legal function which would enforce the rights of individuals and groups who are unfairly or arbitrarily treated by elected managements (Bacharach, 1976, 96). Given their history and their central role in bringing about economic democracy, unions would be the best available guarantors of the maintenance and integrity of the new system.[48] Clearly this would involve a major change in the function and structure of national 'unions'. They would, in fact, become less like unions and more like a kind of elected constitutional 'court'.

A second possibility is that unions could retain an important role in determining wages. There is no reason to think that market forces left to themselves would bring about a significantly more equitable distribution of income under economic democracy than they would under capitalism.[49] As national institutions which have been principally concerned with wage-fixing for much of their history, this would be a natural role for unions. Again, this would involve major changes for the unions. A clear division of authority would have to be established between the new national

[48] Indeed, according to Freeman (1986, 161) unions are already responsible for the generation of an 'industrial jurisprudence system' under the existing capitalist economic constitution.

[49] Arguments along these lines can be found in Gutmann (1980, 206), Dahl (1970, 106), and Horvat (1982, 268–82). Dahl and Horvat emphasize the effect of unequal incomes on consumer sovereignty. Consumers 'vote' on the product market with their dollars. The more dollars they have, the more votes they have.

'unions' and the firm-based self-government bodies to ensure that the former do not encroach on the latter's authority.[50]

It is also possible that after the introduction of economic democracy national unions could combine these roles—both that of constitutional guarantor and that of wage determination. G. D. H. Cole (1920b, 70) envisaged a combined role something like this for his 'Industrial Guild Congress', and related ideas about a socio-economic parliament were debated in early Weimar Germany. One way or the other, then, it should be possible for the labour movement to agree on an appropriate ongoing role for national union leaders, and hence to avoid the 'revolutionary dilemma'.

Intra-actor internal changes cannot increase workers' power in a corporatist system, and hence these changes cannot bring about a process of accumulation. Only inter-actor internal changes and external changes can do that. To begin with I will assume that only internal changes are relevant. Then I will consider whether external factors tend to reinforce or undermine the effects of internal changes. Now imagine that a series of control trade-offs take place in which each trade-off determines the distribution of income, control, and other goods. If external changes are discounted then the only changes that occur between one trade-off and the next will be a function of that trade-off itself. Let me consider the effect of these inter-actor internal changes in game theoretic terms.

The solution to a simple bargaining game is critically dependent on the value of the disagreement point, D. This is true whether we adopt the 'Nash' solution, the maximal 'Schelling' solution, or some other solution. D can be thought of as representing the unilateral power of each party (Schott, 1984, 141). Unilateral power is the power which each party can exercise by itself and without the co-operation of other parties. There are two ways in which unilateral power can be altered to the workers' advantage. First, the workers can increase their punitive power. The workers' punitive power is their unilateral power to impose costs on other

[50] The failure to define clearly who is responsible for the success or failure of a firm was one of the main reasons for the failure of the Hungarian experiment with market socialism which began in 1968 (Kornai, 1986a, 133–5). The legal division of responsibility in Germany between unions on the one hand and works councils and supervisory boards on the other suggests one possible approach to this problem (Berghahn and Karsten, 1987).

parties: in this instance, the capitalists. Second, workers can increase their positive power. The workers' positive power is their unilateral power to achieve gains for themselves.

The effect of these changes on various bargaining solutions is represented diagrammatically in Figure 10. An increase in workers' punitive power is represented by moving D down to D_1. This improves both the Nash and the maximal solution, but not the minimal solution. An increase in the workers' positive power is represented by moving D right to D_2. This improves both the Nash and the minimal solution, but not the maximal solution. An increase in both punitive and positive power for the workers is represented by moving D to D_3. This improves all three solutions.

Now consider a series of control trade-offs. What effect does the outcome of one bargaining game have on the value of D in the next? The outcome of the earlier bargaining game is a control trade-off. That is, the workers gain increased control, and, in exchange, they desist from carrying out their profit threat. Note that what they exchange is not the ability to threaten profits but rather the implementation of that threat. Thus only the transfer of

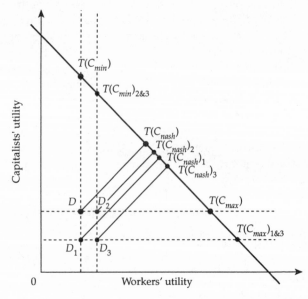

Fig. 10. *The effect of increased workers' power on a simple bargaining game*

control represents a change in the 'holdings' of each side. And therefore, in the subsequent game, the workers' power to threaten the capitalists will be the same as in the earlier game, plus or minus any increase or decrease in power that results from their increased control.

It seems clear that by gaining increased control the workers are increasing their punitive power (Stephens, 1979, 84). The fact that the workers enter into the subsequent bargaining game with additional control means that they can impose additional costs on the capitalists. In effect, they can increase the degree to which the capitalists' profits are threatened. In terms of Figure 10, the increased control gained in an earlier bargaining game will move D down (to say D_1) in a subsequent bargaining game. For example, if the increased control won in the earlier round involved certain rights over health and safety matters, the workers could now threaten to use these rights to delay changes or hold up production, and they could threaten this in addition to their earlier profit threat.

It is not, however, clear that earlier control gains increase the workers' positive power. Although the workers enter into any conflict or disagreement with additional control, they may still lose this control in the course of the conflict.[51] Thus there is no reason to suppose that D will move to the right. Nor, however, is there any reason to suppose that the capitalists can reduce the workers' positive power and move D to the left. The capitalists will enter into a conflict in the same position as before, except for the fact that they will have less control. It may be that the lost control increment was not important to the capitalists' capacity to impose costs on the workers. But this simply means that they can impose the same costs as before, and, hence, that D remains where it was on the left–right (that is, the workers' utility) axis. There is no reason to suppose that the loss of control could increase the capitalists' punitive power.

Thus, if in one bargaining game the disagreement point is at D, then in the subsequent bargaining game it will move to D_1. Consequently the solution of the subsequent game will be a control trade-off to the right of that in the earlier game. As noted above,

[51] The fact that the workers can impose greater costs on the capitalists does not necessarily mean that they can reduce the costs which the capitalists can impose upon them.

this will be true not only for the maximal 'Schelling' solution to which I have been appealing, but also for the Nash solution and the equivalent Zeuthen–Harsanyi solution. This means that, irrespective of which solution we opt for, the workers will be able to win a greater amount of control in the subsequent game than they could in the earlier game. In other words, the workers will be able to accumulate a further increment of control. Since this will be true of each successive pair of bargains in the series, we can conclude that the workers will indeed be able to accumulate greater and greater control until they reach their goal.

I now want to consider whether this conclusion is reinforced or undermined when the possibility of external changes is also allowed. On their own, external changes can both increase and diminish the ability of workers to win control. However, these changes do seem to comply with certain patterns.

I have already suggested that the conditions for a single control trade-off are repeatedly fulfilled. The repeated fulfilment of these conditions ensures that there is a series of control trade-offs, but it is perfectly compatible with a series of trade-offs in which the workers progressively lose (rather than gain) control. To ensure that control is accumulated the conditions must be fulfilled to an 'adequate degree'. In particular, the threat to profits must be at least marginally greater than it was previously.[52] This increase need not be owing to external changes. We have already seen that inter-actor internal changes (in the form of a control trade-off itself) can provide the workers with greater punitive power with which they can threaten profits. Indeed, the profit-threat owing to external changes can actually decrease so long as the decrease is less than the increase due to control gains.

Post-war experience suggests that many of the situations that give workers a profit-threatening exchangeable good repeatedly fulfil the profit-threatening condition to an 'adequate degree' (Schott, 1984, 16–39).[53] For example, situations that require wage restraint in order to contain inflation and situations that require the introduction of new technologies in order to maintain inter-

[52] Obviously this stronger condition entails the weaker condition needed to establish the feasibility of a series.

[53] It should be noted, however, that it is hard to disentangle increases in the threat to profits owing to intra-actor factors (such as the steady increase in the collective organization of workers) from the inter-actor internal factors and the external factors that are relevant here.

national competitiveness have both repeatedly enabled workers to push for new gains. Chapters 7 and 8 are not principally about testing the claim that the conditions for a control trade-off are repeatedly fulfilled to an 'adequate degree'. Nevertheless, by considering situations that are in many ways typical of those that have led to the repeated fulfilment of these conditions, they will hopefully serve to make this claim more plausible.

Periods in which the profit-threatening condition is fulfilled to an adequate degree can be represented diagrammatically by the 'upswings' in Figure 11. In between these periods there can be 'downswings' in which workers lose a great deal of their power. This would seem to undermine the accumulation of control. If control increases are lost during these downswings, then workers will be continually forced to rewin the same gains during upswings, and the possibility of accumulating control will be continually stymied.

Fortunately, there is another effect which militates against the potential for downswings to undermine the accumulation of control. I will call this effect 'control stickiness', by analogy with the

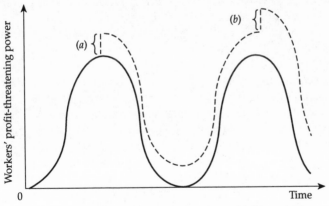

Key: —— Profit-threatening power due to external changes alone
     – – – Profit-threatening power due to both external changes and
           inter-actor internal changes in the presence of control stickiness

(a) = increased power due to an increase in control.
(b) = increased power due to a further increase in control.

FIG. 11. *The effect of control stickiness on cyclical externally produced changes in workers' power*

frequently discussed phenomenon of 'wage stickiness'. A number of economists have noted that since the Second World War, economic downswings have not been accompanied by the reductions in wages that both pre-war experience and neo-classical economic theory would lead one to expect (Schott, 1984, 28–9). This stickiness in a downward direction means that, once given, a wage increase is hard to take away. A similar downward stickiness with respect to control increases has been noted by a number of industrial sociologists.[54]

One of the earliest and most striking examples of this in the post-war period occurred in West Germany. In 1947 unions in the coal and steel industries were able to establish *de facto* a strong form of parity co-determination due to the favourable balance of power in these industries. By the beginning of the 1950s, however, external factors[55] had significantly reduced the power of unions in all industries, and the best that could be achieved generally was a weakened form of co-determination in which only one-third of a company's board of directors were employee representatives. Nevertheless, despite their reduced power, the unions managed to retain strong parity co-determination in the coal and steel industries, and to have it enshrined in legislation during this same period (Gourevitch *et al.*, 1984, 95–102).

There are at least two explanations which contribute to an understanding of downward control stickiness.

The first concerns credible commitment. It is easier to make a credible commitment to maintain gains which have already been achieved than it is to achieve new gains. More specifically, the very existence of a practice strengthens the workers' ideological capacity to credibly commit themselves to it. Typically this is because when the gain is originally achieved, some formula or principle has to be found which enables the capitalists to present the change as justifiable. This then has the effect of legitimizing the change and providing the workers with a principle to which they can credibly commit themselves should the gain be subject to

[54] See, for example, Esping-Andersen (1985), Korpi (1978; 1983), Korpi and Shalev (1980), Sabel (1981), Schott (1984), and Stephens (1979).

[55] These external factors included the onset of the Cold War, the arrival of millions of unemployed refugees from both East Germany and the former German territories that had become a part of Poland and the Soviet Union, and Allied policies in the basic resource industries which they still controlled.

renegotiation in the future.[56] To remove the gain the capitalists would first have to overturn this principle. Furthermore, the workers know that the capitalists have been prepared to accede to their demand in the past, and so will be more confident of taking a stand if the issue comes up again.

The second explanation of downward control stickiness concerns institutionalization of control gains. Once a control gain has been institutionalized it will become more costly for the capitalists to take it back. These costs will increase still further where the gain is enshrined in legislation. Short of investing enormous resources in the uncertain prospect of bringing down the government, it is likely to be impossible to take away legislatively sanctioned control gains during a downswing in workers' power while a pro-labour government remains in power. And even when labour is not in power it is likely to be difficult to take away legislatively sanctioned gains, as to do so threatens established community expectations as well as bureaucratic interests within the state (Weir and Skocpol, 1985, 118).

Control stickiness also seems to obviate the need for the repeated fulfilment of the conditions for a single control trade- off to take place *to an 'adequate degree'*, as defined above. With all previous control gains protected by control stickiness, the workers would be able to accumulate further gains even if their total profit-threatening power were decreasing. However, control stickiness, as its name suggests, is generally only a protection against a short-term decline in workers' power. Control gains are sticky but they are not immovable. If a longer-term decline sets in, they may eventually be prised from the workers. For this reason fulfilment of the 'adequate degree' condition remains necessary over time.

Let me now summarize my discussion of proposition 2. I have been trying to discover a set of conditions that would be jointly sufficient to substantiate the proposition that a series of trade-offs in which workers accumulate greater and greater control until they finally achieve full economic democracy is feasible in a

[56] Indeed, it often seems to be the case that the longer a practice is maintained the greater its legitimacy becomes. Medieval peasant revolts were typically sparked by alterations of long-standing practices and customs (Hilton, 1973, 118–19).

corporatist industrial relations system. There appear to be three such conditions:

1. single control trade-offs must be unstable over time,
2. the conditions for the feasibility of a single control trade-off must be repeatedly fulfilled to an 'adequate degree', and
3. control stickiness must protect control gains during downswings in workers' power.

The fulfilment of conditions 1 and 2 would ensure that there were a series of control trade-offs.[57] The fulfilment of conditions 2 and 3 would ensure that external changes reinforced the inter-actor internal changes that make accumulation of control possible.

The discussion of proposition 1 also led to three conditions. In that case I promised to consider whether or not the three conditions are fulfilled in the economic environment that has prevailed in recent years. I will not undertake an analogous procedure in the case of proposition 2. Given that we cannot be certain about what future economic environments will be like, this would be an extremely complex if not impossible task. Nevertheless, in introducing the three conditions that are jointly sufficient to substantiate proposition 2, I have suggested a number of reasons why, given what we do know, each seems *likely* to be fulfilled.

[57] Although a weaker version of condition 2—namely, a version that required only that the conditions for a single control trade-off be repeatedly fulfilled (to whatever extent)—would suffice for this purpose.

7

Stagflation

In the last chapter I set out three conditions which are jointly sufficient to ensure the feasibility of a control trade-off. I argued that to establish whether or not a control trade-off is feasible in any given period, I have to establish whether or not these conditions have been fulfilled in the economic environment that prevails in that period. What, then, is the kind of economic environment that has prevailed in recent years?

For more than two decades following the end of the Second World War the advanced capitalist world experienced a 'golden age' (Marglin and Schor, 1990) of sustained growth and near full employment. But around the beginning of the 1970s this golden age came to an end and the advanced capitalist countries found themselves in a very different economic environment. Since then two broadly defined periods can be distinguished. The first, from the mid 1970s to the early 1980s, was dominated by the need to tackle stagflation. The second, from the mid 1980s onwards, has been dominated by the need for structural adjustment. This chapter will be concerned with the first period. The next chapter will be concerned with the second. Both, however, will involve the same basic tasks.

In both chapters, and for both periods, my principal task will be to show that the three conditions for the feasibility of a control trade-off are fulfilled in the prevailing economic environment. But I will also consider, as a subsidiary task, whether a control trade-off is still feasible if, instead of assuming that workers want increased control, we assume that workers are solely concerned with their material well-being. Finally, I will briefly point to the recurring nature of the problems that emerge during each of the periods, and to the potential for further control trade-offs in the future.

Let me begin my discussion of the stagflationary period with a brief summary of its main characteristics. The economic environment in the advanced capitalist countries changed radically

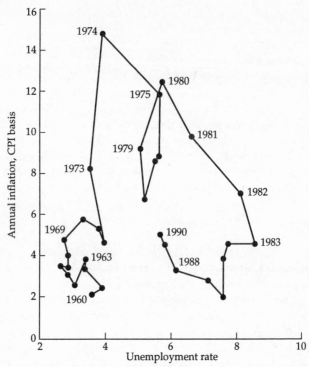

Source: Bruno and Sachs, 1985; OECD, 1993.

FIG. 12. *Unemployment and inflation in the large OECD economies, 1960–
1990*

around the time of the first 'oil shock'—the massive fourfold
increase in the price of oil—that occurred in 1973 (Keohane, 1985,
89). The chief characteristics of the new economic environment
were low or stagnant growth which brought with it rising unemployment, and simultaneously rising inflation. Hence the name
'stagflation'. Previously it had seemed that there was a stable
'Phillips curve' trade-off between unemployment and inflation,
and throughout the 1960s, as Figure 12 shows, the evidence
seemed to bear this out. But after 1969, and most certainly after
1973, this was clearly no longer the case. In the period from 1973–
5 inflation in the OECD countries averaged 11.5 per cent, up from
6.7 per cent in 1971–3. Unemployment rose from 2.5 per cent to 5.0
per cent in the same two periods. Further large rises in both

unemployment and inflation were experienced between 1979 and 1982 (Bruno and Sachs, 1985, 2, 157; OECD, 1990a).

The causes of stagflation are, of course, controversial.[1] It is clear, however, that the advanced capitalist countries experienced two important shocks around the time of its onset. Both drove up the price of supply factors. The first shock was the wave of industrial unrest that spread through Europe in the late 1960s and early 1970s. Beginning perhaps as early as 1966 with wildcat actions that led to riots in Amsterdam (Flanagan *et al.*, 1983, 117), this wave of unrest gained enormous momentum from the French strikes which took place in May 1968 and the Italian 'hot autumn' of 1969. The result was a wage explosion which led to a major shift in income distribution towards labour and away from profits. This in turn helped to bring about low growth. The second shock was a sharp rise in the price of certain raw materials. The first oil shock of 1973 was followed by a further large increase in the price of oil in 1979. And although oil was the most important commodity to experience these rises, it was not the only one. The price of agricultural commodities, for example, also rose sharply in the early 1970s. Coming on top of a wages explosion, these price rises fed into higher inflation.[2] With profits already squeezed before 1973 and real wage levels remaining firm, consumer prices were forced up.

Are the three conditions for the feasibility of a control trade-off fulfilled in a stagflationary environment such as the one just described? To answer this question I will consider these conditions in the following order. First I will consider whether the workers have an exchangeable good that threatens the capitalists' profits. Second I will consider whether a corporatist industrial relations system is compatible with the requirements of national economic management. And third I will consider whether a control trade-off is compatible with the requirements of national economic management.[3]

[1] Good general accounts of the rise of stagflation can be found in the introduction and Chapter 8 of Bruno and Sachs (1985), in Chapter 1 of Flanagan *et al.* (1983), in Glyn *et al.* (1990), in Keohane (1985), and in Maier (1978). My account is close to that of Bruno and Sachs.

[2] See Figure 12.

[3] Note that the order in which the second and third conditions were presented in the previous chapter has been reversed, since it seems sensible to deal with the more general system-wide condition before considering specific trade-offs. How-

First, then, in a stagflationary economic environment, do the workers have a profit-threatening exchangeable good? Even from the brief description of stagflation above it must already be clear that they do. The threat of large wage increases is a paradigmatic exchangeable good. And the wages explosion of the late 1960s and early 1970s demonstrated that workers could credibly threaten to increase their real wages to levels that would seriously reduce profitability. Their threat to do so was credible because they repeatedly carried it out. Whether measured in terms of the share of value added or in terms of the rate of return to capital, profitability fell sharply in the early 1970s (Bruno and Sachs, 1985, 162–3; Flanagan *et al.*, 1983, 10; Glyn *et al.*, 1990, 76–83; Marglin, 1990, 19; OECD, 1990b, 78). By the end of the 1960s, the profit share in Europe had fallen from a 'golden age' high of 25 per cent to 15 per cent. In the United States it fell from 20 per cent to 15 per cent (Marglin, 1990, 19). By 1973, profit rates for the business and manufacturing sectors in the capitalist world's seven largest economies had fallen to around half their 'golden age' peak (Glyn *et al.*, 1990, 74–83). Of course a profit-threatening exchangeable good can exist without there being any evidence of falling profitability, since the threat does not need to be (and indeed must not be) carried out in order to be exchanged. Nevertheless, the claim that workers have a profit-threatening exchangeable good is powerfully reinforced by the evidence that profits do in fact fall when the threat is carried out and the exchangeable good (in this case a wage rise) is retained rather than exchanged.

What about the second condition? Is a corporatist industrial relations system compatible with the requirements of national economic management in a stagflationary environment? I want to spend a little longer on this point.

In order to answer these questions we need first to identify just what are the requirements of national economic management in a stagflationary environment. As stagflation began to bite,

ever, neither condition entails the other. A corporatist system may be compatible with the requirements of national economic management even if the only trade-off that is compatible is, say, a tax trade-off, or even if there are no trade-offs at all that are compatible. On the other hand, a control trade-off may be compatible with the requirements of national economic management even if there are other aspects of a corporatist system such as, say, some form of labour market rigidity, which are incompatible.

two criteria came to dominate public assessment of economic performance. One was the level of unemployment and the other was the level of inflation. The priority placed on these two problems differed according to the country. In Sweden, for example, priority was given to tackling unemployment, while in Germany priority was given to tackling inflation (Hibbs, 1987, 11). But, in most of the advanced capitalist countries, as stagflation continued the public gave greater and greater priority to tackling inflation (Lindberg, 1985, 35). And it seems likely that this was especially true of the swinging voters whose assessment of economic performance is the most electorally significant (Hibbs, 1987, 297). On the other hand, the core constituency of the pro-labour parties remained principally concerned with unemployment. Thus, for the pro-labour parties, national economic management had to simultaneously tackle both inflation and unemployment.

Orthodox Keynesian demand management was unable to meet this requirement, since it further exacerbated inflation. Instead, a policy to restrain aggregate real wage increases became the essential requirement of national economic management. There were four main reasons for this. First, of the two main supply factors that were causing inflation, only wages were fully subject to the influence of national governments. The price of raw materials was largely outside their influence. Second, once inflationary expectations became entrenched, a wages–prices spiral ensued as workers sought ever higher wages for the higher prices they had come to expect. These wage rises themselves fed into production costs, thereby pushing up prices still further and leading to demands for further wage rises to compensate. Since widespread interference in the price-fixing system would have undermined the integrity of the product market (Kornai, 1986b, 1700, 1729), governments were forced to turn their attention to wage-fixing in order to break the wages–prices spiral. Third, wage restraint would help to tackle unemployment, since, by allowing increased profits, it would fulfil one of the preconditions for job-creating investment. Fourth, wage restraint would enable governments to adopt moderately expansionary policies designed to stimulate growth, and hence employment, without further exacerbating inflation. In summary, only through a policy of restraining wage increases could governments simultaneously tackle inflation as well as unemployment. Hence wage restraint was the main requirement of national economic management.

The question, then, is whether corporatism is compatible with this requirement. I will argue that it is. Indeed, I will argue that both theoretical and empirical considerations suggest that corporatism is one of only two industrial relations systems that is compatible with the need for wage restraint.

The theoretical considerations that I have in mind have been forcefully presented by Mancur Olson (1982). Arguments along a similar line have subsequently been developed by Crouch (1985), Lindberg and Maier (1985), Goldthorpe (1987), OECD (1987), Calmfors and Driffill (1988), Pohjola (1992), and others.

Olson (1982, 41–6) points out that where there are a large number of independent unions, each of which organizes only a small proportion of a nation's workforce, then each of these unions has little incentive to consider the overall macro-economic cost of its wage demands.[4] Each union will gain the full benefit of a wage increase while bearing only a fraction of the costs, in terms of, say, the inflation and unemployment, which will result. Furthermore, each union will share the costs of other unions' wage increases, even if it does not demand a wage increase for itself.[5] Thus unions organized in an industrial relations system of this sort—call it pluralism—will be most unlikely to agree to wage restraint. Olson suggests that there are only two ways out of this situation. One involves moving to a more *laissez-faire* industrial relations system. The other involves moving to a corporatist industrial relations system.

If taken far enough, a move towards a *laissez-faire* system would have the effect of weakening the power of unions to such an extent that they would become unable to win wage increases above the market rate. There is, however, a limit to how far the advanced capitalist countries can be pushed in this direction. The outcome of the Second World War drew a line across the political economic terrain which no government could cross. Since the suppression of independent labour organizations was one of the

---

[4] I am not concerned here with Olson's larger claim that stagflation arises from a kind of 'institutional sclerosis' which tends to develop in all stable societies.

[5] The unions can be thought of as being in a Prisoners' Dilemma with respect to each other. See Sutcliffe (1982) and Lange (1984).

hallmarks of fascism, the right of workers to organize became an important symbol of what was free about the 'free world'. The Communist suppression of organized workers from 1953 in Berlin to 1981 in Poland reinforced this symbol. Thus the most that a *laissez-faire* oriented government can hope for is an American-style neo-liberal industrial relations system. And even this may be a peculiarly American possibility. American and European experience of the Second World War was very different. In the United States, which had no direct experience of fascism at home, business was able to launch a major and successful attack on union rights immediately after the war, at a time when, throughout Europe, labour had unprecedented power. In 1979 the Thatcher government in Britain launched the most sustained European attempt to weaken union power. Ten years later it was clear that British unions still retained the power to win inflationary wage increases (Kessler and Bayliss, 1992, 46–8, 193–5).

Whereas the success of a move towards *laissez-faire* depends on forcing unions to accept wage restraint, the success of a move towards corporatism depends on unions' voluntarily accepting wage restraint. The possibility of voluntary restraint arises in a corporatist system because the unions are 'encompassing'. Olson argues that 'the incentives facing an encompassing special-interest organization are dramatically different from those facing an organization that represents only a narrow segment of society' (1982, 48). This is because the more encompassing an interest organization is the closer its interests will be to society as a whole. In the terminology that I have been using, an encompassing organization is basically a centralized organization. But although it is this characteristic of corporatism that features most prominently in Olson's discussion, the other characteristics are also necessary. Encompassing (or centralized) organization only creates the possibility of voluntary wage restraint (Olson, 1982, 52, 92). In order to actually achieve wage restraint there will also have to be corporatist relationships between the industrial relations actors. At least on the issue of wages there must be class co-operation between labour and capital.[6] And public

---

[6] Employers can also start an inflationary wages–prices spiral by competing with each other to pay higher wages for limited staff. Something like this occurred in Sweden in the late 1980s.

involvement will play an important role in clearing information channels, altering pay-offs, and providing guarantees.

So theoretical considerations suggest that, to be compatible with the need for wage restraint, the industrial relations system must be either neo-liberal or corporatist. A number of empirical studies seem to bear this out. Empirical studies of the relationship between industrial relations systems and macro-economic performance can take two forms. They can compare periods in the history of one country, or they can make an inter-country comparison. In Chapter 9 I will draw some lessons from the different episodes in Australian industrial relations history. Here, however, I want briefly to mention the particular case of Britain before moving on to consider some recent cross-national comparative studies.

Britain entered the stagflationary period with a pluralist industrial relations system. Its experience illustrates how corporatism and neo-liberalism became the only available options. Throughout the 1950s and 1960s Britain's pluralist 'free collective bargaining' system was sustained by growing national prosperity. A continually expanding economy was able to absorb workers' demands for higher wages without squeezing profits.[7] But once stagflation struck, wage restraint became a matter of urgency for the government. The Labour governments of 1974–9 attempted to draw the unions into a corporatist system. When this failed the Conservative government that came to power in 1979 began to vigorously pursue a neo-liberal approach, intervening in union affairs with successive waves of legislation designed to undermine their power.

There are a growing number of cross-national comparative studies of the relationship between different industrial relations systems and macro-economic performance. Typically these studies see the structure of the industrial relations system as an important determinant of macro-economic performance.[8] A variety of indices are used to distinguish between different industrial relations systems, but most depend on some measure of labour's

[7] For an account of the period see Crouch (1979), Chapters 1 and 2, especially pp. 32–4.
[8] Although the OECD (1988, 34–5) has cautioned against trying to explain too much through sole reference to systems of industrial relations.

organizational centralization, and this, in turn, is usually equated with corporatism.

Some of these studies provide evidence which directly supports the Olsonian theoretical claim that only neo-liberalism and corporatism are compatible with the requirements of national economic management in a period of stagflation. Calmfors and Driffill (1988), for example, compare a number of indices which rank OECD countries according to their degree of centralization, with a number of measures of macro-economic performance. Their findings suggest that 'both highly centralized and highly decentralized economies are likely to do better than intermediately centralized ones' (Calmfors and Driffil, 1988, 47). This conclusion is supported by Freeman (1988), who uses wage dispersion and union density as a proxy for corporatism. He considers these to be better proxies than the notoriously 'judgemental' indices of centralization.[9] Freeman concludes that 'both highly centralized and highly decentralized labour market arrangements outperform intermediate cases' (Freeman, 1988, 75).[10] Pohjola (1992) also finds a U-shaped relationship between corporatism and various measures of employment performance, and the OECD (1989, 45, 53–4) finds a U-shaped relationship between corporatism and real wage flexibility.

However, other studies, notably those of Bruno and Sachs (1985) and Tarantelli (1986), find that corporatist systems outperformed all others during the period of stagflation. They provide evidence that the more corporatist a system the better it performed against a 'misery' index based on a composite of inflation and unemployment performance. Similar findings based solely on employment performance appear in Bean *et al.* (1986), Newell and Symons (1987), and Soskice (1990).

This second set of studies is not necessarily incompatible with the Olsonian prediction that neo-liberal as well as corporatist systems are compatible with the requirements of national economic management. They may simply indicate that, at least during

[9] Although it is difficult to see how he can deal with a country like Austria which is both highly centralized and has high wage dispersion. Compare with Rowthorn (1992).

[10] This conclusion is based solely on employment performance, but work by Peter Smith and Stephen Thomas (1988), based on UK data, also finds a negative relationship between wage dispersion and inflation.

the period of stagflation from the mid 1970s to the early 1980s, no advanced capitalist country (with the possible exceptions of the United States and Canada) was able to introduce a sufficiently *laissez-faire* industrial relations system. A further set of studies provides some support for this interpretation. Cameron (1984), Crouch (1985), Jackman (1989), Rowthorn and Glyn (1990), and Layard *et al.* (1991) all find that, once union power rises above some threshold, the more corporatist a system, the better it performs in terms of wage restraint and one or both of unemployment and inflation.

However, whatever the final assessment of neo-liberalism, the most important point for present purposes is that all of these studies find that corporatism is compatible either with wage restraint or with the inflation and employment objectives that are the reason for pursuing wage restraint.[11] In short, the empirical evidence supports the theoretical claim that corporatism is compatible with the requirements of national economic management in a period of stagflation.

Indeed, there is some empirical evidence to suggest that, for a pro-labour government, a corporatist system is the only system which is compatible with the requirements of national economic management. According to Lange and Garrett (1985), good macro-economic performance requires both centralized union organization and pro-labour party control of government. When either of these variables is only weakly present there is a negative impact on economic performance. Similar findings appear in Paloheimo (1988). The dependence of a pro-labour government on union centralization is not surprising. It is difficult to imagine such a government successfully opting for a neo-liberal system given that such a system would require the government to seriously weaken the union movement to which it is linked historically, ideologically, and probably institutionally and financially as well. The dependence of union centralization on a pro-labour government serves to emphasize the importance of

[11] It is true that the evidence for inflation alone is weaker than the evidence either for unemployment (or employment) alone, or for a combined inflation plus unemployment index. In fact, some studies deny that there is a positive relationship between corporatism and low or improving inflation. But they do not deny that corporatism is compatible with these objectives. Rather, they suggest that the inflation performance of different countries cannot be distinguished in terms of different industrial relations systems (OECD, 1988; Pohjola, 1992).

the public involvement aspect of corporatism: an aspect which is most likely to be fully developed under a such government.

That leaves the third condition. Is a control trade-off compatible with the requirements of national economic management? In part, the answer to this question has been implicit in the discussion of the previous condition. The reason why corporatism is compatible with the requirements of national economic management is because it enables wage restraint to take place. And one of the ways it does this is by facilitating economy-wide trade-offs in which workers exchange wage increases for other goods (such as control). Thus, so long as the acquisition of these other goods is compatible with the requirements of national economic management, then the trade-offs will also be compatible.

In the case of a control trade-off, it is the acquisition of an incremental increase in control that must be compatible with these requirements. Now there are two ways that the acquisition of a control increment may prove *not* to be compatible with the requirements of national economic management. First, it may lead to counter-productive wage increases in the immediate future. Recall that the need to meet the requirements of national economic management arose because of the need to ensure that a control trade-off did not threaten the government's re-election prospects. Thus the government is likely to want to maintain wage restraint for a number of years, and at least until the time of the next election. Second, the acquisition of a control increment may lead to worse inflation and unemployment by another route. The requirement for wage restraint exists because of the importance, in a stagflationary environment, of simultaneously tackling inflation and unemployment. Thus a control trade-off could still be incompatible with the requirements of a national economic management if the control increment for which wage restraint was exchanged led to worse inflation and unemployment, albeit by a different route.

Note that the question of whether or not the acquisition of a control increment is compatible with the requirements of national economic management is different from the question of viability (or type 3 feasibility) which I discussed briefly in Chapter 3 before setting it to one side. There I was concerned with whether a wholly democratic economy is compatible with the overall requirements of economic efficiency. Here I am concerned with whether a partial move towards a democratic economy is compatible with the particular requirements of national economic management in a period of stagflation. Eventually, as we make the final moves towards full economic democracy, these questions will tend to merge.[12] However, during the period of stagflation here under consideration they remained clearly distinct. Amongst the control increments that were acquired during that period, even the most far-reaching were a long way short of achieving complete economic democracy. Thus, here, we need only be concerned with these partial increases in control.

In Chapter 6 I mentioned that there are two ways of increasing control over a firm. One, typified by co-determination, seeks to usurp the control rights associated with ownership. The other, typified by pension and other worker-controlled funds, seeks to acquire the control rights associated with ownership. The first can be characterized as 'control against ownership', the second as 'control through ownership'. In the stagflationary period which we are considering, the German move to near-parity co-determination is the best example of an increase in control against ownership, and the Swedish move to establish wage earner funds is the best example of an increase in control through ownership. There were many other moves towards economic democracy of each sort, but these two deserve special attention because they were the most far-reaching in each category. Both also took place in a country with a long history of incrementally increasing workers' control. If the degree of economic democracy achieved in Germany and Sweden is compatible with the requirements of national economic management in a period of stagflation, then it seems likely that lesser degrees of economic democracy will also be compatible.

I propose first to discuss increased control against ownership and then to discuss increased control through ownership. In each case I will try to do three things. First, I will consider the specific example mentioned above and present some *prima facie* evidence that it is compatible with the requirements of national economic management in a period of stagflation. Secondly, I will present some general theoretical considerations that support the claim

---

[12] Although the second question, which is concerned with the particular requirements of a given period, will only ever raise a subset of the concerns raised by the first question.

that control increments of that sort are compatible with these requirements. And thirdly, I will present some empirical evidence to back up these claims. Unfortunately, in the case of control increments, the kind of econometric studies to which I appealed when considering the compatibility of corporatism are few and far between. However, the evidence, such as it is, is generally positive.

The German move to near-parity co-determination in 1976 was probably the most far-reaching increase in control which workers won anywhere in the advanced capitalist world during the period of stagflation.[13]

German employers protested vigorously and challenged the move in the federal Constitutional Court. But in the short to medium term their loudly proclaimed fears proved unfounded. Wage bargaining was generally restrained in the late 1970s and early 1980s, and both inflation and unemployment continued to decline until the country was hit by the second oil shock (Gourevitch *et al.*, 1984, 166, 174). Fears that, in the longer term, parity co-determination will lead to a situation in which workers sacrifice investment and future jobs for present consumption also seem unfounded. A system of genuine parity co-determination has operated in the German coal and steel industries since 1951. But, since then, wages in those industries have advanced no more rapidly than in others, and labour directors have generally supported company investment programmes (Flanagan *et al.*, 1983, 291).

There are a number of general theoretical considerations which suggest that co-determination rights, and other forms of control against ownership, will improve the productivity and profitability of a firm. Recall that one of the main reasons for wage restraint is to increase profitability in order to increase investment and hence employment, without increasing inflation. Firstly, a greater upward flow of information may give managers more detailed and more reliable access to knowledge which can only be gained from those on the shopfloor (Freeman, 1986). Secondly, a

[13] On the details of German co-determination see Abb (1977), Almanasreh (1977), Streeck (1984a, 1984c), Gourevitch *et al.* (1984), Markovits (1986), Berghahn and Karsten (1987), and Federal Minister of Labour and Social Affairs (1991). For an overview see Archer (1992, 144–57). During the period of stagflation significant co-determination rights were also won in Holland, Sweden, Norway, and Denmark.

more credible downward flow of information may make it more likely that workers will accept difficult decisions (Nuti, 1987, 24). Thirdly, co-determination may provide a better check against managerial opportunism than that which shareholders are able to provide (Smith, 1990). And fourthly, greater scope for self-realization and a sense of shared responsibility may lead workers to be more committed to the goals of their firm (Putterman, 1990, 162).[14] Each of these factors should help to improve the profitability of co-determined firms, and hence help to fulfil the requirements of national economic management.

There is an accumulating body of empirical evidence to support this claim. For example, there are a number of studies which focus specifically on the performance of German co-determination. Cable and Fitzroy (1980) and Nutzinger (1983) find that it has affected the performance of firms positively. Svejnar (1982) finds that it has had no measurable effect: a finding which still supports the claim that co-determination is compatible with the requirements of national economic management. At a more basic level of control against ownership, there is evidence from the United States that the productivity of unionized firms is greater than that of non-unionized firms (Freeman and Medoff, 1984; Kelly *et al.*, 1991).

Let me now turn to Sweden and the wage earner funds. As we will see towards the end of this chapter, there is reason to believe that the most likely form of control trade-off in a period of stagflation is one that involves increased control through ownership: typically in the form of a worker-controlled pension fund. The original proposal for wage earner funds was far more ambitious than a worker-controlled pension fund. However, in the end, the outcome was not so different.

The original proposal for wage earner funds which was adopted by Sweden's blue collar union federation, LO, in 1976, was known as the Meidner plan after its principal author.[15] The

---

[14] Against this it can be argued that co-determination may give workers greater scope for 'shirking' or free-riding (Alchian and Demsetz, 1986). But this assumes that workers will be unable to develop their own system of supervision (Putterman, 1990, 168; Elster and Moene, 1989, 28–9).

[15] There is a large number of books and articles which discuss the Meidner plan. Amongst those which I have found useful are Meidner (1978), Esping-Andersen (1985), Gourevitch *et al.* (1984), Pontusson (1987), Madsen (1980), Higgins and Apple (1983), von Otter (1985), Swedish Ministry of Finance (1984), and LO (1988). Plans that are similar to the Meidner plan have been considered in Germany, Holland, and Denmark.

main motivation for the plan was the need to bolster wage restraint. By the early 1970s the success of LO's solidaristic wages policy was facing objections from those who worked in highly profitable sectors of the economy, and especially in the metal industry. The solidaristic wages policy required workers in these sectors to keep their wage increases in line with increases in other less profitable sectors, thus guaranteeing extra profits for some capitalists. At the same time there was a renewal of a long-standing concern about insufficient investment.[16] Consequently workers in the most profitable sectors objected that the only effect of their restraint was to further concentrate wealth in the hands of a few capitalists.

The Meidner plan proposed the establishment of employee investment funds in order to address these objections. According to the original plan, each firm with over 50 employees would be required to transfer 20 per cent of its profits, per annum, to the funds, in the form of new shares. The voting rights attached to these shares would be exercised partly by a fund management board appointed by the central union organizations, and partly by the firm's workers through their local union organization (Meidner, 1978, 99). Each year that the firm made a profit the funds would acquire a further 20 per cent, so that eventually, over a period of 20 to 70 years, depending on its profitability (Meidner, 1978, 59), the workers would control a majority of the firm's shares. Since the growth of these funds depended on a firm's profitability, they offered the workers in highly profitable sectors the possibility of some assurance that the extra profits they were forgoing would be reinvested. Almost as a by-product, this would lead the workers to move gradually towards the achievement of economic democracy.

The original Meidner plan went through a number of incarnations and was eventually implemented in a much watered down form in legislation passed in 1983.[17] Under this legislation five

[16] This is best described in Gourevitch *et al.* (1984, 268–78).

[17] There are numerous reasons why the original Meidner plan was not implemented (Pontusson, 1987). But two factors stand out in terms of my analysis of the feasibility of control trade-offs. One is the absence of a unified labour movement position. The Social Democratic government and unions failed to co-ordinate their objectives (Pontusson, 1987, 19, 30). The other is that the original plan seemed to be trapped in the revolutionary dilemma. Of all the propaganda deployed against the plan, the most potent charge was that the funds would lead to an overly centralized economy which concentrated too much power in the hands of the central union officials (Madsen, 1980, 282).

regionally based employee investment funds were established (Swedish Ministry of Finance, 1984). The funds were established within the framework of an already existing pension scheme. They were required to make a return of 3 per cent in real terms, which they had to transfer to the pension scheme. The funds received revenue from a 0.2 per cent payroll tax and a 20 per cent tax on profits over a certain level, and could use these revenues to purchase shares. But the revenue was only to be accumulated until 1990, and each fund could acquire no more than 8 per cent of the shares in any one firm. Local union organizations could exercise half of the voting rights attached to any shares which were purchased.

Precisely because the Swedish wage earner funds were so ambitious, they were highly controversial, and took a long time to implement even in their ultimate watered down form. Indeed, the best opportunity for a control trade-off had already been lost by the time that they were finally implemented. In 1983, at the insistence of metal industry employers, the metal workers union pulled out of LO's central bargaining structure and concluded a separate deal. It seems that pressure for higher wages from the union's membership had by then built up to such an extent that the union leadership did not feel that it was able to sustain sufficient support for industrial action to force the employers back into the centralized system (Lash, 1985, 222). Despite various attempts to reintroduce centrally bargained agreements, many see this as marking a decisive break from more than a generation of highly centralized industrial relations (Lash, 1985; Lundberg, 1985; Peterson, 1987; Ahlen, 1989; Archer, 1992).

Nevertheless, three years after the funds had been established LO could legitimately point to *prima facie* evidence that these funds had been compatible with the need to restrain wages and to lower unemployment and inflation (LO, 1988, 37–44). During this period unemployment fell from 2.9 per cent to 2.2 per cent, and inflation was halved to 4.3 per cent (OECD, 1990a). I have not been able to discover any econometric study which attempts to isolate what influence, if any, the wage earner funds had on this result. However, clearly the most important influence was the major currency devaluation which the Social Democrats undertook on returning to office in 1982. The introduction of wage earner funds was seen at the time as a trade-off to ensure that workers would not undermine the effect of the devaluation by seeking to retain the real value of their wages.

Again there are also a number of general theoretical considerations which suggest that worker-controlled funds and other forms of control through ownership will increase the productivity and profitability of a firm, and hence are compatible with the requirements of national economic management. Over and above the other effects that may result from increased workers' control, employee share ownership may generate important material incentives. In particular, it is often argued that by linking some of a worker's present or future income to the profitability of his or her firm, the worker is given a powerful incentive to work harder and reduce supervision costs, thereby increasing profitability (Nuti, 1987, 23; Putterman, 1990, 162). In theory, increased profitability should lead to increased investment and hence employment. Moreover, worker-controlled funds are themselves an additional source of investment. Against this argument it is often suggested that, either where the employees' funds are held in common, or where teamwork is involved, the shared nature of the effort needed to increase profitability generates a free rider problem. But at worst this can simply neutralize the putative incentive effect of employee share ownership. So long as increased control through ownership does not worsen the performance of firms, it remains compatible with the requirements of national economic management.

There is some empirical evidence that this is indeed the case. Most of the studies deal with American co-operatives and employee share ownership schemes. For example, Rosen and Klein (1983) studied 43 employee-owned firms and found that employment in these grew nearly three times as fast as in conventional firms. Poole and Jenkins (1990, 4–8) review the productivity and employment performance of firms in a number of other American studies. Most find that employee ownership has either a positive impact or no impact on company performance. Poole and Jenkins' own study of British firms finds a positive relationship between employee ownership and profitability, but they suggest that this may be because profitable firms establish employee share ownership schemes (Poole and Jenkins, 1990, 23, 39). Another British study by Blanchflower and Oswald (1987) concludes that employee share ownership has no effect.

Taken together, then, the evidence of both Germany and Sweden, as well as the more general theoretical and empirical evidence, suggests that control increases—whether achieved against or through ownership—*are* compatible with the requirements of national economic management in a period of stagflation. Indeed, some of the evidence suggests that a control trade-off may be not just compatible with, but may actually help to fulfil these requirements. Moreover, compared with other possible trade-offs, there are some good reasons for the government in particular to prefer a control trade-off.[18] One reason for this is that, unlike most of the alternative, income-related trade-offs, a control trade-off costs the government nothing. Cost considerations will be especially important in a stagflationary environment because of the pressure on governments to maintain a tight budgetary policy. Another reason for preferring a control trade-off is that many of the most widely used alternative forms of compensation are themselves sometimes incompatible with the requirements of national economic management. For example, trade-offs in which tax cuts are exchanged for wage restraint can be counter-productive in this way. If tax cuts are spent rather than saved, inflation might increase (Schwerin, 1980).

My main task in this chapter was to consider whether a control trade-off is feasible in a stagflationary economic environment. To this end I have considered each of the three conditions for the feasibility of a control trade-off. First, I showed that workers' ablility to win wage increases provided them with a profit-threatening exchangeable good. Second, I provided both theoretical and empirical evidence that corporatism was compatible with the requirements of national economic management. And third, I argued that the available evidence suggests that a control trade-off is also compatible with the requirements of national economic management. My conclusion, then, is that all three conditions for the feasibility of a control trade-off are fulfilled in a stagflationary economic environment, and thus that a control trade-off is feasible in such an environment.

Having drawn this conclusion I now want to change tack slightly and consider a subsidiary issue. When the three conditions for a control trade-off were set out in Chapter 6 I always

---

[18] And, of course, the point of view of the government is especially important for the compatibility condition that we are discussing, since it is only because the government's consent is needed that this condition needs to be fulfilled.

assumed that the workers wanted increased control and that this was their top priority. This assumption was justified on the grounds that, in considering the feasibility of a control trade-off, I was considering the feasibility of a trade-off *for the labour movement*. Thus I was asking, not whether the labour movement wanted greater control, but whether, if they wanted it, they could get it. This, I argued, was the right way to proceed in order to establish the feasibility of a strategy and of the steps which contribute to it. And it is on this basis that I have now concluded that control trade-offs are feasible in a stagflationary economic environment.

Nevertheless, a critic could point out that it is not clear that workers want greater control, and that it is most certainly not clear that they want it above all else. Opinion surveys of workers' attitudes would provide the critic with some support. While most opinion surveys show that workers do want increased control, the evidence suggests that this does not have a higher priority than the improvement of wages and other conditions that affect material well-being.[19] Thus it seems unlikely that workers in a stagflationary environment would want to exchange increased wages for increased control. The critic could say that, while control trade-offs are theoretically feasible, it would be unrealistic to expect them actually to take place.

It is possible to respond to this criticism by suggesting that workers' preferences and priorities might change. Perhaps they will change simply in virtue of realizing that a control trade-off is feasible. Perhaps they will change because increases in control will strengthen workers' preference for still further increases in control.[20] Or perhaps they will change for some other reason. Here, however, I will make a different response. In particular I will argue that it is still rational for workers to undertake a control trade-off in a stagflationary environment, *even if they are solely concerned about improving their material well-being*. In the process I hope to shed some light on the kinds of control trade-offs that are likely to succeed in a period of stagflation.

To do this I must first establish why it is rational for workers who are solely materially motivated to undertake any sort of trade-off. Since stagflation has an inimical effect on workers as

[19] See Chapter 6.
[20] There is some evidence that workers' preferences do change in this way (IDE, 1981, 194). See also Drago and Wooden (1991).

well as capitalists, might it not be rational for workers to restrain their wages without a trade-off? A sophisticated argument along these lines has been developed by both Adam Przeworski (1985a; 1985b) and Peter Lange (1984). Both authors use rational choice theory to argue that wage restraint without a trade-off may be rational for workers in a variety of economic conditions.

Przeworski assumes, as I now want to, that workers are solely interested in their material welfare (1985b, 172, 173). He argues that the relationship between these workers and the capitalists is simultaneously one of conflict and one of dependence. The relationship is one of conflict because the working class can only increase its *present* standard of living by increasing wages at the expense of profits (Przeworski, 1985b, 171).[21] But the relationship is also one of dependence because the *future* standard of living of the working class depends on restraining wage increases in order to maintain a certain level of profits. This relationship of dependence is a result of two facts: (1) that future wages depend on future output, which in turn depends on present investment, and (2) that profit is a necessary condition of investment, since, in a capitalist society, most investment occurs out of profits (Przeworski, 1985a, 150; 1985b, 178).

In order to decide whether or not it is rational to restrain their wage increases (and hence their present standard of living), the workers have to assess how much they value the improvement in their future living standards which may result from this restraint. In part, of course, this assessment will depend on the size, or amount, of the improvement that may result. But, according to rational choice theory, in assessing how much they value this future improvement *at present*, workers will discount this amount by a parameter which is a function of both how soon they expect to gain the improvement and how certain they are that it will in fact be gained (McLean, 1987, 135; Axelrod, 1984, 12, 126–32).[22] Thus it can be rational for workers to restrain their present wage increases without trade-offs, so long as the future wage increases which they may gain as a result are large enough, come soon enough, and are certain enough.

[21] This presumes that there is a competitive product market which rules out the possibility of making consumers bear the cost of wage increases.

[22] For Przeworski's treatment of this issue see (1985b, 182–5). For Lange's treatment see (1984, 104–5).

The problem is that while wage restraint without trade-offs can in theory be rational, it is hardly ever observed. Flanagan *et al.* (1983) have made a comprehensive study of incomes policies in nine Western European countries.[23] They list a range of compensatory trade-offs that were used as devices to secure union acceptance of wage restraint. Focusing on the generation of incomes policies that were introduced following the wage explosions of the late 1960s, Flanagan *et al.* conclude that 'in most instances incomes policies, formal or otherwise, employed these devices in various combinations' (1983, 664).

The need for compensation is likely to be especially acute in a period of stagflation. Even in the most stable economic environment, workers will be uncertain about whether and, if so, when capitalists will invest the extra profits that they would acquire as a result of workers' wage restraint. But in a stagflationary economic environment this uncertainty will be especially great (Lange, 1984, 115). In assessing whether to agree to wage restraint, workers will have to weigh a certain loss in the present against a highly uncertain gain in the future. Under these circumstances, rational workers who are solely materially motivated would only be prepared to agree to wage restraint in exchange for a compensatory trade-off. A compensatory trade-off could make wage restraint rational for workers either by increasing the non-wage component of their present income, or by reducing the uncertainty about their expected future income. Both sorts of trade-off have been attempted. Tax cuts and improved social welfare payments are a common example of the first sort of trade-off. Government attempts to act as a 'guarantor' by encouraging investment are an example of the second. However, each sort of trade-off suffers from certain problems.

Tax cuts and social welfare improvements may result in costs as well as gains for workers. Tax cuts may lead do reductions in other forms of government expenditure that favour workers, and social welfare improvements may be taken back from workers in the form of higher taxes. Imposing these costs on the capitalists is not an option, since it would undermine the original rationale for wage restraint. In any case, as we have already noted, governments may not be prepared to offer tax and social welfare con-

[23] The nine are: Austria, the Netherlands, Norway, West Germany, Sweden, the United Kingdom, Denmark, Italy, and France.

cessions in an environment that demands a tight budgetary policy (Flanagan *et al.*, 1983, 670–3).

Government attempts to act as a guarantor may suffer from credibility problems. First, the ability of the government to influence private investment decisions is strictly limited. In an environment of world-wide stagflation, investment decisions may be determined by factors beyond its control (Schott, 1984, 52–4). Second, the value of any guarantees that the government can give is dependent on its re-election prospects. In a volatile economic environment these are likely to be uncertain (Lange, 1984, 111).

However, there is another form of compensatory trade-off that has not yet been mentioned: increased workers' control over investment. As in the case of government attempts to act as a guarantor, this trade-off would be aimed at reducing uncertainty about the future. If workers themselves control the investment of the extra capital which results from their wage restraint, then their assessment of the future is no longer dependent on second guessing what the capitalists will do. This was the explicit logic behind the original Meidner plan.

There are, however, a number of less ambitious alternatives that enable workers to exchange wage restraint for greater control over the investment of the capital that results from that restraint. National Development funds, such as the 'solidarity fund' proposed in the 1980 bargaining round in Italy (Lange *et al.*, 1982, 183) or the National Enterprise Board established in 1974 in Britain (Gourevitch *et al.*, 1984, 59), provide a highly centralized form of control. Employee share ownership plans, which have been widely discussed in the United States and Britain,[24] offer more decentralized control.

However, the most promising option is the establishment or improvement of union-controlled pension funds. The Swedish unions had much less difficulty in setting up the so-called 'fourth AP' pension fund in 1974 than they subsequently had with the wage earner funds. This fourth fund was allowed to purchase shares, unlike the original three, which were limited to purchasing bonds. Sixty per cent of the votes that came with these shares

---

[24] The most notable promoters of this discussion have been Kelso and Co. in the United States, and New Bridge Street Consultants and the trade union bank, Unity Trust, in Britain.

were assigned to the local unions in the company concerned. The fund itself exercised the remaining 40 per cent. Within a couple of years its shareholdings in a few large companies such as Volvo were sufficient to win it board representation (Gourevitch *et al.*, 1984, 271). The Danish cost-of-living fund is another interesting example. A 1976 incomes policy agreement stipulated that deferred wage increases be placed in special accounts administered by the national pension scheme. This capital was later transferred to the worker-controlled cost-of-living fund which is permitted to invest a certain percentage of its assets in shares (Ohman, 1983, 40). A further example of a wages-for-pensions trade-off is considered in Chapter 9.

There are a number of reasons why pension funds are especially promising. Pensions do not suffer from any of the potential drawbacks associated with tax or social welfare trade-offs. Workers do not have to pay extra for a pension-based trade-off with tax increases or with the loss of other publicly funded services. And since the scheme is principally dependent on an exchange between unions and employers, the government does not have to bear the cost of the scheme, and the workers need not fear a change of government. However, the main reason why pensions are especially promising is because they provide a double guarantee against future uncertainty: they offer control over the investment of capital that results from wage restraint, plus an assurance that workers' personal income will be improved after retirement. In fact, then, even if workers are solely concerned with their material welfare, a control trade-off is not only a rational option for them, it can actually be an especially attractive option.

It is unlikely that workers are ever solely concerned with their material welfare. Nevertheless *some* concern with material welfare is likely to be important even where control issues become a powerful motivating force in their own right. Thus, even in the best circumstances that are realistically conceivable,[25] a proposal that bridges a desire both for greater control and for greater material welfare is likely to have the best chance of success. And we have seen that bridging both these desires in a stagflationary period requires a trade-off in which wage restraint is exchanged for control of investment.

---

[25] Best, that is, from the point of view of achieving economic democracy.

The control over investment associated with pension funds and the like is a result of increased control through ownership. But in theory, increased control over investment could also result from increased control against ownership. During the 1970s proposals along these lines were pursued by Italian unions (Lange *et al.*, 1982, 170–1), as well as by some German and British unions (Gourevitch *et al.*, 1984, 51, 59, 139, 158). With a few exceptions (such as in the German Chemical industry and in the British division of Chrysler), these proposals were not implemented; and even where they were, they did not last long.

In practice, lasting increases in control over investment were mostly acquired the other way: as a result of increased control through ownership. This suggests that it was easier to acquire total control over a small portion of investment capital than it was to acquire even partial control over the overall investment process. Moreover, from the point of view of workers who are mostly concerned with their material welfare, control through ownership has the advantage of being able to target increased control specifically at the capital which results from their wage restraint. And, in the form of pension funds, it offers these workers the additional advantage of improved personal income. These kinds of considerations suggest that the control trade-offs that are most likely to succeed in a stagflationary environment are those that seek control through ownership, especially in the form of pension funds.

Throughout this chapter I have been concerned with the specific economic environment that prevailed during the stagflationary period of the 1970s and 1980s. In some ways this period was unique. But in other ways it was just the latest manifestation of certain recurrent problems. The need to pursue a policy of wage restraint in order to achieve acceptable inflation or employment outcomes has been an ongoing theme of the postwar world. Prior to the outbreak of stagflation, incomes policies designed to achieve wage restraint were repeatedly utilized in Western Europe from 1945 onwards (Flanagan *et al.*, 1983, 1–3). Moreover, more recent evidence (OECD, 1990) suggests that the need for wage restraint is a concern which, while sometimes overshadowed by other priorities, is likely to continue in the future. Because of this, it is possible to suggest tentatively that the conclusions of this chapter have more general applicability.

The ability of unions to win wage increases that destabilize national economic performance is likely to make recurrent appearances as one of the central concerns of national economic management. If inflation and employment outcomes are central to these concerns, then the evidence of this chapter suggests that, each time this happens, control trade-offs will again be feasible.

8

Structural Adjustment

Between the early and mid 1980s the economic environment changed as stagflation began to wane. Inflation fell steadily in the OECD countries and GDP growth began to pick up. After 1986 even the unemployment rate began to improve.[1] The period of stagflation was followed by a period of structural adjustment (or industrial restructuring). Indeed, it is sometimes suggested that failure to instigate a process of structural adjustment earlier was the root cause of stagflation (Glyn *et al.*, 1990, 89).

It is difficult, however, to provide concise evidence that structural adjustment is taking place. Unlike in the case of stagflation, one cannot simply point to two or three well established indicators of macro-economic performance. There have been various attempts to formulate indicators of structural adjustment. Many of these attempts have focused exclusively on technological change (Sorge and Streeck, 1988, 21), although some have sought to capture the process as a whole (OECD, 1989, 131). But, either way, the complexity and the changing nature of the phenomena[2] that need to be measured have ensured that none of the proposed indicators has won general acceptance.

Nevertheless, it can hardly be denied that widespread structural adjustment has taken place since the mid 1980s. At the most general level structural adjustment involves the modernization of the production process. The production process involves both workers and their tools, and, as we saw briefly at the beginnning of Chapter 6, there are three aspects to its modernization, each of

---

[1] See Figure 12. Note that the sudden improvement in the unemployment rate between 1983 and 1984 is partly due to a break in the series of statistics collected in Britain and Germany.

[2] So, for example, as technology changes, the measure of technological change also changes. Whereas twenty years ago the presence of a large central computer may have been a good measure of the extent to which new technology had been adopted by a firm, research now tends to highlight the use of micro-electronic equipment (such as computer numerical control machines) in the production process. Compare Blau and Schoenherr (1971) with Batstone *et al.* (1987).

which leads to a characteristic concern. First there is the modernization of the work-force itself, which typically leads to issues about training and skills. Second there is the modernization of the tools, which typically leads to questions about new technology and technological change. And third there is the modernization of the relationships between the workers themselves[3] and between the workers and their tools, which typically leads to issues about the organization of work. Modernization is an ongoing process; nevertheless, it is clear from a wide range of sources— from company and regional case studies to more general analyses—that particularly intensive and far-reaching changes have recently been taking place in each of these issue-areas.[4]

The most influential analysis of the causes of this burst of structural adjustment has been provided by Sabel (1982, 194–9) and Piore and Sabel (1985, 184–93, 258–63). According to these authors the post-war prosperity of the advanced industrial countries was based on the mass production of low-cost, standardized consumer goods. But by the 1970s, partly because of the very success of this 'Fordist' model of production, a series of developments had emerged which tended to undermine it. First, the market in the advanced capitalist countries for mass-produced consumer durables had become more or less saturated. For example, by 1970 in the United States 99 per cent of households had television sets, refrigerators, radios, and electric irons (Piore and Sabel, 1985, 184). Second, imitators in newly industrializing countries began to compete for customers in the market that remained. Low wages and the absence of environmental and other government regulations gave these countries a good chance of success. Third, consumer tastes in the advanced capitalist countries began to change. Consumers began to demand a greater variety of more customized, less standardized goods, and were increasingly prepared to pay a premium for quality. Fourth and finally, technological developments enabled producers to respond to these demands for greater variety and quality without pricing themselves out of the market. For example, reprogrammable computer

---

[3] This includes the relationship between managers and rank and file workers.
[4] Amongst a multitude of possible sources, evidence for this assertion can be found in Allen (1990), Batstone *et al.* (1987), Daniel (1987), Gustavsen (1986), Hyman and Streeck (1988), Knights *et al.* (1985), Murray (1985), OECD (1987), OECD (1989), Piore and Sabel (1985), and Sabel (1982).

numerically controlled machines make it possible to produce a series of small batches of goods just as cheaply as one large batch of goods produced according to Fordist principles.

Firms can respond to these developments in one of two ways (Sabel, 1982, 199; Streeck, 1989, 90). Either they can attempt to compete directly with the newly industrializing countries by undertaking a down-market structural adjustment towards a low-wage, unregulated economy; or they can attempt to satisfy changing consumer tastes by undertaking an up-market response. In most of this chapter I will be concerned with this second, up-market response.

Firms which opt for an up-market structural adjustment need not only to produce new goods but also to produce them in different ways. They must adjust their production process in order to increase the *quality* of their products, in order to *diversify* their output to meet the more specialized tastes of consumers and in order to *innovate* more rapidly as those tastes change. That is, they must adjust from a cost-competitive standardized model of production to a quality-competitive customized model of production (Sorge and Streeck, 1988, 29).

Piore and Sabel claim that these changes may portend more than a mere modernization of Fordism (Sabel, 1982, 200–31; Piore and Sabel, 1985, 251–80). Rather, they suggest that in the advanced capitalist countries Fordism may be being replaced by a whole new model of production based on small, high-technology workshops reminiscent of the craft model of production which Fordism itself replaced. Piore and Sabel call this new model 'flexible specialization'. Some writers have challenged the idea that we are witnessing a wholesale transition from Fordism to flexible specialization (Pollert, 1988; Glyn, 1990). And even if a wholesale shift to flexible specialization is taking place, this need not involve a return to low-volume cottage industries (Sorge and Streeck, 1988, 30). But whether Fordism is being replaced or merely adapted, the essential point remains that through the 1980s and into the 1990s many firms have been required to undertake far-reaching structural adjustment.

Are the three conditions for the feasibility of a control trade-off fulfilled in an environment of structural adjustment such as the one just described? As in the previous chapter, I will consider these conditions in the following order. First I will consider whether the workers have an exchangeable good that threatens the capitalists' profits. Second I will consider whether a corporatist industrial relations system is compatible with the requirements of national economic management. And third I will consider whether a control trade-off is compatible with the requirements of national economic management. Then, again as in the previous chapter, I will consider as a subsidiary question whether a control trade-off is still feasible if we assume that the workers are solely concerned with their material well-being. Finally I will briefly point to the recurring nature of structural adjustment and the potential for further control trade-offs in the future.

First, then, in an environment of structural adjustment, do the workers have a profit-threatening exchangeable good?

Before the advent of Fordism, craft workers had a certain amount of decision-making power about what to produce and how to produce it. In contrast, Fordism attempted to vest all such powers in the hands of managers. A sharp distinction was made between the conception of tasks (which was the prerogative of managers) and their execution (which was the duty of workers). The objective was to minimize costs by specifying precisely what was required of the occupant of each job.[5] Once workers came to accept this general division of responsibilities, unions began to focus their efforts on building various conditions into these job specifications which restricted who could do a job, what they could be required to do, and when they could be required to do it (Fox, 1974, 193). These 'restrictive work practices' became the main vehicle through which workers exercised control on the shop floor.

This way of organizing work was always something of an obstacle to adjustment, since any change had to be preceded by a process of negotiation and, if that was successful, by the codification of a new set of work practices. But in a period of structural adjustment like the one described above, the very system of negotiating restrictive work practices becomes a problem, because changing consumer demand requires not just a once-off change but rapid and continual change. In these circumstances there is

---

[5] That this aspiration was never completely fulfilled is clearly shown by the fact that unions have often used 'work to rule' campaigns as an industrial weapon to impose costs on employers.

simply no time to continually renegotiate and codify new work practices. Over time, firms which are not able to adjust quickly enough will lose their customers and hence their profits. Thus, in any period of structural adjustment, and especially in the present period, restrictive work practices are a profit-threatening exchangeable good in the hands of the workers. Note, moreover, that this remains true even in those countries where unions have tended not to resort to restrictive work practices, since even where they do not exist, restrictive work practices, like wage rises, can be threatened.[6] For example, German unions began to make these kinds of threats in the late 1970s and early 1980s, despite their long commitment to supporting constant innovation (Streeck, 1981, 152).

What about the second condition? Is a corporatist industrial relations system compatible with the requirements of national economic management in an environment of structural adjustment? As in the case of stagflation, we need first to identify what the requirements of national economic management are. But unlike in the case of stagflation, it is not so easy to point to one or two criteria, like 'inflation' or 'unemployment', which dominate public assessment of economic performance during a period of structural adjustment. Sometimes the balance of trade, or more generally the balance of payments, becomes the focus of public attention. Sometimes a variety of other measures of international competitiveness are invoked. Sometimes public attention is not focused on a measurable indicator at all. Occasionally, for example, the general project of modernization gets a grip on the public imagination, as it did in Britain as a result of Harold Wilson's 'white heat of technology' theme in the 1964 election campaign.[7]

But whatever the specific criteria, there are only two main routes open to the government. It can either foster up-market structural adjustment in an attempt to retain a place in the league of high-wage, advanced capitalist countries, or it can foster down-market structural adjustment in an attempt to compete with the

---

[6] Indeed, the threat to impose restrictive work practices is likely to be even more credible than the threat to raise wages, since all that workers have to do to implement the first threat is simply to persist with the *status quo*. Unlike, for example, in a strike over wages, it is the management, not the union, that has to mobilize the workforce to undertake tasks that differ from their normal routine.

[7] The theme was first raised in his 1963 conference speech.

newly industrializing countries. Presumably the government will be under electoral pressure to take the up-market route. Therefore, henceforth, when I speak of structural adjustment I will solely be concerned with up-market structural adjustment.

But to achieve either sort of structural adjustment in a market economy the government must enable individual firms to update the way in which they deploy their resources as well as the quantity and quality of these resources. Moreover, each firm needs to make these changes on the basis of the particular circumstances that are affecting it, and to do so repeatedly as these circumstances themselves continuously change. Thus the promotion of 'flexibility' becomes the main requirement of national economic management. And the flexibility that is of most concern in considering the compatibility of corporatism is 'labour market flexibility'. Hence for present purposes I will focus on labour market flexibility as the key requirement of national economic management in a period of structural adjustment.

So is corporatism compatible with labour market flexibility? It became commonplace in the 1980s to hear that the answer is 'no'. Labour market flexibility, according to this line of argument, requires a decentralized industrial relations system, and hence is incompatible with corporatism. Indeed, according to some, the future of unionism itself may be in jeopardy (Piore, 1986b).

However, before jumping to conclusions, we need to clarify exactly what is meant by 'labour market flexibility'. The call for greater flexibility has become something of a catch-cry. But a closer look shows that there are many different sorts of flexibility. Indeed, there are at least five major categories of labour market flexibility, which can be grouped as follows under three headings:[8]

wage flexibility:	(1) aggregate wages
	(2) differential wages
numerical flexibility:	(3) labour mobility
functional flexibility:	(4) skills and training
	(5) organization of work.

[8] My typology of labour market flexibility draws on those of OECD (1986a), OECD (1986b), Brunhes (1989), Boyer (1988), National Labour Consultative Council (1987), and Piore (1986a).

These five categories are often further divided into subcategories. For example, wage differentials can be measured with respect to regions, industrial sectors, company productivity or skill. Similarly, labour mobility is concerned with mobility between jobs, occupations, and geographical regions, as well as with legislatively imposed job security.

Now some of these categories and subcategories are more important for successful up-market structural adjustment than others. And some are more compatible with corporatism than others. For example, as we saw in the last chapter, corporatism is well equipped to deliver aggregate wage flexibility. But its centralized bargaining structures seem less well equipped to deliver differential wages which are flexible with respect to company productivity. However, while aggregate wage flexibility remains important in determining the level of inflation and unemployment, it is not clear that these macro-level outcomes are important for the success of the micro-level process of structural adjustment. On the other hand, wage differentials, along with labour mobility, are often seen (especially by employers) as crucial to this process (OECD, 1986a, 23; OECD, 1986b, 9).[9] So now I want to focus first on these two categories of labour market flexibility. Since aggregate wage flexibility is compatible with corporatism it causes no problem for my argument, even if it is required for successful structural adjustment.

Wage differentials are appealing to employers in a period of structural adjustment because they help to facilitate a rapid redistribution of the existing work-force in the short-term. Successful companies, for example, can buy in the workers they want by making an offer that is too good to refuse, and unsuccessful companies can lower wages in order to keep making a profit. But from a longer term, society-wide point of view, just how important are wage differentials for successful structural adjustment? Skill-based differentials can certainly play an important role by

---

[9] Note, however, that the precise effect of wage differentials and company productivity is controversial. Labour is only one of the factors which feeds into company productivity, and so unless there is full self-government and workers are responsible for investment decisions, the updating of machinery and all other relevant factors, it could be counter-productive to tie wage differentials to company productivity. Workers who have done nothing may get substantial rises, while workers who have been intensively improving their performance may get nothing.

providing an incentive for workers to upgrade their skills in line with changing requirements (OECD, 1986a, 23). But it can also be argued that regional, industrial, or company-based differentials hinder structural adjustment by creating incentives for workers to resist change. If, for example, there are high differentials between industrial sectors—as there are in the United States, where steel workers earn approximately three times as much as textile workers—relatively highly paid workers in declining industries (like steel) are likely to resist being redeployed.[10] What matters, then, is not differentials *per se*, but their effect on labour mobility. In Sweden the level of labour mobility between companies remained unchanged despite a major reduction in wage differentials between the late 1960s and the early 1980s (Faxen *et al.*, 1987, 49–51).

So of all the various subcategories of differential wage flexibility, only skill-based differentials are unambiguously important to the success of structural adjustment. But the process of updating skill-based differentials depends on a categorization and certification of skills which can usually only be accomplished at industry-wide or even at economy-wide level. And processes that require industry-wide or economy-wide agreement are well suited to, and are certainly compatible with, a corporatist industrial relations system. Chapter 9 discusses a recent example of the re-establishment of skill-based differentials in Australia that clearly demonstrates this point.

Labour mobility also has an ambiguous effect on the success of structural adjustment. Labour mobility is certainly important if workers are to be redeployed from firms, industries, and regions which are declining to those which are growing. But there is no simple relationship between the level of labour mobility and successful structural adjustment (OECD, 1986a, 56). Workers can change jobs for a whole range of reasons that have nothing to do with the requirements of structural adjustment. They may move for better pay, better conditions, a better environment, in order to marry: the list is endless. Moreover, each of these moves involves additional 'transaction costs'. Thus, for example, turnover in car assembly plants is seen as a major problem rather than as a sign of necessary adjustment. Furthermore, while job security legislation

---

[10] I owe this point to Claes-Erik Odhner.

(such as expensive redundancy provisions) may in itself have the potential to hinder labour mobility, its effect will be negligible if workers are prepared to voluntarily change jobs where structural adjustment is necessary. Labour mobility is high in both Sweden and the United States even though the laws governing job security in these two countries are poles apart (OECD, 1986a, 58).

This last point provides the seeds of an answer to the question of whether corporatism is compatible with that labour mobility which *is* necessary for structural adjustment. The fastest and most effective structural adjustment will occur in countries where workers voluntarily move when structural adjustment is necessary. But voluntary adjustment will only take place if the workers are confident that they will find suitable employment elsewhere and will not have to bear the transaction costs of the move. Such confidence can only be generated by a central policy that is not dependent on the fortunes of any particular firm, industry, or region. But only where unions are organized in a corporatist industrial relations system (that is, only where they are centrally organized and engaged in society-wide bargaining) are they in a position to apply pressure for the development of a central policy. The best-known example of the kind of policy I have in mind is the Swedish 'active labour market policy' (Lundberg, 1985, 19). The policy was (until 1991) institutionalized in a tripartitely governed Labour Market Board which organized the retraining and redeployment of displaced workers. It seems, therefore, that corporatism is certainly compatible with the labour mobility that is required for structural adjustment. Indeed, it may even play an important role in facilitating it. For a worker to have security that is compatible with mobility, a key theme of the OECD (1986b), there has to be a source of security at a central level that stands above the particular firm, industry, or region in which he or she works. And since workers will typically turn to their unions to achieve security, this mobility-compatible security can only be achieved if unions are able to operate effectively at such a level.

Although employers have made their loudest complaints about wage differentials and labour mobility, it is in fact functional flexibility that is the most important element of labour market flexibility for successful structural adjustment. Wage differentials and labour mobility are principally directed at facilitating the redistribution of the work-force. But it is no good having a perfect distribution mechanism if you do not have the right work-force to distribute or if you do not know how to organize it once it has been distributed. Functional flexibility is concerned with precisely these two issues: skills and training, and work organization.[11]

In the short term, some firms might be able to prosper by paying higher wages to poach workers with the skills they need or by hiring and firing at will. But in the long term, and for society as a whole, structural adjustment will only succeed if there is a widespread diffusion of new skills and successful organizational methods.[12] It may even be that there is a trade-off between short-term and long-term success. Brunhes (1989, 16–36) notes that it is countries with the least short-term flexibility (such as Germany and Sweden) that have the greatest long-term flexibility, and that it is countries with the most short-term flexibility (such as Britain) that pay the least attention to long-term flexibility.

Let me now consider both of the elements of functional flexibility in more detail.

A functionally flexible work-force must constantly acquire new skills. And the acquisition of new skills requires training. But training poses a problem for market economies because it is subject to market failure (Streeck, 1989, 94). The root cause of this failure is the 'free employment contract' which enables workers to leave one firm and join another, taking their skills with them. For this reason firms will be reticent to invest in training their workers for fear that other firms will poach them before the cost of the training has been recovered. In effect, training becomes a public good. Even though each firm recognizes the importance of investing in training, each attempts to free ride for fear of others free riding on its investment.

Not all training is affected by a free rider problem. In particular, a firm can invest in training its workers in firm-specific skills, as opposed to marketable skills, without the fear that other firms will have an incentive to poach its workers (Finegold and Soskice,

[11] Note that they cover two of the three key issues of modernization cited earlier. The third, technological change, is not directly relevant to the labour market, but it has a strong indirect influence over the kinds of skills that workers need, and over the ways in which work should be organized.

[12] Moreover, if there is a shortage of skilled labour, widespread poaching could drive the economy back into the wage-induced inflationary problems of the stagflationary era.

1988). Firm-specific skills are only of use in a particular firm, whereas marketable skills can be used in a number of different firms. The trouble is that many of the skills which firms require are marketable, and this is becoming more rather than less the case in the current period of structural adjustment. As we have seen, in order to meet the challenges of structural adjustment, firms need both to diversify their products and to be able to innovate rapidly. As a result, they need workers with general or multi-purpose skills which can be rapidly adapted to producing a variety of new products. But just because these skills can be adapted to a variety of tasks, they are likely to be useful in a variety of firms.

A corporatist industrial relations system can solve the free rider problem that afflicts investment in marketable skills by providing a mechanism that ensures that all firms invest in training and that this training meets uniform standards. In particular, a centrally co-ordinated union movement has both an interest in disciplining free riding firms and the power to do so, either directly by way of industrial action or indirectly by eliciting government intervention. A centrally co-ordinated employers' association would share a similar interest. Corporatism, then, is not only compatible with the skill and training requirements of a functionally flexible work-force, it actually removes one of the main obstacles to the fulfilment of these requirements. Of course it may not be the only system that can remove this obstacle. Public sector provision of training through the school system may provide an alternative solution to the free rider problem, although it has been argued that most training is best undertaken in the workplace (Piore, 1986a, 165; Streeck, 1989, 99). Franco-German comparisons, in particular, seem to support this argument (Maurice *et al.*, 1986; Lane, 1989). Whereas the French have tended to rely on public sector provision of training, the Germans have tended to opt for a firm-based approach. In any case, however many systems there are that are compatible with the skill and training requirements of a functionally flexible workforce, corporatism is certainly one of them.

Note also that skill and training issues make it easier to legitimize the exercise of centralized union power in a period of structural adjustment than it is to legitimize the exercise of centralized union power in a period of stagflation. In a period of stagflation it is possible to argue that the unions are the source of the problem that they are trying to solve. If workers did not have the power to push up wages in the first place, then there would be no need to centralize their power in order to restrain wages. But in a period of structural adjustment it is not a failure of the workers but a failure of the capitalists that the unions are seeking to solve. At least with respect to skills and training, workers' interests and the public interest coincide.

The second element of functional flexibility concerns the organization of work. The question of how work is organized is distinct from the question of what skills the work-force has. Rather, the former is concerned with how workers and their skills are deployed: that is, it is concerned with the relationship between different workers and between workers and their tools (or machines). Should workers be organized in work teams or on assembly lines? Should they work flexitime or standard hours? Should they have broad or narrow job classifications? These are all typical questions concerning the organization of work.

Is a corporatist industrial relations system compatible with the flexible organization of work? A centralized union movement certainly has the power to impose restrictive work practices that would hinder a firm's ability to organize work flexibly. But so does a more decentralized (British-style) union movement. However, whereas decentralized union movements have an incentive to impose restrictions at the level of the firm because it is only at that level that they can exercise power, centralized union movements have no such incentive. As you would expect, given these incentives, more corporatist countries like Germany and Sweden have greater flexibility in the organization of work than less corporatist countries like Britain and France (Brunhes, 1989).

This does not mean that all agreements reached under a corporatist system of industrial relations will necessarily be compatible with the need for flexibility in the organization of work. But some certainly are. In particular, it is possible for centralized union movements to make 'framework agreements' with centralized employers' organizations which set out basic principles while leaving the details to separate negotiations between individual employers and firm-based worker representatives. In countries like Germany and Sweden, framework agreements have become increasingly common over the last decade.

So far I have been trying to establish that condition two is fulfilled by showing that corporatism is compatible with each of the elements of labour market flexibility that is important for successful structural adjustment. There is, however, a more general theoretical argument that suggests that corporatism is compatible with labour market flexibility and with structural adjustment taken as a whole. The argument that I have in mind is essentially the same Olsonian argument to which I appealed in the case of stagflation. According to Olson (1982, 48), encompassing interest organizations, such as those in a corporatist industrial relations system, have an incentive to consider the general interests of a society which more narrowly specialized interest organizations do not have. Wolfgang Streeck (1984a) has shown that this same argument can be applied to the case of structural adjustment.[13]

Even if structural adjustment is in the interests of society as a whole, workers organized in small groups may have an interest in resisting it, since their share of the costs of failed adjustment is negligible compared with the gains which they alone can make from successfully resisting it. The same is true of small groups of organized capitalists. By contrast, Streeck (1984a, 141) argues: 'Corporatist systems of industrial relations exclude from articulation sectional interests that stand to profit from preservation of the *status quo* in spite of resulting sub-optimal performance of the industry or economy. Because of the way corporatist organizations aggregate process and transform the interests of their members, they allow for a good deal of flexibility of the productive apparatus and a high rate of efficient adjustment and restructuring.'

Of course increased centralization of the industrial relations actors is not the only way to avoid Olson's problem. It may also be possible in some societies to decentralize the actors to such an extent that they lose their power to resist change. Thus, just as in the case of stagflation, we would expect both corporatist and *laissez-faire* systems to have the best record of structural adjustment.

However, unlike in the case of stagflation, empirical confirmation of this hypothesis is hard to come by. In part this is a

[13] See especially the introduction and Chapter 8.

function of the fact that labour market flexibility and structural adjustment are difficult to measure. Boyer (1988, 228), for example, provides a table of over thirty ways of measuring different elements of labour market flexibility. Nevertheless, such evidence as there is, both from inter-country comparisons and company-level studies, tends to confirm our theoretical expectations. John Zysman (1985, 168), for example, provides evidence that successful structural adjustment requires either a neo-liberal system (such as in the United States) or a corporatist system (such as in Germany and Sweden, where labour is included, or France and Japan, where it is largely excluded). Britain, he claims, failed to adjust successfully because it was unable to commit itself to one or another of these systems and remained somewhere in between. Streeck (1984a) himself uses a case study of Volkswagen to provide empirical backing for his claim that corporatism in particular is compatible with structural adjustment.

Let me now move on to the third and final condition for the feasibility of a control trade-off. Is a control trade-off compatible with the requirements of national economic management? In discussing the first condition I identified restrictive work practices as a profit-threatening exchangeable good. Clearly these practices can be exchanged for a variety of other goods. For example, during the round of 'productivity bargaining' in Britain in the 1960s they were frequently exchanged for higher wages. The question here is whether restrictive work practices can be exchanged for greater control in a way that is compatible with the requirements of national economic management. I will argue that the acquisition of greater control that would result from such a trade-off is not just compatible with the requirements of national economic management, but actually fosters their fulfilment.

We saw in Chapter 2 that employment involves a worker not just in a contractual (or exchange) relationship, but also in an authority relationship with a firm. The exchange relationship only enables the firm to buy the potential for labour (or what Marx calls 'labour power'). The firm uses the authority relationship to turn this potential labour into actually performed labour (or what Marx calls 'labour'). The Fordist model of production seeks to make maximum use of this authority relationship. As we saw earlier while considering the first feasibility condition, a sharp distinction is drawn between the conception of tasks and their execution. The conception of tasks is the function of an élite of 'management scientists' whose job is to specify precisely what series of actions each worker should undertake, when they should undertake each action, and how long it should require. The execution of these precisely specified actions is the function of shop-floor workers, and a hierarchical system of management control is imposed to ensure compliance. Thus every effort is made to minimize the discretion of shop-floor workers. According to the leading theorist of the Fordist model, Frederick W. Taylor, the workers must 'do what they are told promptly and without asking questions or making suggestions . . . it is absolutely necessary for every man in an organization to become one of a train of gear wheels' (Fox, 1974, 193).

Low levels of discretion are related to low levels of skill and low levels of commitment. The Fordist employer's underlying assumption is that workers are neither able nor willing to make appropriate use of discretion. Whether or not workers are able to make appropriate use of discretion depends on whether or not they are skilled. By definition skilled workers have mastered certain general principles which they can apply to solve particular problems (Sabel, 1982, 23). Thus, by its very nature, skilled work requires a degree of discretion and a certain blurring of the division between conception and execution. But even when skilled workers are available, whether or not they are willing to make appropriate use of discretion depends on whether or not they are committed to the objectives of their firm (Walton, 1985). Even when skilled workers are available, Fordist employers seek to minimize discretion because they doubt the commitment of their workers. This is a question of trust.

Now trust tends to be reciprocal and self-reinforcing. In the case of the employment relationship this means that if employers do not trust their workers, then the workers in turn will tend not to trust their employers (Fox, 1974, 67, 97). Since workers are likely to interpret an employer's attempt to reduce their discretion as a manifestation of low trust, they will tend to respond to it in kind by attempting to reduce the employer's discretion in areas which they consider of particular importance (Fox, 1974, 69). Thus in a Fordist firm workers will attempt to impose restrictive work practices if they have the power to do so. But this, in turn, is likely to further lower the employer's trust of his or her workers, leading to a further reduction in their discretion. The result is a downward spiral of ever-declining trust (Fox, 1974, 102–13).

We have already seen that restrictive work practices are profit-threatening goods in a period of structural adjustment. Here, however, I want to draw attention to the fact that even if workers are not able to credibly threaten to impose restrictive work practices, key features of the Fordist model of production are incompatible with the requirements of structural adjustment. At the beginning of this chapter we saw that there are a number of developments that seem to require the advanced capitalist economies to move away from a cost-competitive standardized model of production (such as Fordism) towards a more quality-competitive customized model. This latter model has three key features. It seeks to improve quality, to increase diversity, and to speed up innovation. Contrary to the Fordist model, each of these features requires a blurring of the distinction between conception and execution, and thus at least some degree of discretion for shop-floor workers. Discretion, in turn, requires the skills, commitment, and trust needed to make it work. I will briefly consider each of these features in turn.

Where there is a rigid Fordist division of conception and execution, shop-floor workers have no motive to pay special attention to the quality of what they produce. Their job is to follow orders: no more and no less. At the same time, these workers cannot help but observe the production process in which they are engaged, and, as a result, they begin to build up a store of knowledge which could be used to improve it but is unknown to those responsible for conceiving the process. Giving workers greater discretion helps to solve both these problems. It fosters greater commitment, which provides workers with a motive to identify and avoid mistakes, and it opens up the possibility of tapping the workers' unused knowledge to improve the production process. When autonomous work teams were given responsibility for quality control in the Lineout project of the Swedish engineering firm Saab-Scania, the quality level improved by 50 per cent (Berggren, 1980, 247).

The more diversified or customized a firm's products become, the smaller each batch of products will have to be. And the smaller the batch size the more frequent will be the need to retool, reset, replan, reprogramme, and redesign in order to adapt to the different specifications of each batch. But the more frequent this process of adaptation the more difficult it is for the firm to centrally plan all the actions of each worker while maintaining the continuity of production (Sorge and Streeck, 1988, 25). This problem is compounded by the requirements of innovation. Firms need to be able to produce not just one diverse set of products, but a continually changing diverse set of products. 'The more frequently products and processes are changed, the less time there is to translate conceptions into reliable, mechanically applicable routines. The more imperfect the routines, of course, the more interpretation and initiative they require from workers at all levels' (Sabel, 1982, 210). In other words, the requirements of diversity and innovation force firms to rely, at least to some extent, on the discretion of their workers. To this extent, firms must increase the area in which workers execute their work according to their own conception.

The distinction between conception and execution is the conceptual correlative of the distinction between choice and action which I used to develop the conceptions of freedom and authority which are discussed in Chapter 1.[14] By increasing the area in which workers' own conceptions (that is, their choices) govern the tasks that they execute (that is, their actions), the direct control which those workers exercise over their firm is increased at the expense of the authority of the capitalist employer.

This is not to say that the demands of quality, diversity, and innovation threaten the higher levels of authority in a capitalist firm. Even the most far-reaching changes, such as those in the Volvo plant in Kalmar in Sweden, have not led to increases in the control above the third level of Stephen's diagram[15] (Berggren, 1980, 245). However, in most, if not all, of the advanced capitalist countries, significant increases in control can be achieved even if they are restricted to these lower levels.

In summary, then, my discussion of the third condition runs as follows. Structural adjustment requires a move from cost-competitive standardized production to quality-competitive customized production. But quality-competitive customized production requires that workers have greater discretion. And

[14] See Figures 2 and 3.
[15] See Figure 7. Note, though, that control of pension funds has also led to worker representation on Volvo's board of directors.

greater worker discretion involves increasing the extent to which workers exercise direct control over their firms. Thus a control trade-off would not only be compatible with the requirements of national economic management in a period of structural adjustment, but it would actually help to fulfil these requirements.

So each of the three conditions for the feasibility of a control trade-off are satisfied in an environment of structural adjustment. First, I showed that workers' ability to impose restrictive work practices provides them with a profit-threatening exchangeable good. Second, I provided evidence that corporatism is compatible with the requirements of national economic management. And third, I showed that a control trade-off is not only compatible with the requirements of national economic management but would actually help to fulfil these requirements. I conclude, therefore, that a control trade-off is feasible in such an environment.

Having shown this, I have fulfilled the main purpose of this chapter. However, as in the previous chapter, I now want to briefly consider a subsidiary question. In formulating the three conditions for the feasibility of a control trade-off I assumed that workers wanted increased control. But is it still rational for workers to opt for a control trade-off in an environment of structural adjustment if they are solely concerned about improving their material well-being? Answering this question will enable me to shed some light on the kind of control trade-offs that are likely to succeed in a period of structural adjustment.

The material well-being of workers is usually taken to include both wages and working conditions. In the previous chapter it was possible to make a straightforward argument about the rationality of a control trade-off for materially motivated workers on the basis of wage considerations alone. Here, however, I will appeal to both factors.

The developments which have brought about the need for structural adjustment will ensure that the advanced capitalist countries can only be high wage countries by becoming high skill countries (Streeck, 1989, 90). In particular, workers will have to acquire the skills which are needed both to produce a diverse range of quality goods and to be able to rapidly adjust to producing a new range of such goods. These skills will mostly be marketable skills. But, as we saw earlier, employers cannot be relied on to provide training in marketable skills. Hence workers have a material incentive, based on their desire to earn a high wage, to exercise some control over their firm's training activities.[16] A good example of a union-led attempt to introduce co-determination over training activities during the present period of structural adjustment is considered in the next chapter. Moreover, the significance of control over the training system may be greater than it at first appears. According to Maurice *et al.* (1986), the training system is a crucial determinant of the overall distribution of authority within a firm.

Working conditions are intimately affected by the organization of work. In a Fordist system workers responded to proposed changes in the organization of work by seeking to negotiate the introduction of a new regime of work practices. But as we have seen, this option is no longer available. The negotiation and implementation of a new regime of work practices takes too long, and once implemented it hinders a firm's ability to rapidly make further adjustments. Since continual rapid adjustments are now required there are only two options open to the workers. They can either withdraw from the regulation of their working conditions altogether or they can seek to institutionalize their influence, not by seeking to introduce a rigid code to govern each new issue as it arises, but rather by ensuring that they share some control over the process by which all these issues are decided. The 1984 agreement between IRI[17] and the Italian unions is a good example of the latter strategy. The agreement established joint union–management committees which could make binding judgements about industrial restructuring initiatives (Negrelli, 1988, 94).

More generally, it is becoming harder for workers to insulate the regulation of wages and working conditions from the regulation of a firm's overall strategy. The need to respond rapidly to changing product markets is forcing firms to increase their flexibility by integrating the regulation of wages and working conditions into a comprehensive commercial strategy.[18] Thus

[16] Control over training activities would also have the advantage of providing a partial guarantee against an owner-initiated attempt at a down-market adjustment to a low wage, low skill economy.

[17] IRI is the main group of state-controlled enterprises in Italy.

[18] The primary importance of the product market and the subordinate role of labour market considerations in dictating employers' overall strategies is borne out by a series of case studies conducted by Batstone *et al.* (1987, 210–13) which focus on decisions to introduce new technologies.

workers will also be forced to develop an integrated strategy simply in order to maintain some influence over the wages and conditions that are central to their material well-being (Sorge and Streeck, 1988, 42).

Now I noted in the previous chapter that improved material well-being is likely to remain important for workers even if they are independently interested in increased control: independently, that is, of its effect on their material well-being. Thus, even where workers are independently committed to achieving greater control, a proposal that links control gains with material gains is likely to have the best chance of success.

In the previous chapter I suggested that control trade-offs that sought 'control through ownership' rather than 'control against ownership' were best able to make this link in a stagflationary environment. The above considerations suggest that the reverse is true in an environment of structural adjustment. They suggest, that is, that in such an environment an extension of co-determination (especially in the organizations of work and training) and other forms of control against ownership (rather than control through ownership) are likely to be typical.

Throughout this chapter I have been concerned with a process of structural adjustment that has taken place over recent years. What marks this period out is the intensity and scope of the structural adjustment that has been taking place. Some have even suggested that we are at the beginning of a new Kondratiev cycle[19] (Jacobi, 1988; Coombes, 1984; Freeman, 1984; van Duijn, 1983). But though of differing intensity and scope, bouts of structural adjustment are an ongoing feature of the advanced capitalist economies. So it may well be possible to repeat the kind of control trade-off that I have been advocating here during future bouts of structural adjustment.

Many unionists fear that trading off hard-won restrictive work practices is a foolish, once-only possibility that will leave them seriously weakened in the future. This fear has been especially prevalent in Anglo-Saxon countries, where restrictive work practices have been one of the main expressions of union power. However, as we will see in the next chapter, even in these countries the fear can be overcome. According to those imbued

---

[19] Kondratiev identified a series of long waves of development beginning with the emergence of capitalism and each lasting approximately half a century.

with this fear, trading off restrictive work practices is like abandoning a defensive trench which has been slowly built up over the years and is a precondition for further advance. This perspective suggests that once workers have traded off their restrictive work practices further control trade-offs during future periods of structural adjustment will not be feasible. However, there are reasons to doubt this perspective. For one thing, restrictive work practices do not have to exist in order to trade off the threat to impose them. In this respect they are just like wage increases. For another, it is unlikely that even the most well entrenched restrictive work practices can be defended indefinitely in the face of a hostile employer. In this respect the ultimate defeat of the London print workers in 1987 is instructive.

But quite apart from these considerations, the fear of trading off restrictive work practices is fundamentally misconceived. Recall from Chapter 5 that the labour market has three historical features and four intrinsic features which lead to a power imbalance between individual capitalists and individual workers. Organization can counter some of these features, and so enable workers to rectify this imbalance and even to accumulate a surplus of power. But while organization can counter some of these features it cannot counter them all. In particular, it has no effect on two intrinsic features of labour and capital: their 'range of applicability' and their 'ease of transformation'. These features disadvantage labour since, relative to capital, labour has a small range of applicability and is difficult to transform. But while these features are intrinsic they are not immutable. By replacing restrictive work practices with high discretion, multi-purpose skills, labour can increase its range of applicability. And by establishing a flexible training system that can top up and redirect these more generally based skills, labour can increase its ease of transformation. Thus the task for labour is not to prohibit the introduction of flexible skills and flexible training arrangements but rather to control it. If labour can manage the introduction of this flexibility without allowing flexibility to undermine its organization, it will actually strengthen its position by weakening two intrinsic disadvantages which are beyond the reach of organization alone.

9

An Unexpected Case of Corporatism

Since the first election of the Hawke government in 1983, the Australian labour movement has purposefully gone about building up a corporatist industrial relations system. The system which has been established is based on a *Statement of Accord by the Australian Labor Party and the Australian Council of Trade Unions Regarding Economic Policy* (ALP/ACTU, 1983). The 'Accord', as it came to be known, was centred on an incomes policy. However, by now its original prescriptions have been altered so many times that the government and the unions refer instead to the 'Accord process'.

The bipartite origins of this process have ensured that a high degree of public involvement and a highly centralized union movement have become the most distinctive feature of Australian corporatism. Both formal and informal negotiations between the government and the ACTU play a fundamental role in setting macro-economic policy. However, this process has in turn brought about greater class co-operation, leading, for example, to a radical reduction in strike activity. In the late 1980s explicitly negotiated class co-operation between unions and employers also began to emerge.

In the early years of the Labor government many commentators dismissed the emergence of corporatism in Australia as an aberration which would soon fall into line with an international trend towards less centralized industrial relations systems. But when the Labor party was re-elected for an unprecedented third term in July 1987, and then went on the win a fourth term in March 1990, it became clear that the Australian labour movement had genuinely bucked the international trend and established a lasting corporatism in the 1980s.[1]

[1] The Labor Party was subsequently re-elected for a fifth term in March 1993 under the new leadership of Prime Minister Keating.

This chapter is divided into three sections. Sections two and three deal with the performance of Australian corporatism. Section two deals with the period of stagflation and section three deals with the period of structural adjustment. In each section, I focus on evidence that both corporatism and a control trade-off have been compatible with the requirements of national economic management. I also point out that the control trade-offs that have taken place are precisely those that the argument of the previous two chapters would lead us to expect.

Section one sets out the background which is needed to understand Australian industrial relations. But it also raises a separate question which is important in its own right. In order to show that it is feasible for the labour movement to undertake a control trade-off, I had to show that it is feasible for the labour movement to *maintain* a corporatist system. But until now I have said nothing about whether it is feasible for the labour movement to *establish* a corporatist system where one did not previously exist.[2] Yet this is what I must do if I want to claim that the corporatist trade-off strategy is feasible in *all* the countries of Western Europe and Australasia. Now although I do not intend to address this question directly, I do want to lend plausibility to the claim that the establishment of corporatism is feasible in all these countries. To do this I will criticize what I take to be the most typical counter to this claim. According to this counter-claim, while the establishment of corporatism is feasible in countries like Germany, Austria, and Sweden, it is not feasible in Anglo-Saxon countries like Britain. This is said to be so because the establishment of corporatism is only feasible in countries where certain traditions are already well embedded. If this counter-claim were true it would not be feasible for the labour movement to establish a corporatist system in all of the countries of Western Europe and Australasia. I will argue that the counter-claim is false.

1. CHOOSING CORPORATISM

Is it possible for a society to choose its industrial relations system? And in particular, is it possible for a country without a tradition of

---

[2] See Chapter 6.

corporatism to opt for a corporatist system? The work of some industrial sociologists suggests that it is not. Colin Crouch (1986, 177), for example, argues that in Europe corporatism can only be successfully established in countries which have a tradition of sharing political space, and that these traditions were established 'some time in the eighteenth or nineteenth centuries'. Drawing on the work of Charles Maier (1984, 29), he highlights the importance of the 'liberal parenthesis' that existed between the era of the guilds and the *standestaat*, and the era of organized capitalism and organized class interests. During this parenthesis parliamentary states attempted to monopolize political space.[3] In some countries the parenthesis lasted longer than in others. And in some countries the political monopoly that inaugurated it proved more difficult to establish than in others.[4] According to Crouch these two factors established a tradition which continues to determine whether a country has a liberal or a corporatist industrial re-lations system. His central thesis is that 'the longer the interval, or the sharper the breach, between the destruction of ancient guild and *standestaat* institutions and the construction of typically "modern" interest organizations, the more committed did the state become to liberal modes of interest representation, and the less likely to tolerate sharing political space' (1986, 182). So whether a country is prepared to share political space, and hence whether it is prepared to countenance corporatism, is a function, not of contemporary choices, but of long-established traditions. I will refer to this type of claim as the 'tradition-boundness thesis'.

Now I have been dwelling on this point because, *prima facie* at least, Australia seems to provide a decisive counter-example. Of course it is not a counter-example of Crouch's particular thesis, since in the history of white Australia there is no pre-parenthesis period. But it does seem to provide a counter-example to the general line of argument that corporatism can only arise as a function of long-established tradition. For Australia's long-estab-

[3] The liberal parenthesis is better known as the era of *laissez-faire* capitalism. As Crouch points out, state attempts to monopolize political authority were directly linked to the defence of a *laissez-faire* market. To defend a *laissez-faire* market the state must not only keep itself out of the economic system; it must also monopolize political space to keep economic actors out of the political system, for this would also have the effect of politicizing the market.

[4] The difficulty was especially great in those countries where the Catholic church had a long-established claim to political space.

lished industrial relations tradition is generally thought of as a variant of the British liberal tradition. This is reflected in almost every attempt to rank countries according to their degree of corporatism. Australia is typically grouped near the bottom of the list with the other Anglo-Saxon countries—Britain, the United States, Canada, and New Zealand.[5] But if this is so, the emergence of corporatism in the 1980s can hardly be a product of tradition. The liberal industrial relations tradition of the Anglo-Saxon world is widely seen as the antithesis of a corporatist tradition.

In response it might be said that white Australia does not provide a counter-example to the tradition-boundness thesis because it is simply so young that it has no traditions and hence should be ruled out as an exceptional case. We should be wary of this argument. As with most advanced capitalist countries, Australia has a tradition of organized industrial relations dating back well over a century. The tradition is a product of both its British inheritance and a reaction against it. If the tradition-boundness thesis is true, the emergence of Australian corporatism must be a product of this tradition. To see if Australia is really a counter-example we will have to identify the elements of this tradition and assess whether they helped or hindered the rise of corporatism.

One way in which a country's tradition manifests itself is through its dominant ideologies.

Two ideologies dominated the first century of white settlement in Australia. The first was a version of English radical liberalism. The second was the distinctively Australian ethos of 'mateship'.

The Australian colonies were among the world's first democracies. Between 1850 and 1858 the main points of the constitutional programme of English radicalism were put into effect. Manhood suffrage and vote by ballot were adopted a generation before the third Reform Act brought them to England. Economically, the radicals focused on the question of land distribution. By promoting the development of a class of small independent

---

[5] See, for example, Cameron (1984, 165), Crouch (1985, 119), Bruno and Sachs (1985, 226), and Schott (1984, 2). Schmitter (1981, 294) does not include Australia, but as Crouch (1985, 118) points out, Schmitter's criteria would place it 'at or near the bottom of his ranking'. The one exception is Calmfors and Driffill (1988, 17–20), who give Australia an intermediate ranking. This is partly because of their attempt to take into account the developments of the early years of the Accord.

farmer–settlers they hoped to provide the new democracy with a solid foundation. This aspiration was shared by many miners, who began to look for alternative ways of safeguarding their independence once the gold rush of the early 1850s began to wane (Gollan, 1960, 15–16). The radicals won the legal battle with the passage of the Land Acts of 1860–1 in the colonies of New South Wales and Victoria. But the 'squattocracy' (named both for the way in which they originally acquired their vast land holdings and their aristocratic pretensions) retained overall control of the pastoral industry, and it became increasingly clear that wage-labour rather than self-labour would be the norm. So lucrative was the pastoral industry, however, that in the early twentieth century Australia had the highest standard of living in the world.

Alongside these radical liberal initiatives a different ideology was emerging amongst the bush workers of the outback: the ethos of mateship. Mateship grew up amongst the semi-nomadic drovers, shepherds, shearers, bullock-drivers, stockmen, bound-ary-riders, and station-hands, who were collectively known as bushmen. These men did not deny the value of individual inde-pendence stressed by the radical liberals. But they placed a special emphasis on egalitarian values and on the importance of soli-darity or fellowship. Mates were equals, and mateship was a fellowship of equals. These values were rooted both in the hard-ship and loneliness of life in the outback, and in the convict origins of the earliest bushmen (Ward, 1965, 2, 10, 27, 78). Al-though it seems likely that 'the main features of the new tradition were already fixed before [the begining of the goldrush in] 1851' (Ward, 1965, 11), it was in the 1880s that they came to have enormous national significance, when a movement of writers and poets began to promote mateship and the values of the bush as definitive of a new Australian national identity.[6]

---

[6] One of the most forceful and influential advocates of this new identity, *The Bulletin*, defined it like this: 'By the term Australian we mean not those who have been merely born in Australia. All white men who come to these shores—with a clean record—and who leave behind them the memory of the class distinctions and the religious differences of the old world; all men who place the happiness, the prosperity, the advancement of their adopted country before the interests of Imperialism, are Australian. In this regard all men who leave the tyrant-ridden lands of Europe for freedom of speech and the right of personal liberty are Australians before they set foot on the ship which brings them hither. Those who

The point to note is that neither radical liberalism nor mateship is straightforwardly propitious for the development of corporatism. The first is clearly hostile, placing a premium on individual independence; while the second is more ambiguous, valuing both a collective and an individual identity.[7]

But ideologies are not the only manifestations of traditions. Traditions are also carried by long-established institutions. To get a clearer picture of Australia's industrial relations tradition, we need to look at each of the institutions that has played a significant role in establishing it. To assess the tradition-boundness thesis we will have to consider whether these institutions have helped or hindered the emergence of corporatism. I will first consider the institutions of the labour movement (that is, the unions and the Labor Party), then those of the employers, and finally those of the state.

Embryonic workers' organizations began to appear in the 1830s, but it was only in the 1850s, after gold brought new prosperity to the colonies, that stable unions were formed. These were unions of skilled workers based on craft divisions, and they set a pattern of craft unionism which continues to exist. They were joined by new unions of unskilled and semi-skilled miners, shearers, and waterside workers in the 1880s. These unions drew strength from the mateship ethos of the bush. According to the first president of the Shearers' Union, W. G. Spence: 'Unionism came to the Australian bushman as a religion. It came bringing salvation from years of tyranny. It had in it that feeling of mateship which he understood already, and which always characterized the action of one "white man" to another. Unionism extended the idea, so a man's character was gauged by whether he stood true to Union rules or "scabbed" it on his fellows' (Crowley, 1980, 78). The new unions faced their first trial of

fly from an odious military conscription; those who leave their fatherland because they cannot swallow the worm-eaten lie of the divine right of kings to murder peasants, are Australians by instinct—Australians and Republicans are synonymous. No nigger, no Chinaman, no Kanaka, no purveyor of cheap coloured labour is an Australian' (*The Bulletin*, 2 July 1887; cited in Clark, 1955). Australians combined a vituperative racism with an image of themselves as egalitarian, prosperous, and free.

[7] Bushmen exhibited a '"manly independence" whose obverse side was a levelling, egalitarian collectivism, and whose sum was comprised in the concept of mateship' (Ward, 1965, 167).

strength during the depression of the early 1890s. Under the banner of 'freedom of contract', employers, supported by police and troopers, took on the seamen, the shearers, and the miners. In each case the workers were decisively defeated.

These defeats encouraged unions to consider the benefits of direct involvement in parliamentary politics. From 1890 onwards the Trades and Labour Councils that co-ordinated union activity in the various colonies began to form parties to contest seats in their respective parliaments. By 1895 the New South Wales Labor Party held the balance of power. And in 1899 the world's first labour government was formed in Queensland, although it was out of power by the end of the week. However, there was little to distinguish Labor parliamentarians from other progressives. The representatives of labour were deeply committed to liberalism and parliamentary government, and only a minority saw socialist or collectivist ideas as distinguishing themselves from other liberals (Gollan, 1975, 206). Those socialist ideas that did exist were heavily influenced by Edward Bellamy's justly forgotten *Looking Backward*, which mingled them with a populist belief in a semi-mystical entity called 'the money power' which conspired against 'the people'. In general, however, there was little attention to doctrine of any kind. Anticipating federation in 1901, the colonial Labor parties met the year before to establish the Australian Labor Party (ALP). Its objectives were established at its first full-scale national conference in 1905. By 1910 majority Labor governments were in power both federally and in New South Wales.

Neither the unions nor the Labor Party were developing in a way that was propitious for corporatism.

I will begin with the unions. The one factor which is almost universally agreed upon as a precondition for corporatism is a strong, centralized union movement. Indeed, a number of writers see the centralization of organized labour as coextensive with corporatism.[8] As we saw in Chapter 4, centralization has three attributes: membership density, organizational unity, and concentration of power.[9] These were illustrated in Figure 5. Only on

[8] This is especially true of the economists who have recently attempted to quantify corporatism. See, for example, Calmfors and Driffill (1988).

[9] Cf. Cameron's (1984, 164–6) 'organizational power of labour', and Schmitter's (1981, 294) 'societal corporatism'.

the first of these dimensions do Australian unions score well prior to the 1980s.

Membership density refers to the extent to which unions have succeeded in organizing workers. In the first decades of this century, Australia became the most unionized country in the world. By 1920 over 53 per cent of all employees belonged to a union. During the depression this dropped to a low point of 42.6 per cent in 1934, and then steadily rose to an all-time high of 63 per cent in 1953. During the 1960s and 1970s membership density settled down to around the 55 per cent mark.

Organizational unity refers to the extent to which unions are themselves organized into peak councils. The lowest scores go to countries with a multiplicity of peak councils and numerous unions. The craft origins of Australian unionism led to the formation of a plethora of unions, each jealously protective of its craft base. There have been well over 300 unions for most of this century. In 1983 the figure still stood at 319.[10] After a number of unsuccessful attempts many of these unions joined to form the Australian Council of Trade Unions in 1927. But its coverage was far from universal. The Australian Workers Union, built on the base of the old Shearers' Union, claimed the status of an alternative peak council and refused to join until 1967. Moreover, white collar and public sector unions were organized into two separate peak councils. These merged with the ACTU in 1979 and 1981 respectively. The formation of a single peak council has certainly helped the development of corporatism. But with over 300 unions and three or four peak councils until the beginning of the 1980s, organizational unity can hardly be considered part of the industrial relations tradition.

Concentration of power refers to the extent to which a peak council is able to control the industrial activities of its affiliates. In Australia intrastate industrial disputes are managed either by the union concerned or by the state's Trades and Labour Council. Although the Trades and Labour Councils are branches of the ACTU, they retain significant independent powers reflecting their early growth and importance during the colonial period. Formally, the ACTU has the power to take over the management

[10] Of these the largest 14 unions (each with more than 50,000 members) represented 44.6% of unionists, while the smallest 105 (each with less than 500 members) represented just 0.6% (Hancock Committee, 1985, 23).

of interstate industrial disputes. But in reality, unless its assistance is sought, disputes remain outside its control. It is the affiliates that control strike funds and, on the whole, it is the affiliates that initiate and manage disputes.

What about the Labor Party? There are three factors concerning socialist parties which have been thought to help the development of corporatism. None of them seems to apply in Australia.

The first concerns the original relationship between the party and the unions. Corporatism has prospered where parties and unions developed at the same pace. But it has proved difficult to establish either where parties reached maturity before unionism became firmly established, as in France and Italy, or where unionism preceded party formation, as in Britain (Maier, 1984, 54–5; Valenzuela, 1992, 55, 60–3, 70, 83). We have seen that it is this latter, British-style relationship that pertains in Australia. The unions established the Labor Party to put their delegates in parliament, and they considered their influence over the party a matter of right rather than one of negotiation.

Second, corporatism has been most sustained in those countries in which socialist parties have played a dominant role in government (Schmitter, 1981, 313–14; Panitch, 1977). Clearly, 'unions will be more prepared to enter into political bargaining, and will have greater confidence in eventual gains from it, where they possess close ideological as well as organizational ties with the ruling party' (Maier, 1984, 49). However, in Australia, despite its early success, the Labor Party did not become a natural party of government, as in Sweden, or even a natural partner of government, as in Austria. The 1949 defeat of the Labor government which had led the country through the Second World War inaugurated 23 years of continuous conservative rule. In 1972 Labor regained government for just 3 years before the conservatives were returned to office, where they remained until 1983.

Third, it seems that it is not just the predominance of socialist parties that matters; it is the predominance of socialist parties of a certain type. In particular, corporatism seems to be best fostered by German-style social democratic parties with a Marxist-influenced past (Goldthorpe, 1984b, 327; Lehmbruch, 1984, 77). Having resigned themselves to operating within a capitalist economy, the Marxist heritage of these parties fostered class-wide corporate identities and a more political unionism. We have seen that the Australian Labor Party was built on essentially liberal ideological foundations. The speed with which the newly formed Labor parties moved into a position of power forced them to turn their attention immediately to the exigencies of running a capitalist economy, and left little room for the development of radical political ideas. Marxist ideas, in particular, were thin on the ground. According to a contemporary commentator, Labor leaders 'know little or nothing of Marxian theories. Few of them know even by title the principal text books of continental social-ism.'[11] It is true that in 1921 the ALP adopted 'the socialization of industry, production, distribution, and exchange' as its objective, but, by then, 'socialism without doctrine' was already well entrenched.[12]

In summary, neither of the two main institutions of the Australian labour movement carried traditions which were pro-pitious to the development of corporatism. The unions did have a high membership, but were otherwise weakly centralized. They were established well before the Labor Party, and the party itself failed to predominate. Marxist ideas had very little influence. In each of these respects the Australian labour movement looked very similar to its British counterpart, and a similar industrial relations tradition could be expected.

Employer organizations have also been unfavourable to the development of corporatism. The employers have even less of a tradition of strong centralized organization than do the unions. Their early organizations were either trade associations or were formed for specific purposes such as combatting the 1890 strikes. When national organizations began to emerge after federation, their role was restricted to making legal challenges to the emerg-ing industrial relations system. Ultimately two stable organiz-ations took root: one co-ordinated employers' federations, the other co-ordinated chambers of commerce. Employers remained deeply divided between the two until the 1960s. A merger was

---

[11] V. S. Clark, *The Labour Movement in Australasia*, Westminster, 1906. Cited in Pons (1984, 118).

[12] In this regard it is interesting to note the role of communists in providing the legitimizing framework for the Accord within the union movement. Australia's most prominent communist union official, Laurie Carmichael, repeatedly empha-sized that the Accord was a class policy designed to protect the interests of all workers, not just the sectional interests of those who happened to have industrial muscle.

finally achieved when the Confederation of Australian Industry was formed in 1977. But the unity was short lived. In 1983 a second national employer organization—the Business Council of Australia—was formed. And in the latter half of the 1980s the CAI's claim to be a national peak council was further undermined as one after another of its main industry groups chose to operate independently.

Finally, I want to look at the institutions of the state. Australia's origins as a penal colony bequeathed it centralized and interventionist administrative institutions. Following self-government, these institutions were turned to entrepreneurial tasks in order to promote rapid colonial development. Large-scale assisted immigration programmes were launched to import labour from Britain (de Lepervanche, 1975), and the colonial governments raised huge capital loans on the London Bond Market which they invested in railways, roads and bridges (H. V. Evatt Research Centre, 1988, 17). So widespread and so widely supported was this public economic intervention that it is often referred to as a kind of 'colonial socialism'. After federation in 1901 an interventionist approach was also adopted by the federal government. It was most clearly articulated in the 'New Protection' policy which restricted immigration to whites, and imposed tariffs and bounties to protect local manufacturers, and some agricultural producers, from overseas competition. However, in the realm of industrial relations it was much more difficult for the federal government to act.

The new Australian constitution specified the powers of the Commonwealth (or federal government) and left all other powers with the States (which took over from the old colonial governments). In the area of industrial relations the Commonwealth's powers are severely restricted. Section 51(xxxv) of the constitution empowers it 'to make laws for the peace, order and good government of the Commonwealth with respect to ... Conciliation and Arbitration for the prevention and settlement of industrial disputes extending beyond the limits of any one State'. The power to legislate about incomes, working conditions, and all other industrial relations matters rests with the States.[13] With such limited powers the federal government does not seem well

[13] Wartime, and the Commonwealth's own employees, are exceptions to this.

equipped to foster corporatism. In fact, however, this peculiar constitutional situation led to the establishment of a unique conciliation and arbitration system which some have seen as a form of proto-corporatism. Anyone wanting to claim that the Accord is a product of Australian traditions would emphasize its continuity with the arbitration system. Since the arbitration system provides defenders of the tradition-boundness thesis with their strongest argument, I want to consider it in more detail.

The outcome of the industrial struggles of the 1890s convinced the labour movement that some sort of state machinery was necessary to enforce union recognition and fair wages and conditions. In 1904, with Labor Party backing, the federal government used its limited constitutional power to establish a Court of Conciliation and Arbitration which was later renamed the Conciliation and Arbitration Commission. When a dispute occurs, the Commission is first required to encourage conciliation between the parties. If the parties manage to reach an agreement, the Commission will usually register it as a 'consent award'. But if the parties fail to agree, arbitration is compulsory and the Commission must convene a hearing and make an award itself. Either way the outcome is an award which is legally binding on both parties. Penalties can be imposed on those who fail to comply with an award, but in reality these are only used against employers.[14]

By 1912 similar industrial tribunals had been established in all the States. Gradually the federal tribunal became predominant. In the 1907 Harvester case, the founder of the federal arbitration system, Justice Higgins, established a needs-based criterion for setting the basic (or minimum) wage that should be paid to an unskilled worker. Skilled workers would be awarded 'margins' over and above the basic wage. Arguing that an average man must support himself, his wife, and three children, Higgins set the basic wage at 42 shillings a week. Since this was above the prevailing minimum rate being offered by the State tribunals, many unions sought to be covered by a federal award. Ultimately

[14] Attempts to fine striking unionists in the 1960s led to the jailing of the tram workers' leader Clarrie O'Shea. The unions responded with a national strike and refused to pay all further fines. Since then penalties for direct action by unionists have not been imposed.

almost the entire work-force was covered by either Federal or State awards.[15]

There is no doubt that the Arbitration system 'is deeply entrenched in [Australian] society'. These are the words of the Hancock Committee (1985 (vol. 2), 4), which was established in 1983 by the Hawke government to conduct the first comprehensive review of the industrial relations system since its inception. The Hancock Committee essentially recommended a continuation of the existing system, and public opinion seemed to support this recommendation.[16]

Now there are a number of objections to the claim that the Arbitration Commission has fostered the development of corporatism. Firstly, it can be argued that, both by taking on the mantle of the public interest and by protecting the existence of a plethora of small craft-based unions, the Commission has hindered the development of an encompassing, strategically thinking union movement. Why should unions consider the public interest when the Commission is there to mediate between their claims and the public interest? Secondly, some economists have suggested that the Commission has no long-term effect at all. This is a controversial point, but those who support it argue that Commission decisions simply mimic the changing market strength of employers and unions.[17] Thirdly, it is often emphasized that it is a mistake to juxtapose the arbitration system with free collective bargaining, since one of the main aims of the system's founders was to achieve recognition of collective bargaining. In particular, 'it is wrong to equate "conciliation and arbitration" and centralization and to equate "collective bargaining" and decentralization. . . . it is possible to have highly centralized collective bargaining

[15] The first official survey of award coverage in 1954 showed that 89.5% of the work-force were covered by awards. 42.5% were covered by federal awards, while the remaining 47.0% were shared out between the six states.

[16] The Hancock Committee commissioned a poll in 1984 which showed that 56% of people thought that the Arbitration Commission did a good job at national wage fixing, while 16% thought it did a poor job (Hancock Committee, 1985 (vol. 3), 212). In another poll that year, people were asked whether the Commission should continue in its major role of determining wages and working conditions. 76% answered yes; 14% answered no; and 10% did not know (Hancock Committee, 1985 (vol. 2), 227).

[17] The Hancock Committee rejects this view (1985 (vol. 2), 156 and n. 10). For a review of some of the literature see Gill (1987a).

systems and highly decentralized arbitral systems' (Hancock Committee, 1985 (vol. 2), 212).

This third objection is especially telling given the pivotal role of centralized bargaining in a corporatist system. Consider wage bargaining, for example. A cursory look at the historical record shows that the arbitration system has coexisted with a wide variety of wage fixing systems. Figure 13 summarizes the history of Australian wage fixation prior to the Accord. It is clear that early on the Arbitration Commission developed into a unique centralized forum which based its awards on national criteria

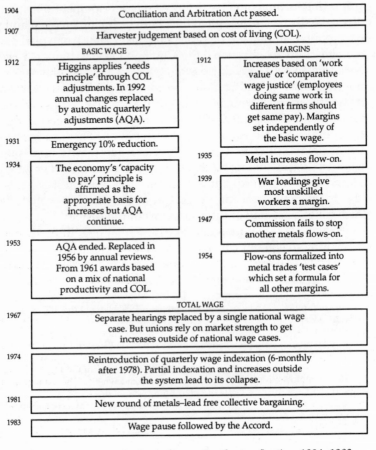

1904	Conciliation and Arbitration Act passed.		
1907	Harvester judgement based on cost of living (COL).		

	BASIC WAGE		**MARGINS**
1912	Higgins applies 'needs principle' through COL adjustments. In 1992 annual changes replaced by automatic quarterly adjustments (AQA).	1912	Increases based on 'work value' or 'comparative wage justice' (employees doing same work in different firms should get same pay). Margins set independently of the basic wage.
1931	Emergency 10% reduction.		
		1935	Metal increases flow-on.
1934	The economy's 'capacity to pay' principle is affirmed as the appropriate basis for increases but AQA continue.	1939	War loadings give most unskilled workers a margin.
		1947	Commission fails to stop another metals flows-on.
1953	AQA ended. Replaced in 1956 by annual reviews. From 1961 awards based on a mix of national productivity and COL.	1954	Flow-ons formalized into metal trades 'test cases' which set a formula for all other margins.

	TOTAL WAGE
1967	Separate hearings replaced by a single national wage case. But unions rely on market strength to get increases outside of national wage cases.
1974	Reintroduction of quarterly wage indexation (6-monthly after 1978). Partial indexation and increases outside the system lead to its collapse.
1981	New round of metals–lead free collective bargaining.
1983	Wage pause followed by the Accord.

FIG. 13. *Key events in Australian national wage fixation, 1904–1983*

such as the the needs principle, the economy's capacity to pay, and the doctrine of comparative wage justice. But the important point to note is that the Commission later showed itself to be quite compatible with a highly decentralized system closely resembling British-style free collective bargaining. In particular, in the late 1960s and early 1970s the Commission's national wage decisions had become little more than a guaranteed minimum for weakly organized workers, and the most important wage rises were achieved in individual award changes negotiated outside the arbitration system. Evidence for this can be seen in the sharp rise in consent awards (which are simply ratified by the Commission) and overaward payments (which are paid completely independently of the Commission), and in increased strike activity.[18] By the financial year 1974–5 the contribution of National Wage Cases to increases in average male award wages had fallen to just 21.2 per cent (Howard, 1977, 271). After a period of centralized indexation there was a further period of decentralized free collective bargaining in the early 1980s.

This is very damaging for the tradition-boundness thesis. In its strongest form, the thesis claims that certain tradition-carrying ideologies or institutions exist which in themselves are a sufficient condition for the development of corporatism. We have seen that amongst the ideologies there are no candidates for this role, and that amongst labour, employer, and state institutions, only the Arbitration Commission is a viable candidate. But at times, and indeed immediately prior to the Accord, the Arbitration Commission has coexisted with liberal wage fixing arrangements, so it can hardly be a sufficient condition for corporatism. However, to finally lay the tradition-boundness thesis to rest we also have to tackle the weaker claim that the Commission was a necessary condition for corporatism. To test this weaker claim we need to identify what were the main conditions which led to the emergence of the Accord. If the Commission is not among them then the claim is false.

A comprehensive analysis of the conditions which led to the emergence of the Accord would be a major task. But briefly we can say that the Accord came about because the labour movement

---

[18] On consent awards see Gill (1987b, 8). On overaward payments and strike activity see Hancock Committee (1985 (vol. 2), 193, 54).

adopted it as a policy at a time when it had the power to implement it.

The policy developed out of new ideas which began to emerge during the late 1970s and early 1980s in both the political and industrial wings of the labour movement. A National Committee of Inquiry began a systematic reappraisal of Labor Party policies in 1978, and in the same year the metal workers union began publishing a series of booklets on alternative ways of dealing with Australia's growing economic crisis. In particular, they identified the social wage and industry development as industrial issues that required unions to negotiate not only with employers but also with government. It was these changing attitudes within the unions—especially powerful left-wing unions like the metal workers—that were crucial.

A peculiar combination of boom and bust ensured both that these unions committed themselves to the Accord and that they had a powerful voice in setting the terms of the agreement. The 'boom' was a phoney resources boom in 1980–1 which strengthened the negotiating position of the unions which, led by the metal workers, won huge wage rises in the market. This also strengthened the unions' hand in negotiating the terms of the Accord with the Labor Party. Labor urgently required a coherent alternative to the Liberal government's monetarist-inspired 'fight inflation first' strategy if it was to avoid a fourth successive defeat at the impending elections. And this required an agreement with the unions on wage restraint. The left-wing unions used their bargaining strength to widen the Accord to include social wage issues and an interventionist industry development policy. The 'bust' was the 1982 recession, which soon made it clear that the unions' underlying strength was being seriously eroded. Massive lay-offs and soaring inflation reinforced the unions' commitment to the Accord. In the 12 months to May 1983, employment in the metal and engineering industries fell by 17 per cent.[19]

[19] The crucial importance of the recession in cementing the Accord supports Maier's contention (1984, 50) that it is their 'sense of potential economic vulnerability' that drives small, highly developed countries towards corporatism; and, more generally, highlights Katzenstein's thesis (1985) that small open economies tend to adopt corporatism because of their extreme vulnerability to external shocks. During the early years of the Accord, Bob Hawke liked to dramatize the crisis confronting Australia, by comparing his task with that of the wartime Labor Prime Minister John Curtain.

The Accord was an agreement between Labor and the unions. The Arbitration Commission played no role in formulating it. Of course, because of the constitutional division of power, the newly elected Labor government had to turn to the Commission to implement the Accord's income policy. But this hardly suggests that the Commission was a necessary condition. On the contrary, if it were not for Australia's peculiar constitutional division of powers, the government could have simply implemented its policy directly. In a sense the Commission was an impediment. It was an independent party outside the original Accord agreement which had to be convinced of the agreement's probity. This is not to suggest that there were no advantages to operating through the Commission. It did, for example, provide a ready-made forum for national wage fixation, and it released the unions and the government from some of the responsibility for policing the system. But this is a long way from being a necessary condition for corporatism. Being helpful is not the same as being necessary. Australia's newly emerged corporatism is a product, not of tradition, but of the choices made by the labour movement in response to the circumstances of the 1980s. The *prima facie* observation was right: Australia does provide a counter-example to the tradition-boundness thesis.

2. DEALING WITH STAGFLATION

In Chapter 7 I claimed that a corporatist industrial relations system is compatible with the requirements of national management in a period of stagflation. As evidence for this claim I presented various cross-country comparisons of the actual performance of different industrial relations systems. But it is also possible to test this claim by examining alternating corporatist and non-corporatist episodes within a single country. This is what I intend to do in the case of Australia. Since wage restraint is the main requirement of national economic management in a period of stagflation, I will focus attention on the wage-fixing component of industrial relations.

Australia has experienced a number of more or less centralized wage-fixing 'episodes' since the onset of stagflation in 1972. We have already seen that decentralized free collective bargaining was the order of the day in the early 1970s. In 1975 this was replaced by centralized quarterly wage indexation which gradually broke down and was followed in 1981 by a renewed bout of decentralized bargaining. To complete the picture we need to consider the wage-fixing arrangements that have prevailed since 1983 under the auspices of the Accord.

The Accord was explicitly designed to deal with stagflation. It identified 'simultaneously high levels of unemployment and inflation' as 'the fundamental feature' of the crisis afflicting Australia in the early 1980s (ALP/ACTU, 1983, 1). The Accord rejected the monetarist solutions adopted by the Liberal government and noted that the OECD countries which have dealt best with stagflation are those that 'have eschewed monetarism and have instead placed substantial importance on developing prices and incomes policies by consultation' (ALP/ACTU, 1983, 2). An incomes policy is vital, according to the Accord, because, by restraining wage increases, it will allow the government to pursue expansionary policies designed to promote economic and employment growth, while retaining control of inflation. Without wage restraint, 'economic recovery will soon lead to increased inflation, thus forcing the government to adopt contractionary anti-inflation policies which will truncate the recovery and prevent any restoration of full, or near full employment' (ALP/ACTU, 1983, 1).

Thus wage restraint is a fundamental prerequisite for 'the parties' prime objective of full employment' (ALP/ACTU, 1983, 1). The Accord attempts to combine this with a second key objective; namely, 'to ensure that the living standards of wage and salary earners and non-income earning sectors of the population requiring protection are maintained and through time increased with movements in national productivity' (ALP/ACTU, 1983, 4). To achieve both these objecives—employment growth through wage restraint and the maintenance of living standards—the Accord advocated a return to a centralized wage-fixing system based on full cost-of-living adjustments. Increases could also be sought on the basis of increased national productivity, and reduction to the emerging 38-hour-week norm could continue, but otherwise unions must make no extra claims. The Accord partners also reached agreement on price surveillance, taxation, and a number of 'supportive policies' covering industrial development and the social wage (Archer, 1988, 216–18). Here, however, I will concentrate on the incomes policy commitments which are at the heart of the Accord.

The final years of the Fraser Liberal government were marked by escalating social conflict. This was forcefully brought home to the public in 1982 when a demonstration by recently retrenched steel workers forced its way past police and broke down the doors of Parliament House. During the 1983 election campaign Labor leader Hawke contrasted this conflict with his call for consensus and national reconciliation. Having won the election, Hawke immediately convened a National Economic Summit of State and Federal governments, unions, and business leaders, and won from it endorsement for a return to centralized wage fixing. Against this background the ACTU, supported by the government, applied to the Arbitration Commission for the estab-lishment of a centralized wage-fixing system based on the pro-visions of the Accord. The Commission agreed to a system of twice-yearly hearings at which full cost-of-living increases would be granted unless extraordinary circumstances persuaded it to the contrary, and so long as unions gave a commitment to make no extra claims.

This system remained in place until September 1985, when, in an agreement with the government known as the 'Accord Mark II', the unions agreed to trade off wage rises due to cost-of-living and productivity increases for tax cuts and the introduction of employer-funded occupational superannuation. But a much big-ger change was on its way.

In May 1986 the Treasurer, Paul Keating, publicly suggested that Australia was threatening to turn into a 'banana republic'.[20] The Treasurer's comment inaugurated a huge shift in public per-ceptions, and conveniently marks the beginning of a new period in which the government pursued policies that were fundamen-tally at odds with the original Accord agreement. Stagflation was replaced by the balance of payments deficit as the main focus of economic strategy.

Figures 14, 15, and 16 show the different components of the balance of payments crisis confronting Australia by mid 1986. The terms of trade were deteriorating rapidly as key export com-

[20] Interview broadcast on Sydney radio station 2GB, 14 May 1986.

modity prices fell by about 10 per cent (Figure 14). In a country where primary produce accounted for approximately 80 per cent of export earnings this had a dramatic effect. Foreign indebtedness rose sharply (Figure 15). So did import penetration (Treasury, 1988a, 38–41). All this contributed to a large and worsening current account deficit (Figure 16).

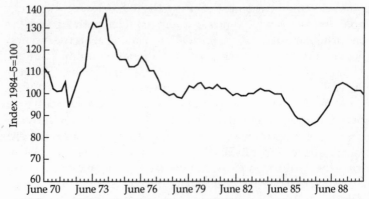

Terms of trade measured by the ratio of the implicit price deflator for exports of goods and services to the implicit price deflator for imports of goods and services.
Source: Treasury, 1988 and 1993.

FIG. 14. *Terms of trade in Australia, 1970–1990*

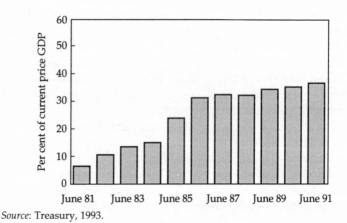

Source: Treasury, 1993.

FIG. 15. *Net external debt in Australia, 1981–1991*

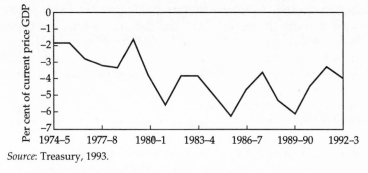

Source: Treasury, 1993.

FIG. 16. *Balance on current account in Australia, 1974–1992*

In June 1986 Prime Minister Hawke responded to the balance of payments crisis with a National Economic Statement that called for cuts in real wages and deep cuts in public spending. The contractionary budget that followed made it clear that even the Accord's basic commitment to reducing unemployment had been dropped. Hence both the key objectives of the original Accord—reduced unemployment and the maintenance of living standards—were no longer being pursued by the government. This was a crucial juncture for the Accord. The ACTU could easily have returned with righteous indignation to the old-style politics of opposition. Instead it chose to push ahead with the 'Accord process'. Two days after the 1986 Budget, when it became clear that the old wage-fixing system would not survive, the ACTU began formulating a workable alternative: the Accord Mark III. The ACTU proposed a new 'two-tier' system which was accepted by the Arbitration Commission in March 1987. Under the first tier the Commission awarded a flat-rate A\$10 increase to all workers. Under the second tier workers with industrial muscle could win increases up to a maximum of a further 4 per cent by making enterprise level productivity agreements. This partial decentralization was reinforced by the August 1988 national wage case which awarded increases that were conditional on unions agreeing to a 'structural efficiency' principle which foreshadowed industry and enterprise level negotiations with employers aimed at radically revising and modernizing all awards. This was widely viewed as a decisive shift away from centralized wage-fixation, and this shift was confirmed in October 1991 when the Commission adopted an 'enterprise bargaining' principle which was backed by both the government and the unions (Macklin *et al.*, 1992, 38–43).

In summary, then, there have been at least five wage-fixing episodes since the onset of stagflation. These are shown in Table 1 below.

So has the Accord improved Australia's macro-economic performance? Figures 17 and 18 and Tables 2 and 3 show movements in some of the main indicators over the period of stagflation. A cursory examination seems to support the public perception that the Accord brought some significant improvements. Clearly, in judging whether the Accord was successful in tackling stagflation, its first three years are of special significance. For it was only during this period that stagflation was the focus of the government's policy and that the Accord's stagflation-oriented incomes policy was being pursued.

Both unemployment and inflation improved markedly in the early years of the Accord. In two years inflation was halved from its 1982–3 high of 11.5 per cent, although it then began to rise again (Figure 17). This was accompanied by strong employment growth. The government met its promise to create 500,000 jobs in its first three years, and by the end of 1987–8, over 1 million jobs had been created. Increased participation (notably by women)

TABLE 1. *Australian wage-fixing systems since the onset of stagflation*

Period	Degree of centralization	Key events
1972–4	decentralized	rapid wage increases
1975–81	centralized	wage indexation: undermined by discounting CPI adjustments and lack of government support
1981–2	decentralized	further rapid wage increases
1983–7	centralized	wage pause followed by CPI indexation: some discounting in exchange for social wage benefits
1987–91	partially decentralized	two-tier system and structural efficiency reviews

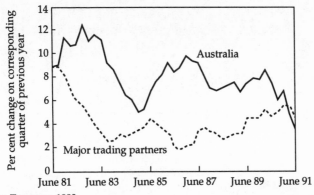

Source: Treasury, 1993.

FIG. 17. *Consumer price inflation in Australia and major trading partners,*
1981–1991

reduced the impact of employment growth on the rate of unemployment. Nevertheless, by June 1986 unemployment had fallen
from a peak of 10.2 per cent to 7.8 per cent (Figure 18). The new
jobs were fuelled by strong growth in the Gross Domestic Product. Negative growth in 1982–3 was followed by strong GDP
growth to the end of the decade (Table 2). The contractionary
policies announced in the 1986 budget can be seen in reduced
GDP growth and a slight increase in unemployment during 1986–
7. Later a sharp rise in unemployment again occurred during the
international recession of the early 1990s.[21]

All in all the first three years of the Accord seem to provide
strong *prima facie* evidence of the advantages of corporatism.
However, the evidence of international comparisons is more ambiguous. While there is no doubt that Australian GDP and employment growth were remarkably strong by international
standards (Tables 2 and 3), neither inflation nor unemployment
compare especially favourably with OECD norms. As Figure 17
shows, the fall in inflation that occurred during the Accord's first
two years parallels a similar fall in the inflation rates of Austra-

[21] In what follows I want to maintain a focus on the stagflationary period
discussed in Chapter 7. The recession of the early 1990s was not 'stagflationary' as
it coincided with low and falling inflation. Moreover, unlike in the stagflationary
recessions of 1974–5 and 1982–3, wage increases do not seem to have been a factor
in the recession and unemployment of the early 1990s (Treasury, 1993, 2.33).

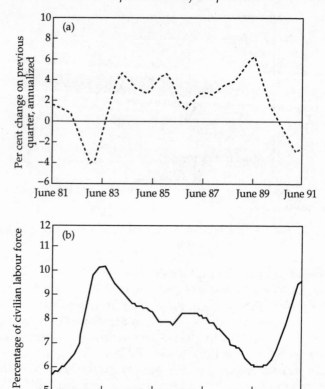

Panel A: Growth in employment (non-farm)
Panel B: Unemployment rate

Source: Treasury, 1993.

FIG. 18. *Labour market aggregates in Australia, 1981–1991*

TABLE 2. *Growth of real GDP in Australia and the OECD, percentage change from previous year, 1982–1992*

	1982	1983	1984	1985	1986	1987	1988	1989	1990	1991	1992
Australia	−0.1	0.7	7.5	4.8	1.9	4.4	4.4	4.6	1.4	−0.8	2.0
Total OECD	0	2.7	4.4	3.3	2.9	3.3	4.4	3.3	2.5	0.8	1.7

Source: OECD (1993).

TABLE 3. *Employment and unemployment in Australia and the OECD,*
1982–1992

Panel A: Employment growth, percentage changes from the previous period

	1982	1983	1984	1985	1986	1987	1988	1989	1990	1991	1992
Australia	0	−1.8	3.0	3.1	4.1	2.2	3.7	4.4	1.6	−1.9	−0.5
Total OECD	−0.5	0.5	1.7	1.3	1.5	1.7	1.9	1.9	1.3	0	−0.3

Panel B: Unemployment rates (OECD Standardized), per cent of total labour force

	1982	1983	1984	1985	1986	1987	1988	1989	1990	1991	1992
Australia	7.1	9.9	8.9	8.2	8.0	8.0	7.2	6.1	6.9	9.5	10.7
Total OECD	8.1	8.5	8.0	7.8	7.7	7.3	6.7	6.2	6.1	6.8	7.5

Source: OECD (1993).

lia's major OECD trading partners (that is, the G7 countries plus New Zealand) which occurred more than a year earlier. Moreover, in 1985–6 Australia's inflation rate rose sharply while that of its major trading partners was stable and falling. Table 3 shows that since receiving a boost from the 1982 recession, Australia's unemployment has never managed to fall below the OECD average.

Here, however, I want to focus on comparing the performance of the different wage-fixing systems that have operated *in Australia* under stagflationary conditions. The Accord's strategy for tackling stagflation is built on the assumption that wage indexation will restrain the aggregate growth of real wages. As we saw in Chapter 7, this is the main requirement of national economic management in a period of stagflation. Hence whether indexation does in fact reduce aggregate real wage results is the main test of whether the Accord is compatible with the requirements of national economic management during this period.

Lewis and Kirby have conducted such a test by developing a theoretical model of the wage determination process which attempts to estimate the equilibrium real wage which could be expected on the basis of labour supply and demand. They conclude that over the first two years of the Accord 'equilibrium real

wages were over 5 per cent below what would have been expected from previous experience' (Lewis and Kirby, 1987).[22]

A number of studies draw similar conclusions about the
earlier 1975–81 indexation period. In particular, Gregory (1986)
measures the difference between actual average weekly earning
outcomes and those that would be expected if the Arbitration
Commission were simply a veil for market forces. Two wage
equations are developed to estimate expected market outcomes.
One is based on unemployment and the other is based on over-
time data. Both suggest that 'overall, the 1975–81 indexation experiments kept the rate of growth of nominal wages below levels
that might have been expected'. Furthermore, 'these gains were
not lost in a subsequent wage rebound' (1986, S70). Dornbusch
and Fisher (1984) reach a similar conclusion about the rate of
growth of real wages. They estimate that indexation reduced real
wages by a little more than 2 per cent in the period from 1975–80.
This is similar to Lewis and Kirby's (1987) finding that equilibrium real wages were reduced by 2.6 per cent during 1975–81,
with little evidence of a subsequent 'catch up' effect.

If these studies hold up for the 1975–81 indexation period, they
provide important support for the claim that the 1983–7 indexation period was also effective in reducing real wages. For during
the 1975–81 period, wage drift outside the system reduced the
downward effect of indexation on real wages and ultimately undermined it. Partial discounting of full CPI indexation which
began just 12 months after the system was introduced put
pressure on unions to make up the difference outside the system.
During the 1983–7 period the Commission has explicitly sought
to minimize wages drift by rigorously enforcing its 'no extra
claims' ruling. And when discounting of full CPI indexation has
taken place the lost wages have generally been offset by social

[22] Simes and Richardson (1987) and Pissarides (1987) have produced alternative
wage equations which challenge these results. According to Simes, Lewis and
Kirby have failed to adequately specify labour market pressures. However, Simes
himself has been criticized by John Beggs. Beggs believes that Simes's own work
would show that the Accord had been effective if he based his results on a non-
parametric test. Further support for Lewis's conclusion comes from a series of
studies by Bruce Chapman which use five different statistical models of the
Australian economy. The results of these studies are reported in the *Australian
Financial Review*, 20 December 1989.

wage improvements,[23] thereby taking pressure off unions to move outside the system. Furthermore, the 1983–7 indexation period did not end in a decentralized wages explosion like its predecessor, but rather in a managed partial decentralization which maintained a cap on aggregate wage outcomes. It seems reasonable to suggest, therefore, that the Accord has been at least as effective as the 1975–81 system in reducing real wages.

So the evidence from intra-country comparisons of different wage episodes in Australia supports the evidence from the inter-country comparisons discussed in Chapter 7. It thereby strengthens the conclusion that corporatism is compatible with the need for wage restraint, and, hence, that it is compatible with the requirements of national economic management in a period of stagflation.

Given the assumption that employment growth is, at least in part, a function of real wage restraint,[24] this conclusion implies that the Accord has been responsible for at least some of the 1.6 million jobs that had been created under its auspices by the end of the 1980s. A comparison of Australian employment growth with that of the major OECD economies (Table 3) suggests a similar conclusion. In 1988 Treasurer Keating could claim that 'our rate of job growth is unmatched in the Western world' (1988, 2).[25]

Of course, in the Accord's own terms, job creation was only one of two key objectives. With falling real wages, the second key objective—the maintenance of living standards—seems to be out of reach. But this ignores the importance of the social wage trade-offs mentioned above. In fact the government is keen to point to

---

[23] Tax cuts, pensions, family allowances, and the introduction of occupational superannuation and universal health insurance have been prominent examples of social wage improvements which have been traded off for reduced real wages.

[24] In the late 1970s this assumption was hotly debated in Australia, but by the late 1980s it was widely accepted. See the *Australian Financial Review*, 26 September 1988.

[25] A study by Chapman, Dowrick, and Junakar argues that, on a conservative estimate, at least one-fifth of the jobs created since 1983 can be credited to the Accord. See the *Australian Financial Review*, 28 November 1989. Further supportive evidence for the efficacy of the Accord comes from two studies by Beggs and Chapman (1987a; 1987b), who argue that it has significantly reduced strike activity. Through both an international comparison and a model of previous Australian experience, they show that changing macro-economic conditions account for only 40 per cent of the decline in strike activity during the first three years of the Accord.

TABLE 4. *Wages and household income in Australia, percentage change on previous year, 1982–1988*

	1982–3	1983–4	1984–5	1985–6	1986–7	1987–8	1988–9(a)
At constant (1984–5) prices (c)							
Average award rates of pay	0.2	−1.9	−0.6	−3.3	−3.6	−3.0(a)	−1
Average earnings (national accounts basis) (b)	2.0	−2.4	0.8	−1.9	−1.9	−0.6	1¼
Household disposable income	−0.2	3.9	2.3	2.8	0.2	2.1	3
Household disposable income (per capita)	−1.8	2.6	1.1	1.4	−1.3	0.6	1½

(a) Forecast.

(b) Non-farm sector.

(c) Deflated by the private consumption deflator.

Source: Treasury (1988).

the statistics in Table 4, which show that while both award rates and average earnings have fallen in real terms during the life of the Accord, average real household disposable income, and (except for one year) average real household disposable income per capita, have shown reasonable growth.

However, even measuring the performance of the Accord with respect to both employment growth and the maintenance of average living standards is somewhat restrictive. Bob Rowthorn (1992), for example, has suggested that wage dispersion should also be taken into account. He rightly argues that people do not only want work. They want well paid work.

There has been a wide-ranging and inconclusive debate about whether the Australian arbitration system has led to more egalitarian wage dispersion.[26] Current official wisdom holds that there is nothing especially unique about the structure of Australian wage relativities.[27] And it is certainly not clear that periods of

[26] For reviews of the literature see Gill (1987a) and Hancock Committee (1985 (vol. 3), appendix II).

[27] See Hancock Committee (1985 (vol. 3), 11–15) and National Labour Consultative Council (1987, 14).

centralized wage fixation have compressed wage relativities *vis-à-vis* other periods. For example, there is evidence that relativities widened in 1953–67, when the basic wage plus margins system might have been expected to compress them; that they were compressed in 1967–74, when the relatively free reign of market forces might have been expected to widen them; and that they widened again in 1975–82.[28]

However it does seem that the Accord halted the expansion of relativities that preceded it. Peetz (1985, 20) has shown that during its first two years the Accord maintained existing relativities. Flat dollar increases like those awarded in the 1987 and the 1988 national wage cases should slightly compress wage relativities. But even if they do not, it is not necessarily appropriate to criticize the Accord for failing to generate a more egalitarian wage dispersion. This is because what really matters is the dispersion of total income. Given that the willingness of the Accord partners to trade off real wage reductions for social wage improvements has been an important feature of the Accord's success, this is of fundamental importance. Indeed, the original Accord sees fiscal rather than wages policy as the main vehicle for achieving redistributive measures. In light of this, wage dispersion is not really an appropriate measure of the Accord's success.[29] More work needs to be done in order to establish whether the Accord has compressed or widened total income dispersion. *Prima facie* the government's record is ambiguous. Some initiatives, such as the introduction of Medicare, where a flat rate premium for health insurance was replaced by a fixed rate percentage of income, have had a progressive effect on income dispersion. Others, such as income tax cuts, where the top marginal rate was reduced from 60 per cent to 49 per cent and the bottom rate from 25 per cent to 24 per cent, have been regressive.

[28] For the first two periods see Gill (1987b). Presumably part of the compression in 1967–74 is due to the Arbitration Commission's implementation of equal pay for women in the early 1970s. For the third period see Peetz (1985, 16–23 and appendix C). Unfortunately Peetz does not distinguish between the contributions of the 1975–81 and the 1981–2 periods to the widening of relativities, although evidence of a regressive change in income distribution from 1978–9 to 1981–2 suggests that the latter period made an important contribution, as might be expected.

[29] This also casts doubt on Freeman's (1988) attempt to link corporatism, or even just centralized wage bargaining, with low wage dispersion.

Finally, in this section, I want to draw attention to the fact that
the Australian experience also confirms that a control trade-off
can be compatible with the requirements of national economic
management in a period of stagflation. Recall that the 'Accord
Mark II' agreement in 1985 involved a trade-off in which the
unions exchanged a wage increase—a 3 per cent wage increase
to be precise—for an equivalent contribution to newly created
industry-wide superannuation funds. The trustees of these funds
are mostly appointed jointly by the relevant industry's unions,
and employer associations, although a few are controlled by the
unions alone. Since then a further wages-for-superannuation
trade-off has been incorporated into the 'Accord Mark VI' agreement in 1990, and the ACTU is seeking to increase the total
employer contribution to 12 per cent by the end of the 1990s.[30]

Note that a superannuation trade-off is precisely the kind of
control trade-off which was predicted to have the best chance of
success in a stagflationary period. It links greater control with the
kind of greater well-being that is likely to concern workers in a
period of stagflation. The establishment of superannuation funds
addresses workers' material concerns in two ways. First, it helps
to secure their personal retirement income, and second, it reduces
their dependence on the savings and investment behaviour of
capitalists. But the funds also deliver increased control. At present
they are still mostly managed by private financial institutions, but
the potential for direct union management is clearly present. At
the 1989 ACTU Congress, the Treasurer, Paul Keating, urged
unionists to begin managing the rapidly growing funds themselves as soon as possible so that they can supplement their
industrial muscle with 'institutional muscle' should they find
themselves in a 'hostile political environment'.

In 1987 the unions proposed the basis for an even more
ambitious control trade-off which again linked control issues with
the material concerns of a stagflationary period, and, in particular, with concerns about the low level of capitalist investment
which persisted in spite of the increased profits flowing from real
wage reductions. The unions called for the establishment of a

[30] In a tentative move towards employer support for a fully tripartite corporatism, the Business Council of Australia sought ACTU support for an agreed target
for employer contributions in return for which it would help to enforce the deal on
recalcitrant employers.

National Development Fund which would invest in new industrial capacity (ACTU/TDC, 1987, 21–3). The fund would draw up
to 20 per cent of the income of the superannuation funds and
would be controlled by a tripartite body including government,
unions, and employers. The National Development Fund
proposal is clearly inspired by the Swedish experiments with
economic democracy discussed in Chapter 7. There are certain
advantages to having a second bite at the cherry. The Accord was
a successful adaptation by the Australian labour movement of
failed British efforts to institutionalize a social contract. In time,
maybe the same can be done with failed Swedish efforts to in-
augurate economic democracy.

3. STRUCTURAL ADJUSTMENT

In the mid 1980s stagflation started to fade in the OECD countries
as both unemployment and inflation slowly declined. Instead, as
we saw in Chapter 8, the advanced capitalist countries entered a
period of far-reaching structural adjustment.

In Australia this general imperative was given special urgency
by the balance of payments deficit: what Treasurer Keating (1988,
4) called 'Australia's number one economic problem'. And few on
either the left or the right disagreed. Even though commodity
prices recovered after a sharp fall in 1985–6, the long-term downward trend meant that Australia could not continue to rely on
its abundant natural resources to support a high standard of
living (Figure 19). Rather, the traditionally complacent and highly
protected manufacturing sector would have to become more
internationally competitive in order both to find new export
markets and to fend off growing import penetration.[31] The
government recognized that this required a wholesale micro-
economic reform programme of industrial restructuring that
aimed to improve the productivity of individual firms. And, in
order to allow firms to make these adjustments, the government
placed a high priority on achieving greater labour market
flexibility (Department of Industrial Relations, 1988).

[31] By the early 1990s there was evidence that exports of high value-added
products from the manufacturing sector had indeed grown strongly (McKinsey
Report, 1993).

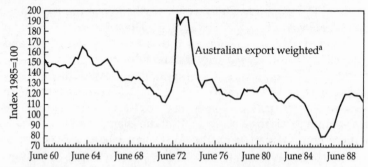

[a] Nominal $US non-fuel commodity prices weighted by Australian export values deflated by the United Nations $US index of manufactured export unit values.

Source: Treasury, 1988.

FIG. 19. *Real commodity prices, 1960–1990*

In Chapter 8 I focused on labour market flexibility as the main requirement of national economic management in a period of structural adjustment, and I argued that, contrary to expectations, corporatism is indeed compatible with this requirement. The Australian experience bears this out. In fact the extraordinary thing about Australia is that Accord-style corporatism proved to be not merely compatible with the requirements of structural adjustment. It actually became the driving force in bringing them about.

To understand how this has been possible requires an understanding of the crucial role played by the unions. And this in turn requires an understanding of the fundamental transformation of the union movement that the Accord has set in place. Ten years ago the Australian union movement looked quite similar to its British counterpart. This provides a benchmark against which the extent of the transformation of Australian unionism can be measured. Whereas in Britain the Thatcher government thought industry could only be modernized by undermining the unions, the Hawke government showed that modernization could be achieved with the unions in the driver's seat.

The Accord has made the unions more confident and forward-looking. The old defensive unionism was left behind and replaced by a new agenda-setting unionism which aimed, in the words of one of its architects, to provide 'a fundamental challenge for leadership to the nation' (Carmichael, 1986). The decision to shift to the two-tier wage-fixing system of the Accord Mark III was a key expression of this transformation. In particular it was an expression of both the importance which the ACTU attached to its role as a national agenda-setter, and its willingness to adapt to the continually changing conditions imposed by the world economy in order to maintain that role.

But the shift to the two-tier system was not the only expression of this transformation. More important, in a way, was the ACTU's 1986 Mission to Western Europe. Senior unionists visited Sweden, Norway, Austria, Germany, and Britain. In a comprehensive report entitled *Australia Reconstructed* they highlighted the advantages of the Swedish and Norwegian industrial relations systems and emphasized the importance of 'strategic unionism'. Strategic unionism requires the development of an integrated long-term strategy. To this end *Australia Reconstructed* recommended that 'Australian unions should continue to develop the co-ordinated national approach to policy formulation and implementation under the umbrella of the ACTU' (ACTU/TDC, 1987, 189). At its 1987 biennial conference the ACTU adopted the recommendations of *Australia Reconstructed* as its policy.

Australia Reconstructed also served to re-emphasize union concern with industry development. Industry policy has been an abiding theme of the unions in the Accord period (Ewer, 1988). In the early years of the Accord, special importance was attached to the formulation of tripartite industry plans in which employer and union commitments were given in return for government assistance. Later in the 1980s, however, the unions shifted their focus from negotiations with government to direct negotiations with employers, in order to reach agreement on plans to modernize production at both an industry and an enterprise level.

For its part, the government believed that this sort of employer–union co-operation was essential to the success of structural adjustment. Confrontation between workers and employers would not only slow structural adjustment and increase its costs. More importantly for the government, it would inhibit the development of a 'productive consciousness' in which ongoing changes to improve productivity are widely accepted.

In September 1986 an agreement in principle was reached between the ACTU and the employer peak councils (the CAI and the BCA) on the need to improve efficiency and productivity at an industry and enterprise level. This became incorporated into the two-tier wage system the following year. In order to win the second tier increase of 4 per cent, unions had to offer productivity improvements of an equivalent value. These typically involved giving up so-called 'restrictive work practices'. Later, two further agreements were reached between peak union and employer organizations. The tripartite National Labour Consultative Council (1987) sponsored a report on *Labour Market Flexibility* in the Australian Setting, and the CAI and the ACTU (1988) issued a *Joint Statement on Participative Practices*.

The report by the National Labour Consultative Council (NLCC) examined the implications for Australia of the OECD's (1986a) Dahrendorf report on labour market flexibility. As we saw in Chapter 8, labour market flexibility actually refers to a great many different things. The NLCC report identified six distinct elements of labour market flexibility which are of special relevance to Australia: the general level of wages, relative wages, non-wage labour costs, labour mobility, work practices and work patterns, and education and training.[32] The differences between these elements are crucial. For while some, such as more flexible relative wages, may be incompatible with corporatism, others, such as a more flexible general level of wages, may depend on it. The NLCC report argued: 'In comparison with other countries Australia's experience has been above average in terms of both [external] labour mobility and the responsiveness of wages generally to unemployment and inflation, and on a par with many countries in relative wage flexibility and developments in labour on-costs. . . . However . . . significant deficiencies remain in Australia's education and training systems and in the area of work organization and working patterns' (National Labour Consultative Council, 1987, 1). This assessment was confirmed by the OECD's Economic Survey of Australia (1988).

The government believed that greater flexibility in these two deficient areas did not require wholesale deregulation (Department of Industrial Relations, 1988, pp. ii, 8). On the contrary, it argued that an industrial relations system which is at least par-

[32] See National Labour Consultative Council (1987, 13). The Dahrendorf report also discusses conditions of labour such as employment protection, and regulations relating to the labour market (OECD, 1986a, 9).

tially centralized is needed to maintain aggregate wage restraint, to ensure systematic restructuring of industries, to preserve union co-operation, and to develop national training standards.

To rectify these deficiencies the Accord partners launched a labour market reform programme which had two main elements: reform of post-school education and training, and 'award restructuring'. The first was principally pursued by the government with the support of the unions. The second was principally pursued by the unions with the support of the government. Both took as their starting-point the importance of encouraging the growth of a highly skilled work-force which was seen as a prerequisite for maintaining a high productivity, high wage economy. But again, it was the unions that set the overall agenda. Indeed, according to the *Australian Financial Review*,[33] it was a 'seasoned communist', the ACTU Assistant Secretary Laurie Carmichael, who 'has been responsible over the past year for driving the debate on training and skilling in industry to the centre of the micro-economic reform agenda'.

Post-school education and training reform is focusing both on the higher education system and on enterprise-level training.

Under new funding arrangements the government has sought to make the higher education system more responsive to national economic priorities. Institutions are now required to submit 'educational profiles' outlining their goals and how they relate to national economic priorities, and 'performance indicators' have been developed to measure the achievement of these goals (Department of Employment, Education and Training, 1988a, 29, 85). The government also planned a large expansion of the higher education system. Forty thousand new student places were created in the 1989–91 triennium. As a result, by the end of the triennium, at least 110,000 new places in higher education (an increase of 43 per cent) had been created since the government came to power in 1983 (Department of Employment, Education and Training, 1988b, 3; Keating, 1992). To offset the cost of this growth a special graduate tax was introduced.

On the enterprise level the government has imposed a training levy on employers. Under this scheme employers with an annual wage bill of A$200,000 or more are required to spend 1 per cent of

[33] 6 October 1988.

their wage bill on training from 1 July 1990 rising to 1.5 per cent from 1 July 1992. Employers who do not meet this target will be required to pay the shortfall into a special fund for training.[34] While the training levy is important, the most significant effects on enterprise training are coming about as a result of union-initiated award restructuring.

Awards are legally enforceable documents which contain sets of job classifications, pay rates, and conditions of employment for all individuals employed in an occupation or industry. Many awards contained obsolete classifications and conditions, some dating back to the beginning of the century, which inhibited flexible working patterns and the efficient use of new technology. But the goal of the unions in promoting award restructuring was not merely to update these classifications and conditions. More importantly, the unions were trying to establish the conditions for an internationally competitive high skill and high wage economy. To this end they sought to establish a career structure within each award so that the lowest paid worker can, by obtaining the right qualifications, progress to the highest paid job. Progression along this career path has been linked to the acquisition of clearly established skill levels, and pay rates have been organized so as to create an incentive for each worker to acquire superior skills. This should lead to the emergence of a more highly skilled work-force which will in turn require new, less hierarchical forms of work organization.

Of course by allowing long-established conditions and working practices to be altered the unions are giving up an important source of power. Job classifications have typically been the final trenches into which unions retreat in order to defend their members. For this reason the unions, or rather the metal unions which took the lead, struck an agreement with the employers in which they traded off these restrictive work practices for greater control over the organization of work and training. In March 1990 this agreement was ratified by the Arbitration Commission (now renamed the Industrial Relations Commission) and incorporated into a new metal industry award.[35]

---

[34] The Australian Bureau of Statistics conducted its first survey of training expenditure in the September quarter of 1989. According to this survey, while employers overall devoted 2.2 per cent of the national wage bill to training, only 21 per cent of private employers paid anything for formal training.

[35] For details of the new award I am grateful to Simone McGurk, a West Australian official of the Metal Trades Federation of Unions.

Amongst other things, the new award compels employers to set up workplace-based joint consultative committees which will oversee the introduction of new forms of work organization. In particular, it will oversee the implementation of the new job classification structure[36] and negotiate the introduction of various other kinds of flexibility. Certain kinds of flexibility (especially those relating to hours and leave) can only be introduced if the majority of workers in a workplace agree.

Given that improved training would be pivotal to the success of award restructuring, the unions sought still greater control in this area. The new award provides for workplace training committees with equal representation of employers and employees. These committees will oversee the development of a training plan and the provision of paid training leave.[37] The establishment of training committees marks the first systematic attempt to establish plant level co-determination in the private sector in Australia. The Metal Trades Federation of Unions (1988, 4) sees them as 'the basic building block of industrial democracy'.

In short, the new award incorporates a trade-off in which the unions exchange restrictive work practices for consultation and co-determination committees which would give them greater control over the organization of work and training. It thus confirms the conclusion of Chapter 8 that a control trade-off can be compatible with the requirements of national economic management in a period of structural adjustment. Moreover, the particular control trade-off that the metal unions have pursued is precisely the kind of control trade-off which was predicted to have the best chance of success in such a period.

Between 1988 and 1991 the Arbitration Commission's 'structural efficiency' principle required all unions and employers to commit themselves to industry or enterprise level negotiations to restructure their awards. There is no denying that this, along with the attempt to link pay rates to the skill needs of particular industries, implied a more decentralized wage-fixing system. But did it imply a less corporatist system? Not necessarily. For one thing, wage bargaining was only partially decentralized. Wages were still subject to a maximum aggregate outcome which was a product of centralized negotiations. In the 1988 wage case this

[36] The 360 classifications in the old metal award have been reduced to 14.
[37] The development of a training plan and the provision of paid training leave are new obligations that the award now imposes on employers.

aggregate figure was largely determined by negotiations between the government and the ACTU prior to the Commission's hearings. This occurred again in 1989 and again in 1990.

In any case, the wage fixation system is not the only factor which determines the nature of an industrial relations system. Centrally negotiated framework agreements on productivity, labour market flexibility, participatory practices, and superannuation are also important manifestations of corporatism.

In addition, the organizational unity and hence the centralization of the unions was significantly strengthened in the late 1980s and the early 1990s by a concerted ACTU-led effort to amalgamate as many as possible of the small craft unions into about 20 large industrial unions by the end of the century (ACTU, 1987).[38]

Overall, then, the Australian case reinforces the argument of Chapters 7 and 8. The Australian experience shows that both a corporatist system and a control trade-off were compatible with the requirements of national economic management first during the stagflationary period of the late 1970s and early 1980s, and then again during the period of structural adjustment that followed.

However, I do not want to over-emphasize the importance of the Australian case. The argument of the preceding chapters stands on its own with or without the additional Australian evidence discussed in sections 2 and 3 above. Indeed, to put too much faith in models based on the experience of one country is often a recipe for disappointment. For the experience on which such models are based is invariably superseded by developments that do not always fit with the model.

In Australia, for example, the government and the unions committed themselves to a more decentralized system of 'enterprise bargaining' in the early 1990s. Under the new system awards will

---

[38] This radical programme of amalgamation and membership exchange is in part an attempt to reverse declining union membership by providing improved services through larger, better resourced unions. Ironically, it is the one component of centralization which was historically strong which now appears to be weakening. According to survey data compiled by the Australian Bureau of Statistics, membership density has fallen from 49% in 1982 to 46% in 1986. An alternative official series based on union returns shows membership steady at 55%. The ACTU (1987, 11) believes that 'the lower figure is the more accurate of the two, although it does slightly understate the true figure'.

become minimums which can be bettered in separate enterprise agreements between unions and employers. And national wage rises will only be available to workers who do not have the industrial strength to strike these separate agreements.

It is possible to construe this change as an evolutionary development of Accord-style corporatism. After all, national agreements between the government and the unions continue to set the framework within which enterprise bargaining must take place. And these agreements continue to determine both aggregate wage outcomes and non-wage issues like superannuation.

But it is also possible to construe the move towards enterprise bargaining as foreshadowing a fundamental break with Accord-style corporatism. Even if this proves to be true, however, the Australian experience discussed in sections 2 and 3 remains pertinent. For this experience provides a sustained concrete illustration of how the conditions for the feasibility of a control trade-off can be met.

Here, then, is the corporatist trade-off strategy in action. Not in the 1970s when unions everywhere seemed strong, but in the 1980s when unions everywhere seemed weak. Not in the Scandinavian and Germanic strongholds of corporatism, but in the traditionally anti-corporatist Anglo-Saxon world. Here is the corporatist trade-off strategy in action, just where you would least expect it.

10

Into the Next Century

An economic democracy is a system in which firms operate in a market economy but are governed by those who work for them. In this book I make two main claims about economic democracy. First, I argue that it is a morally desirable goal. And second, I argue that there is a feasible strategy for achieving it in the advanced capitalist countries.

Will these claims still be tenable as we move into the next century?

The claim that economic democracy is a morally desirable goal rests on an appeal to the value of individual freedom. This value requires that control over a firm should be exercised by those who are affected by it. More particularly, it requires that direct, decision-making control over a firm should be exercised by those who are subject to its authority. In a capitalist economy, a firm's workers are its only subjects and hence they should exercise direct, decision-making control over it. Other individuals who are affected by a firm without being subject to it should exercise indirect, constraint-setting control such as that which consumers exercise through the market.

Although the validity of this argument is not itself dependent on the particular historical circumstances of the late twentieth century, it is possible that its rhetorical force may wax and wane with the passage of time.

When, as at present, the ideological climate is heavily influenced by neo-liberal doctrines, a socialist theory which emphasizes its commitment to individual freedom has some important advantages. In particular, such a theory allows socialists to appeal to a similar moral starting-point as neo-liberals in order to draw some very different conclusions. It thus enables socialists to tackle their opponents in an intellectually powerful way.

In saying this, I do not want to suggest that this appeal to the value of individual freedom is the product of an opportunistic shift in the face of a decade or more of neo-liberal ideological assaults. On the contrary, as we saw at the very beginning of this book, it arises from socialism's own Enlightenment roots.

I do want to suggest, however, that we need to consider the possibility that, as we move into the next century, changes in the ideological climate could weaken the rhetorical force of the moral argument for economic democracy which I have pursued in this book. Neo-liberalism is of course only one version of moral individualism. But should the influence of moral individualism in general begin to wane (perhaps to be replaced by nationalism or some other form of communalism), then the intuitive appeal of my emphasis on individual freedom may lessen, and what is taken here as a moral starting-point may have to be further justified.

Given the internationally dominant position of 'Western' values and institutions following the collapse of the Soviet bloc, it seems reasonable to suppose that moral individualism *will* continue to exert a powerful influence in the advanced capitalist countries as we move into the next century. Nevertheless, there are also some contrary trends. It would thus be prudent to keep a weather eye on debates (such as those between 'liberals' and 'communitarians') which concern themselves with the moral foundations of individualism, in case there is indeed an upsurge in support for nationalist or communalist doctrines which challenge the value of individual freedom.

To summarize, then, it seems unlikely that the argument for the moral desirability of economic democracy will weaken as we move into the next century. The validity of the argument is not itself dependent on the particular historical circumstances of the late twentieth century. And although its rhetorical force may in principle wane with the passage of time, this is in fact unlikely in the coming decades.

The second main claim of this book is that there is a feasible strategy for achieving economic democracy. This claim rests on an appeal to the advantages of a corporatist industrial relations system. A corporatist system enables workers to pursue economic democracy through a series of trade-offs in which they agree to help maintain profits in exchange for incremental increases in direct control. Capitalists and governments—even social democratic governments—can block these trade-offs. However, if they are rational, they will agree to them so long as certain

conditions are met. In recent years these conditions have in fact
been met.

Now there are at least two potential problems with this appeal
to the advantages of corporatism which we may encounter as we
move into the next century.

The first stems from possible changes in the economic environment in which the industrial relations actors will operate. We saw
in Chapters 7, 8, and 9 that the conditions for the feasibility of a
control trade-off (including those which make corporatism itself
feasible) have been met both in the stagflationary period of the
1970s and early 1980s and in the period of structural adjustment
that followed. But will these conditions still be met once the
period of structural adjustment has come to an end?

Of course we can never know for certain what the future
will bring, but three points are worth bearing in mind when
considering the next decade or so.

First, it is not clear just when the period of structural adjustment *will* come to an end. There is no evidence that the fundamental pressures which are driving structural adjustment in the
advanced capitalist countries are easing.[1] On the contrary, these
pressures are probably becoming more acute. For example, competitive pressures from the newly industrializing countries of
East and South-East Asia continue to increase. And these may
soon be augmented by similar pressures from Eastern Europe.

Second, some of the problems which were associated with the
period of stagflation—particularly the problem of high unemployment—are returning to the top of the political agenda. For
this reason, the kinds of trade-offs which were typical of that
period may again prove to be feasible.

Third, a century or so of experience with capitalist democracy
suggests that both the problems associated with structural adjustment and the problems of unemployment and inflation recur
repeatedly. This in turn suggests that the kind of economic environment in which the conditions for the feasibility of a control
trade-off are likely to be met may continue to recur so long as the
basic institutions of capitalist democracy remain in place.

In light of these points, it seems reasonable to suppose that,
although the economic environment will undoubtedly keep

[1] These pressures are discussed at the beginning of Chapter 8.

changing, the conditions which make control trade-offs feasible (including those which make corporatism itself feasible) will probably continue to be met into the next century.

This brings me to the second potential problem with my appeal to the advantages of a corporatist industrial relation system. This second problem stems from the fact that changes in the future may not just affect the environment within which industrial relations actors operate: these changes may also affect the nature of those actors themselves. Since an industrial relations system is defined in terms of the organizational characteristics of the actors which comprise it, changes in the nature of the industrial relations *actors* may in turn affect the nature of the industrial relations *system*.

In particular, in formulating my argument for the feasibility of economic democracy, I have simply assumed, as I pointed out in the introduction, that it is possible for organized labour to continue to act in a centrally co-ordinated way. But many commentators (especially in Britain) are increasingly sceptical about whether this kind of labour movement unity will be possible in the future. Since corporatism can only exist where there are centrally co-ordinated industrial relations actors, these commentators are also sceptical about whether corporatism has a future.

It is important to be clear what this scepticism is about: it is not, for the most part, scepticism about the continued existence of unions *per se*; rather, it is scepticism about the continued existence of a union movement which can behave as a unified actor. It is in this vein that Crouch (Baglioni and Crouch, 1990, 359) asks: 'Unions may have a long-term future, but do union *movements*?'

Feeding this scepticism is the perception that fundamental changes are taking place in the nature of work—changes that are structural rather than cyclical—and that these changes are leading to declining union membership, a growing fragmentation of the core working-class interests which unions have traditionally represented, and increasing decentralization of collective bargaining (Visser, 1992).

Fundamental changes in the nature of work are undoubtedly taking place. Among the most important are the growth of white collar and service sector occupations, the increasing number of women in the work-force, and a growing trend towards part-time and less secure forms of work.

But the impact of these changes has been different in different countries. It would therefore be wrong to draw sceptical conclusions about the future of labour movement unity on the basis of these changes alone. In some countries, changes in the nature of work have indeed been accompanied by a growing fragmentation and decentralization of organized labour, but in other countries these same changes have been compatible with the maintenance or even the strengthening of a centrally co-ordinated union movement (IRRR, 1990a and 1990b; Ferner and Hyman, 1992).

This should not be surprising. After all, it is one of the fundamental insights of political sociology that the salience of an interest group is a function not just of socio-economic factors but also of ideological and institutional factors (Sartori, 1969; Pizzorno, 1981; Berger, 1981). Socio-economic factors alone always throw up a plethora of potential interest groups. Ideological and institutional factors are important because they help to pick out which of these potential interests will actually be realized and become politically salient.[2]

Thus, in order to assess the significance of currently emerging changes in the nature of work, what is needed is further research into the relative importance of socio-economic, institutional, and ideological factors, as well as further research into the way in which these factors interact to strengthen or weaken the unity of organized labour.

Some research along these lines is already being conducted. For example, Golden and Pontusson (1992) and Steinmo *et al.* (1992) emphasize the importance of institutional factors in explaining why some union movements have been more successful at maintaining their unity than others.

But even without any further research there is reason to be doubtful about the claims of sceptics who suggest that there is no future for either centrally co-ordinated union movements or centrally co-ordinated industrial relations systems. Take the question

---

[2] For example, at the beginning of the twentieth century Marxism was not just a sociological theory pointing to the rise of the new forms of work which accompanied capitalist industrialization. It was also an ideology which picked out class-wide interests as particularly salient while downplaying the importance of other potential interests: both sectional interests within a class as well as interests which cut across class, such as race or religion.

of the decentralization of collective bargaining which figures prominently in recent literature.

The first point to note is that the sceptics often place undue emphasis on the British experience. Since the collapse of the Labour government's Social Contract in 1979, Britain has indeed experienced a radical decentralization of collective bargaining (Millward *et al.*, 1992).[3] There is no doubt that this experience has left corporatism seriously discredited in Britain. But although it dominates academic and public perceptions there, the British experience is atypical.

While there has certainly been a trend towards less centralized bargaining in a number of European countries, this has not led to the radical decentralization which has been seen in Britain. For example, the decentralization of collective bargaining in Sweden in the early 1990s has been widely noticed given Sweden's role as a corporatist paradigm in much of the earlier literature.[4] But this has only been a partial decentralization which may well leave Sweden with a nationally co-ordinated industry-level bargaining system similar to that which operates in Germany (Archer, 1992, 161). Moreover, in Germany itself as well as in some other countries with relatively centralized bargaining systems, the basic structure of collective bargaining has scarcely altered (Archer, 1992, 154). While in still other countries—such as Spain, Greece, and Portugal—collective bargaining has become more centralized (IRRR, 1990b).

Overall, in the first half of the 1990s, national-level negotiations are continuing to play an important role in most of the countries we have been concerned with in this book. In 1993, for example, with the sole exception of Britain, each of the five largest European countries sought (not always successfully) to win union support for 'social pacts' of various kinds. In Italy and Spain this involved full-scale negotiations aimed at securing wide-ranging tripartite agreements. In Germany it involved informal consultations leading to union and employer support for a 'solidarity pact' on the costs of German unification, while in France it in-

[3] It is, however, important to realize that this was the culmination of a trend which began in the 1950s (Beaumont, 1990; Brown and Walsh, 1991), and which thus might be better attributed to the fragmented institutions of the British union movement than to more recent changes in the nature of work.

[4] This development followed a decade of oscillations between decentralizing and recentralizing episodes (Ahlen, 1989; Kjellberg, 1992).

volved thorough tripartite consultations about the new right-wing government's five-year employment plan. Moreover, in the same year, bipartite or tripartite central agreements involving national union organizations were also reached in Austria, Belgium, Denmark, Finland, Greece, Ireland, the Netherlands, Norway, and Australia (EIRR, 1993).

In addition, the emergence of a European-wide corporatism remains a possibility. When dealing with issues like unemployment or worker participation, the instinct of many in the European Commission is to reach for corporatist-style agreements between European-wide bodies of employers and employees (EIRR, 1993, 237.2). Corporatist deals are appealing both to the Christian democratic politicians who remain at the heart of the process of European union, and to the social democrats who are their main opponents.

In citing this evidence of the ongoing importance of national (and perhaps even supra-national) bargaining institutions, I do not mean to deny that industrial relations systems are experiencing important changes, nor do I mean to deny that the changing nature of work can help to fragment organized labour. As I have said, these are important issues which warrant further research. What I do want to suggest, however, is that, on the evidence which we have at present, it seems reasonable to suppose that centrally co-ordinated union movements and corporatist industrial relations systems will be with us into the next century, and hence that it will continue to be possible, as I have done in this book, to appeal to the advantages of corporatism in order to argue for the feasibility of further moves towards economic democracy.

In brief then, it seems likely that both the main arguments of this book—the argument for the moral desirability of economic democracy and the argument for its strategic feasibility—will still be tenable as we move into the next century.

These arguments aim to convince all those who are influenced by the Enlightenment and its values. But they are especially pertinent for socialists. For they show that as the century draws to a close, the socialist challenge has not yet run its course. In particular, they show that socialists still have at least one programmatic goal—economic democracy—which can and should pose a fundamental challenge to some of the basic institutions of advanced capitalism. Armed with this goal, the socialist movement could return to the centre of political life.

Bibliography

ABB, FRITZ (1977), 'Trade Union Influence on the Distribution of the Social Product in the Federal German Republic', in Heathfield, ed. (1977).

ABELL, PETER (1983), 'The Viability of Industrial Producer Cooperation', in Crouch and Heller, eds. (1983).

ACTU (1987), *Future Strategies for the Trade Union Movement*, D164-87, September.

ACTU/TDC MISSION TO WESTERN EUROPE (1987), *Australia Reconstructed*, Canberra: AGPS.

AHLEN, KRISTINA (1989), 'Swedish Collective Bargaining Under Pressure: Inter-union Rivalry and Incomes Policies', *British Journal of Industrial Relations*, 27, no. 3, November.

ALCHIAN, ARMEN, and DEMSETZ, HAROLD (1986), 'Production, Information Costs, and Economic Organisation', in Putterman, ed. (1986).

ALLEN, CHRISTOPHER S. (1990), 'Trade Union, Worker Participation and Flexibility', *Comparative Politics*, 22, no. 3, April.

ALMANASREH, Z. (1977), 'Institutional Forms of Worker Participation in the Federal German Republic', in Heathfield, ed. (1977).

ALP/ACTU (1983), *Statement of Accord by the Australian Labor Party and the Australian Council of Trade Unions Regarding Economic Policy*, Melbourne: ACTU.

APPLE, NIXON (1988), *The Economy and Industry Development Report to AMWU National Conference*, July, AMWU.

ARCHER, ROBIN (1988), 'The Australian Accord', *International Review of Applied Economics*, 2, no. 2.

—— (1989), 'Really Radical Reform: Economic Citizenship in Hungary', unpublished paper.

—— (1992), 'Lessons from Northern Europe: Collective Bargaining and Economic Performance in Britain, Germany and Sweden', in Peetz *et al.*, eds. (1992).

ARENDT, HANNAH (1963), *On Revolution*, Harmondsworth: Penguin.

ARROW, K. J. (1974), *The Limits of Organisation*, New York: Norton.

AUSTRALIAN CONCILIATION AND ARBITRATION COMMISSION (1988), *National Wage Case*, August, Dec 640/88 M Print H4000.

AXELROD, ROBERT (1984), *The Evolution of Cooperation*, New York: Basic Books.

BACHARACH, MICHAEL (1976), *Economics and the Theory of Games*, London: Macmillan.

BACHRACH, PETER (1969), *The Theory of Democratic Elitism*, London: University of London Press.

BAGLIONI, G., and CROUCH, C., eds. (1990), *Industrial Relations in Europe: The Challenge of Flexibility*, London: Sage.

BATSTONE, ERIC, GOURLAY, STEPHEN, LEVIE, HUGO, and MOORE, ROY (1987), *New Technology and the Process of Labour Regulation*, Oxford: Clarendon.

BAUER, OTTO (1978), 'Political and Social Revolution', in T. Bottomore and P. Goode, eds. (1978).

BEAN, CHARLES, LAYARD, RICHARD, and NICKELL, STEPHEN (1986), 'The Rise of Unemployment: A Multi-Country Study', *Economica*, 53, Supplement, Spring.

BEAUMONT, P. B. (1990), *Change in Industrial Relations: The Organisation and the Environment*, London: Routledge.

BEGGS, JOHN J., and CHAPMAN, BRUCE J. (1987a), 'An Empirical Analysis of Australian Strike Activity: Estimating the Industrial Relations Effect of the First Three Years of the Prices and Incomes Accord', *The Economic Record*, 63, no. 180, March.

—— (1987b), 'Declining Strike Activity in Australia 1983–85: An International Phenomenon?', *The Economic Record*, 63, no. 183, December.

BENN, S. I., and WEINSTEIN, W. L. (1971), 'Being Free to Act and Being a Free Man', *Mind*, New Series, LXXX.

BERGER, SUZANNE, ed. (1981), *Organising Interests in Western Europe*, Cambridge: Cambridge University Press.

BERGGREN, CHRISTIAN (1980), 'Changes in the Rationalisation Pattern and Organisation of Work within Mass Production in the Swedish Engineering Industry', *Acta Sociologica*, 22, no. 4.

BERGHAHN, V. R., and KARSTEN, D. (1987), *Industrial Relations in West Germany*, Oxford: Berg.

BERGSTROM, HANS (1988), 'Election Year '88: Social Democrats Still Going Strong—Incorporating the Green Wave?', *Current Sweden*, Stockholm: Swedish Institute.

BERLE, ADOLF, and MEANS, GARDINER (1932), *The Modern Corporation and Private Property*, New York: Commerce Clearing House.

BERLIN, ISAIAH (1969), 'Two Concepts of Liberty', in *Four Essays on Liberty*, Oxford: Oxford University Press.

BERNSTEIN, EDUARD (1961), *Evolutionary Socialism*, New York: Schocken.

BLANCHFLOWER, DAVID G., and OSWALD, ANDREW J. (1987), 'Shares for Employees: A Test of their Effect', Centre for Labour Economies, London School of Economics, *Discussion Paper* no. 273, February.

BLAU, P. M., and SCHOENHERR, R. A. (1971), *The Structure of Organisation*, New York: Basic Books.

BLUMBERG, PAUL (1968), *Industrial Democracy: The Sociology of Participation*, London: Constable.

BOSTON, J. G. (1983), 'The Theory and Practice of Voluntary Incomes Policies with Particular Reference to the British Labour Government's

Social Contract 1974–79', D.Phil. Thesis, Oxford.

BOTTOMORE, TOM, and GOODE, PATRICK, eds. (1978), *Austro-Marxism*, Oxford: Clarendon Press.

BOWLES, SAMUEL (1986), 'The Production Process in a Competitive Economy: Walrasian, Neo-Mobbesian, and Marxian Models', in Putterman, ed. (1986).

—— and GINTIS, HERBERT (1986), *Democracy and Capitalism*, London: Routledge.

BOYER, ROBERT (1988), *The Search for Labour Market Flexibility*, Oxford: Clarendon.

BRANNEN, PETER (1983), *Authority and Participation in Industry*, London: Batsford.

BROWN, W., and WALSH, J. (1991), 'Pay Determination in Britain in the 1980s: The Anatomy of Decentralisation', *Oxford Review of Economic Policy*, 7, no. 1.

BRUNHES, B. (1989), *Labour Market Flexibility: Trends in Enterprises*, Paris: OECD.

BRUNO, MICHAEL, and SACHS, JEFFREY D. (1985), *Economics of Worldwide Stagflation*, Cambridge, Mass.: Harvard University Press.

BRUS, WLODZIMIERZ (1985), 'Socialism—Feasible or Viable?', *New Left Review*, 153.

BUCHANAN, A. (1982), *Marx and Justice*, London: Methuen.

BULL, M. J. (1988), 'From Pluralism to Pluralism: Italy and the Corporatism Debate', in A. Cox and N. O'Sullivan, eds., *The Corporate State*, Aldershot: Elgar.

BUTLER, DAVID, and STOKES, DONALD E. (1974), *Political Change in Britain*, 2nd edn., London: Macmillan.

CABLE, J., and FITZROY, F. R. (1980), 'Production Efficiency, Incentives and Employee Participation: Some Preliminary Results from West Germany', *Kyklos*, 33.

CALMFORS, LARS, and DRIFFILL, JOHN (1988), 'Centralisation of Wage Bargaining', *Economic Policy*, April, Cambridge: Cambridge University Press.

CAMERON, DAVID R. (1984), 'Social Democracy, Corporatism, Labour Quiescence and the Representation of Economic Interest in Advanced Capitalist Society', in Goldthorpe, ed. (1984a).

CARMICHAEL, LAURIE (1986), *Seminar and Conference Discussion Paper*, AMWU.

CASTLES, F. G. (1978), *The Social Democratic Image of Society*, London: Routledge.

CAWSON, ALAN (1986), *Corporatism and Political Theory*, Oxford: Blackwell.

CHAPMAN, B. J., ISAAC, J. E., and NILAND, J. R., eds. (1984), *Australian Labour Economics: Readings*, 3rd edn., Melbourne: Macmillan.

CLARK, C. M. H., ed. (1955), *Selected Documents in Australian History: 1851–1900*, Sydney: Angus and Robertson.

COASE, RONALD (1986), 'The Nature of the Firm', in Putterman, ed. (1986).

CODDINGTON, ALAN (1968), *Theories of the Bargaining Process*, London: George Allen and Unwin.

COHEN, G. A. (1979), 'Capitalism, Freedom and the Proletariat', in A. Ryan, ed., *The Idea of Freedom*, Oxford: Oxford University Press.

—— (1985), 'Are Workers Forced to Sell Their Labour Power?', in *Philosophy and Public Affairs*, 14, no. 1.

—— (1988), 'The Structure of Proletarian Unfreedom', in *Capitalism, Labour and Freedom*, Oxford: Oxford University Press.

COLE, G. D. H. (1920a), *Social Theory*, London: Methuen.

—— (1920b), *Guild Socialism Restated*, London: George Allen and Unwin.

—— (1960), *Socialism and Fascism*, London: Macmillan.

—— (1972), *Self-Government in Industry*, London: Hutchinson.

—— (1953), *Socialist Thought: The Forerunners*, London: Macmillan.

COMMITTEE OF REVIEW INTO AUSTRALIAN INDUSTRIAL RELATIONS LAW AND SYSTEMS (1985), *Australian Industrial Relations Law and Systems*, (Hancock Report), Canberra: AGPS.

COOMBES, R. W. (1984), 'Long-term Trends in Automation', in Marstrand, ed. (1984).

COX, ANDREW (1988), 'The Old and the New Testaments of Corporatism: Is it a Political Forum or a Method of Policy Making?', *Political Studies*, XXXVI, no. 2, June.

CRESSEY, PETER, ELDRIDGE, JOHN, MacINNES, JOHN, and NORRIS, GEOFFREY (1981), *Industrial Democracy and Participation: A Scottish Survey*, London: Department of Employment.

CROCKER, LAWRENCE (1980), *Positive Liberty*, The Hague: Martinus Nijhoff.

—— (1981), 'Marx, Liberty and Democracy', in John P. Burke, Lawrence Crocker, and Lyman H. Legfers, eds., *Marxism and the Good Society*, Cambridge: Cambridge University Press.

CROUCH, COLIN (1977), *Class Conflict and the Industrial Relations Crisis*, London: Heinemann.

—— (1979), *The Politics of Industrial Relations*, London: Fontana.

—— (1982), *Trade Unions: The Logic of Collective Action*, London: Fontana.

—— (1983), 'Pluralism and the New Corporatism: A Rejoinder', *Political Studies*, 31, September.

—— (1985), 'Conditions for Trade Union Wage Restraint', in Lindberg and Maier, eds. (1985).

—— (1986), 'Sharing Public Space: States and Organised Interests in Western Europe', in John A. Hall, ed. (1986), *States in History*, Oxford: Blackwell.

—— (1988), unpublished paper on the future of organized labour.

—— (1990), 'Generalised Political Exchange in Industrial Relations in Europe During the Twentieth Century', in Bernd Marin, ed. (1990).

—— (1992), 'The Fate of Articulated Industrial Relations Systems', in Mario Regini, ed. (1992).

—— (1993), *Industrial Relations and European State Traditions*, Oxford: Oxford University Press.

—— and HELLER, FRANK A., eds. (1983), *International Yearbook of Organisational Democracy*, Chichester: Wiley.

CROWLEY, FRANK, ed. (1980), *A Documentary History of Australia*, vol. 3, *Colonial Australia 1875–1900*, Melbourne: Nelson.

CUNNINGHAM, FRANK (1987), *Democratic Theory and Socialism*, Cambridge: Cambridge University Press.

DABROWSKI, MAREK (1989), 'Workers' Self-Management and the Polish Economic Reform', unpublished paper.

DABSCHECK, BRAHAM, and NILAND, JOHN (1981), *Industrial Relations in Australia*, Sydney: Allen and Unwin.

DAHL, ROBERT A. (1970), *After the Revolution*, New Haven, Conn.: Yale University Press.

—— (1979), 'Procedural Democracy', in Peter Laslett and James Fishkin, eds., *Philosophy, Politics and Society*, Fifth Series, New Haven, Conn.: Yale University Press.

—— (1985), *A Preface to Economic Democracy*, Cambridge: Polity.

—— and TUFT, EDWARD R. (1973), *Size and Democracy*, Stanford, Calif.: Stanford University Press.

DANIEL, W. W. (1987), *Workplace Industrial Relations and Technical Change*, London: Frances Pinter.

DANIELS, NORMAN (1975), 'Equal Liberty and the Unequal Worth of Liberty', in *Reading Rawls*, New York: Basic Books.

DEERY, S., and PLOWMAN, D. (1985), *Australian Industrial Relations*, 2nd edn., Sydney: McGraw-Hill.

DEIR (1986), *Industrial Democracy and Employee Participation*, Department of Employment and Industrial Relations, Canberra: AGPS.

DE LEPERVANCHE, MARIE (1975), 'Australian Immigration 1788–1940: Desired and Unwanted', in Wheelwright and Buckley, eds. (1975).

DE MENIL, GEORGE (1971), *Bargaining: Monopoly Power versus Union Power*, Cambridge, Mass.: MIT Press.

DEPARTMENT OF EMPLOYMENT, EDUCATION AND TRAINING (1987), *Skills for Australia*, Canberra: AGPS.

—— (1988a), *Higher Education: A Policy Statement*, Canberra: AGPS.

—— (1988b), *A New Commitment to Higher Education in Australia*, Canberra: AGPS.

DEPARTMENT OF INDUSTRIAL RELATIONS (1988), *Labour Market Reform: The Industrial Relations Agenda*, Canberra: AGPS.

DORNBUSCH, S., and FISHER, R. (1984), in R. E. Caves and L. B. Krause, eds., *The Australian Economy: A View from the North*, Washington: Brookings Institute.

DRAGO, ROBERT, and WOODEN, MARK (1991), 'The Determinants of Participatory Management', *British Journal of Industrial Relations*, 29, no. 2, June.

DUNLOP, J. T. (1950), *Wage Determination and Trade Unions*, New York: Kelley.

DWORKIN, RONALD (1986), 'Liberalism', in *A Matter of Principle*, Oxford: Clarendon.

EDWARDS, RICHARD (1986), 'From *Contested Terrain*', in Putterman, ed. (1986).

EIRR (1993), *European Industrial Relations Review*, vols. 228–39.

ELLERMAN, DAVID (1990), *The Democratic Worker-Owned Firm*, Boston: Unwin Hyman.

ELSTER, JON (1985), *Making Sense of Marx*, Cambridge: Cambridge University Press.

—— (1989), *The Cement of Society: A Study of Social Order*, Cambridge: Cambridge University Press.

—— and MOENE, KARL OVE (1989), *Alternatives to Capitalism*, Cambridge, Cambridge University Press.

ELY, JOHN HART (1980), *Democracy and Distrust: A Theory of Judicial Review*, Cambridge, Mass.: Harvard University Press.

ENGELS, FREDERICK (1975), Socialism: *Utopian and Scientific*, Peking: Foreign Language Press.

ESPING-ANDERSEN, GOSTA (1985), *Politics Against Markets: The Social Democratic Road to Power*, Princeton, NJ: Princeton University Press.

—— and KORPI, WALTER, 'Social Policy and Class Politics in Post-War Capitalism: Scandinavia, Austria and Germany', in Goldthorpe, ed. (1984).

EULAU, HEINZ, and LEWIS-BECK, MICHAEL S., eds. (1985), *Economic Conditions and Electoral Outcomes*, New York: Agathou.

EWER, PETER (1988), 'Industry Policy in Australia; Debate and Practice', *International Review of Applied Economics*, 2, no. 2.

—— HIGGINS, WINTON, and STEVENS, ANNETTE (1987), *Unions and the Future of Australian Manufacturing*, Sydney: Allen and Unwin.

FAXEN, KARL-OLOF, ODHNER, CLAES-ERIK, and SPANT, ROLAND (1987), *Wage Formation and the Economy in the Nineties*, unpublished English edition.

FEDERAL MINISTER OF LABOUR AND SOCIAL AFFAIRS (1991), *Co-determination in the Federal Republic of Germany*, Bonn.

FELDMAN, STANLEY (1985), 'Economic Self-Interest and the Vote', in Eulau and Lewis-Beck, eds. (1985).

FERNER, ANTHONY, and HYMAN, RICHARD, eds. (1992), *Industrial Relations in the New Europe*, Oxford: Blackwell.

FINEGOLD, DAVID, and SOSKICE, DAVID (1988), 'The Failure of Training in Britain: Analysis and Prescription', *Oxford Review of Economic Policy*, 4, no. 3.

FINLEY, M. I. (1968), 'Slavery', *International Encyclopaedia of the Social Sciences*, New York: Macmillan.

FISERA, VLADIMIR, ed. (1978), *Worker's Councils in Czechoslovakia 1968–9*, London: Allison and Busby.

FLANAGAN, ROBERT J., SOSKICE, DAVID W., and ULMAN, LLOYD (1983), *Unionism, Economic Stabilisation, and Income Policies*, Washington, DC: Brookings Institute.

FORD, BILL, and PLOWMAN, DAVID, eds. (1983), *Australian Unions: An Industrial Relations Perspective*, Melbourne: Macmillan.

FORD, G. W., HEARN, J. M., and LANSBURY, R. D., eds. (1987), *Australian Labour Relations: Readings*, 4th edn., Melbourne: Macmillan.

FOX, ALAN (1974), *Beyond Contract: Work Power and Trust Relations*, London: Faber.

FREEMAN, CHRISTOPHER (1984), 'Keynes or Kondratiev?', in Marstrand, ed. (1984).

FREEMAN, RICHARD (1986), 'Individual Hostility and Union Voice in the Labour Market', in Putterman, ed. (1986).

—— (1988), 'Labour Markets', *Economic Policy*, April, Cambridge: Cambridge University Press.

FREEMAN, R. B., and MEDOFF, J. L. (1984), *What Do Unions Do?*, New York: Basic Books.

FRENKEL, STEPHEN J. (1988), 'Australian Employers in the Shadow of the Labor Accords', *Industrial Relations*, 27, no. 2, Berkeley, Calif.: University of California Press.

FRIEDMAN, R. (1973), 'On the Concept of Authority in Political Theory', in R. E. Flathman, ed., *Concepts in Social and Political Philosophy*, New York: Macmillan.

GABEL, J. R., and FITZROY, F. R. (1980), 'Productive Efficiency, Incentives and Employee Participation: Some Preliminary Results for West Germany', *Kyklos*, XXXIII.

GALLIE, DUNCAN (1978), *In Search of the New Working Class*, Cambridge: Cambridge University Press.

GARRETT, GEOFFREY M. (1986), 'The Political Economy of Capitalist Democracy: The Politically Desirable, the Economically Feasible and Economic Policy in Britain, France and Sweden since 1974', unpublished paper.

GAY, PETER, (1979), *The Dilemma of Democratic Socialism*, New York: Octagon.

GEARY, DICK (1981), *European Labour Protest 1848–1939*, London: Macmillan.

GERBER, JOHN (1988), 'From Left Radicalism to Council Communism:

244   *Bibliography*

Anton Pannekoek and German Revolutionary Marxism', *Journal of Contemporary History*, 23, no. 2.

GIERKE, OTTO (1900), *Political Theories of the Middle Age*, Cambridge: Cambridge University Press.

GILL, FLORA (1987a), 'Inequality and the Arbitration of Wages in Australia: An Historical Perspective', *The Australian Quarterly*, 59, no. 2, Winter.

—— (1987b), 'Determination of Wage Relativities under the Federal Tribunal 1953–74', *Working Papers in Industrial Relations*, no. 2, Sydney: Deartment of Industrial Relations, University of Sydney.

GLYN, ANDREW (1990), 'Productivity and the Crisis of Fordism', *International Review of Applied Economics*, 4, no. 1, January.

—— A. HUGHES, LIPIETZ, A., and SINGH, A. (1990), 'The Rise and Fall of the Golden Age', in Marglin and Schor, eds. (1990).

GOLDEN, MIRIAM, and PONTUSSON, JONAS (1992), *Bargaining for Change: Union Politics in North America and Europe*, Ithaca, NY: Cornell University Press.

GOLDTHORPE, JOHN H., ed. (1984a), *Order and Conflict in Contemporary Capitalism*, Oxford: Clarendon.

—— (1984b), 'The End of Convergence: Corporatist and Dualist Tendencies in Modern Western Societies', in Goldthorpe, ed. (1984a).

GOLDTHORPE, J. (1987), 'Problems of Political Economy after the Postwar Period', in C. Maier, ed. (1987), *Changing Boundaries of the Political*, Cambridge: Cambridge University Press.

GOLLAN, ROBIN (1960), *Radical and Working Class Politics: A Study of Eastern Australia 1850–1910*, Melbourne: Melbourne University Press.

—— (1975), 'The Ideology of the Labour Movement', in Wheelright and Buckley, eds. (1975).

GOODRICH, CARTER L. (1975), *The Frontier of Control*, London: Pluto.

GOULD, CAROL C. (1988), *Rethinking Democracy*, Cambridge: Cambridge University Press.

GOUREVITCH, PETER, MARTIN, ANDREW, ROSS, GEORGE, BORNSTEIN, STEPHEN, MARKOVITZ, ANDREI, and ALLEN, CHRISTOPHER (1984), *Unions and Economic Crisis: Britain, West Germany and Sweden*, London: George Allen and Unwin.

GRAHAM, KEITH (1982), 'Democracy and the Autonomous Moral Agent', in *Contemporary Political Philosophy: Radical Studies*, Cambridge: Cambridge University Press.

—— (1986), *The Battle of Democracy*, Brighton: Wheatsheaf.

GRAMSCI, A. (1977), *Selections from Political Writings*, London: Lawrence and Wishart.

GRAY, JOHN (1984a), 'Introduction', in Pelczynski and Gray, eds. (1984).

—— (1984b), 'On Negative and Positive Liberty', in Pelczynski and Gray, eds. (1984).

GREEN, LESLIE (1988), *The Authority of the State*, Oxford: Clarendon.

GREENWOOD, GORDON, ed. (1955), *Australia: A Social and Political History*, Sydney: Angus and Robertson.

GREGORY, R. G. (1986), 'Wages Policy and Unemployment in Australia', *Economica*, 53.

GRIFFIN, GERARD, and GIUCA, VINCENT (1986), 'One Union Peak Council: The Merger of ACSPA and CAGEO with ACTU', *Journal of Industrial Relations*, 28, no. 4, December.

GUGER, ALOIS (1992), 'Social Corporatism: Success or Failure? Austrian Experiences', in Pekkarinen *et al.*, eds. (1992).

GUSTAVSEN, BJORN (1986), 'Evolving Patterns of Enterprise Organisation: The Move towards Greater Flexibility', *International Labour Review*, 125, no. 4, July–August.

GUTMANN, AMY (1980), *Liberal Equality*, Cambridge: Cambridge University Press.

HABERMAS, JURGEN (1976), *Legitimation Crisis*, London: Heinemann.

HAGAN, JIM (1981), *The History of the A.C.T.U.*, Melbourne: Longman Cheshire.

HANCOCK COMMITTEE (1985), *see* Committee of Review into Industrial Relations Law and Systems.

HANSON, CHARLES, and RATHKEY, PAUL (1984), 'Industrial Democracy: A Post Bullock Shopfloor View', *British Journal of Industrial Relations*, 22, no. 1, March.

HAREL, ALON (1989), 'The Logic of Industrial Organisation: Firm versus Markets', unpublished paper.

HARRISON, GREG (1988), *Initial AMWU Proposals for Restructuring of Trades Classifications in the Steel Industry*, restrc1.doc, cl/sdi/88, Amalgamated Metal Workers Union.

HARSANYI, JOHN C. (1977), *Rational Behaviour and Bargaining Equilibrium in Games and Social Situations*, Cambridge: Cambridge University Press.

HAYEK, F. A. (1960) *The Constitution of Liberty*, London: Routledge.

—— (1986), 'The Use of Knowledge in Society', in Putterman, ed. (1986).

HEATHFIELD, DAVID F., ed. (1977), *The Economics of Codetermination*, London: Macmillan.

HELD, DAVID (1987), *Models of Democracy*, Cambridge: Polity.

HIBBS, DOUGLAS A. (1987), *The Political Economy of Industrial Democracies*, Cambridge, Mass.: Harvard University Press.

HIGGINS, WINTON (1987), 'Unions as the Bearers of Industrial Regeneration: Reflections on the Australian Case', *Economic and Industrial Democracy*, 8.

—— and APPLE, NIXON (1983), 'How Limited Is Reformism?', *Theory and Society*, 12, Amsterdam: Elsevier.

HILTON, R. (1973), *Bond Men Made Free*, London: Methuen.

HIRSCH, FRED, and GOLDTHORPE, JOHN, eds. (1978), *The Political Economy of Inflation*, Cambridge, Mass.: Harvard University Press.

HIRSCHMAN, ALBERT O. (1970), *Exit, Voice and Loyalty*, Cambridge, Mass.: Harvard University Press.

—— (1981), *Essay in Trespassing*, Cambridge: Cambridge University Press.

HOBSBAWM, E. J (1962), *The Age of Revolution: Europe 1789–1848*, London: Cardinal.

—— (1982), 'Marx, Engels and Pre-Marxian Socialism', in *The History of Marxism, Volume One: Marxism in Marx's Day*, Brighton: Harvester.

HOLMES, STEPHEN (1988), 'Precommitment and the Paradox of Democracy, in J. Elster and R. Slagstad, eds., *Constitutionalism and Democracy*, Cambridge: Cambridge University Press.

HORVAT, BRANKO (1982), *The Political Economy of Socialism*, Oxford: Martin Robertson.

HOWARD, W. A. (1977), 'Australian Trade Unions in the Context of Union Theory', *Journal of Industrial Relations,* September.

HUHNE, C. (1990), 'Germany Prepares for Another Miracle', *Independent on Sunday*, 1 July.

HUNT, RICHARD N. (1974), *The Political Ideas of Marx and Engels, Volume One*, Pittsburgh: University of Pittsburgh Press.

—— (1984), *The Political Ideas of Marx and Engels, Volume Two*, London: Macmillan.

H. V. EVATT RESEARCH CENTRE (1988), *The Capital Funding of Public Enterprise in Australia*, Sydney: H. V. Evatt Foundation.

HYMAN, RICHARD (1992), 'Trade Unions and the Disaggregation of the Working Class', in Regini, ed. (1992).

—— and STREECK, WOLFGANG, eds. (1988), *New Technology and Industrial Relations*, Oxford: Blackwell.

IDE (1981), *Industrial Democracy in Europe*, Industrial Democracy in Europe International Research Group, Oxford: Clarendon.

IRRR (1990a), 'Developments in European Collective Bargaining: 1', *Industrial Relations Review and Report*, 460, 20 March.

—— (1990b), 'Developments in European Collective Bargaining: 2', *Industrial Relations Review and Report*, 465, 6 June.

JACKMAN, RICHARD (1989), 'Where Corporatism Works', LSE Quarterly, 3, no. 2, Autumn.

JACOBI, OTTO (1988), 'New Technological Paradigms, Long Waves and Trade Unions', in Hyman and Streeck, eds. (1988).

——, KELLER, BERNDT, and MÜLLER-JENTSCH, WALTHER (1992), 'Germany: Codetermining the Future', in Ferner and Hyman, eds. (1992).

JENSEN, MICHAEL, and MECKLING, WILLIAM (1976), 'Theory of the Firm: Managerial Behaviour, Agency Costs and Ownership Structure', in Putterman, ed. (1986).

Jones, Peter (1983), 'Political Equality and Majority Rule', in D. Miller and L. Siedentop, eds., *The Nature of Political Theory*, Oxford: Clarendon.

Jordan, Winthrop D. (1969), *White Over Black: American Attitudes Towards the Negro 1550–1812*, Baltimore: Penguin.

Katzenstein, Peter J. (1985), *Small States in World Markets*, Ithaca, NY: Cornell University Press.

Keating, P. J. (1988), *Budget Speech 1988–89*, Canberra: AGPS.

—— (1992), *Economic Statement*, February, Canberra: AGPS.

Kelly, Maryellen, Harrison, Bennett, and Xue, Lan (1991), *Technology Review*, MIT, January.

Keohane, Robert O. (1985), 'The International Politics of Inflation', in Lindberg and Maier, eds. (1985).

Kessler, Sid, and Bayliss, Fred (1992), *Contemporary British Industrial Relations*, Basingstoke: Macmillan.

Kinder, Donald R., and Kiewiet, D. Roderick (1981), 'Sociotropic Politics: The American Case', *British Journal of Political Science*, 11.

Kis, Janos, Koszez, Ferenc, and Solt, Ottilia (1987), *Social Contract*, in G. Demsky, G. Gado, and F. Roszeg, eds., *Roundtable*, Digest of Independent Hungarian Press.

Kjellberg, Anders (1992), 'Sweden: Can the Model Survive?', in Ferner and Hyman, eds. (1992).

Knight, Ian B. (1979), *Company Organisation and Worker Participation*, London: HMSO.

Knights, David, Collinson, David L., and Willmott, Hugh (1985), *Job Redesign: A Critical Perspective on the Labour Process*, Aldershot: Gower.

Kolakowski, Leszek (1968), 'The Concept of the Left', in *Marxism and Beyond*, London: Pall Mall.

—— (1978), *Main Currents in Marxism*, vol. 1, Oxford: Clarendon.

Kolchin, Peter (1987), *Unfree Labour: American Slavery and Russian Serfdom*, Cambridge, Mass.: Belknap.

Kornai, Janos (1986a), *Contradictions and Dilemmas*, Cambridge, Mass.: MIT Press.

—— (1986b), 'The Hungarian Reform Process: Visions, Hopes and Reality', *Journal of Economic Literature*, XXIV, December.

Korpi, Walter (1978), *The Working Class in Welfare Capitalism*, London: Routledge.

—— (1983), *The Democratic Class Struggle*, London: Routledge.

—— and Shalev, Michael (1980), 'Strikes, Power and Politics in Western Nations, 1900–1976', *Political Power and Social Theory*, 1.

Kyloh, Robert (1985), 'Overaward Payments and Wage Flexibility', *Wages and Incomes Policy Research Paper*, no. 5, Canberra: Department of Employment and Industrial Relations.

LANE, CHRISTEL (1989), *Management and Labour in Europe*, Aldershot: Edward Elgar.

LANGE, PETER (1984), 'Unions, Workers and Wage Regulation: The Radical Bases of Consent', in Goldthorpe, ed. (1984a).

—— and GARRETT, GEOFFREY (1985), 'The Politics of Growth: Strategic Interaction and Economic Peformance in the Advanced Industrial Democracies', *Journal of Politics*, 47, no. 3, August.

—— ROSS, GEORGE, and VANNICELLI, MAURIZIO (1982), *Unions, Change and Crisis: French and Italian Union Strategy and the Political Economy, 1945–1980*, London: George Allen and Unwin.

LASH, SCOTT (1985), 'The End of Neo-Corporatism?: The Breakdown of Centralised Bargaining in Sweden', *British Journal of Industrial Relations*, 23, no. 2, July.

—— and URRY, JOHN (1987), *The End of Organised Capitalism*, Cambridge: Polity.

LASKI, HAROLD (1967), *A Grammar of Politics*, 5th edn., London: Allen and Unwin.

LAYARD, R., NICKELL, S., and JACKMAN, R. (1991), *Unemployment, Macroeconomic Performance and the Labour Market*, Oxford: Oxford University Press.

LEHMBRUCH, GERHARD (1979), 'Consociational Democracy, Class Conflict and the New Corporatism', in Schmitter and Lehmbruch, eds. (1979).

—— (1982), 'Introduction: Neo-Corporatism in Comparative Perspective', in Lehmbruch and Schmitter, eds. (1982).

—— (1984), 'Concertation and the Structure of Corporatist Networks', in Goldthorpe, ed. (1984a).

—— and SCHMITTER, PHILIPPE C., eds. (1982), *Patterns of Corporatist Policy-Making*, London: Sage.

LEWIS, PHILIP E. T., and KIRBY, MICHAEL G. (1987), 'The Impact of Incomes Policy on Aggregate Wage Determination in Australia', *The Economic Record*, 63, no. 181, June.

LEWIS-BECK, MICHAEL S., and EULAU, HEINZ (1985), 'Economic Conditions and Electoral Outcomes in Transnational Perspective', in Elau and Lewis-Beck, eds. (1985).

LINDBERG, LEON N., and MAIER, CHARLES S., eds. (1985), *The Politics of Inflation and Economic Stagnation*, Washington: Brookings Institute.

LINDBLOM, CHARLES E. (1977), *Politics and Markets*, New York: Basic Books.

LINDSAY, A. D. (1962), *The Modern Democratic State*, Oxford: Oxford University Press.

LIPSET, S. M. (1983), *Political Man*, expanded edn., London: Heinemann.

LO (1988), *Three Years with Employee Investment Funds: An Evaluation*, Stockholm: LO.

LUCE, DUNCAN, and RAIFFA, HOWARD (1957), *Games and Decisions*, New York: John Wiley.

LUKES, STEVEN (1973), *Individualism*, Oxford: Blackwell.

—— (1974), 'Socialism and Equality', in Leszek Kolakowski and Stuart Hampshire, eds., *The Socialist Idea: A Reappraisal*, New York: Weidenfeld & Nicolson.

—— (1979), 'The Real and Ideal Worlds of Democracy', in Alkis Kontos, ed., *Powers, Possessions and Freedom*, Toronto: Toronto University Press.

—— (1984), *Marxism and Morality*, Oxford: Oxford University Press.

LUNDBERG, ERIK (1985), 'The Rise and Fall of the Swedish Model', *Journal of Economic Literature*, XXIII, March.

MCKINSEY AND COMPANY (1993), *Emerging Exporters: Australia's High Value-Added Manufacturing Exporters*, Melbourne: Australian Manufacturing Council.

MACKLIN, ROBERT, GOODWIN, MILES, and DOCHERTY, JIM (1992), 'Workplace Bargaining in Australia', in Peetz *et al.*, eds. (1992).

MCLEAN, IAN (1987), *Public Choice*, Oxford: Blackwell.

—— and RICHARDSON, SUE (1986), 'More or Less Equal? Australian Income Distribution in 1933 and 1980', *The Economic Record*, 62, no. 176, March.

MCLENNAN, G. (1984), 'Capitalist State or Democratic Polity? Recent Developments in Marxist and Pluralist Theory', in G. McLennon, D. Held, and S. Hall, eds., *The Idea of the Modern State*, Milton Keynes: Open University Press.

MACPHERSON, C. B. (1973), *Democratic Theory*, Oxford: Clarendon.

MCPHERSON, MICHAEL (1983), 'Efficiency and Liberty in the Productive Enterprise: Some Recent Work in the Economics of Work Organisation', *Philosophy and Public Affairs*, 12, no. 4, Fall.

MADSEN, HENRIK JESS (1980), 'Class Power and Participatory Equality: Attitudes towards Economic Democracy in Denmark and Sweden', *Scandinavian Political Studies*, 3, New Series, no. 4.

MAIER, CHARLES S. (1985), 'The Politics of Inflation in the Twentieth Century', in Lindberg and Maier, eds. (1978).

—— (1981), 'The Fictitious Bounds of Wealth and Law: On the Theory and Practice of Interest Representation', in Berger, ed. (1981).

—— (1984), 'Preconditions for Corporatism', in Goldthorpe, ed. (1984a).

MARGLIN, STEPHEN (1986), 'What Do Bosses Do?', in Putterman, ed. (1986).

—— (1990), 'Lessons of the Golden Age: An Overview', in Marglin and Schor, eds. (1990).

—— and SCHOR, JULIET, eds. (1990), *The Golden Age of Capitalism*, Oxford: Oxford University Press.

MARIN, BERND, ed. (1990a), *Governance and Generalised Exchange*, Boulder, Colo.: Campus Westview.

MARIN, BERND (1990b), 'Generalised Political Exchange', in *Generalised Political Exchange*, Boulder, Colo.: Campus Westview.

MARKOVITS, ANDREI S. (1986), *The Politics of West German Trade Unions*, Cambridge: Cambridge University Press.

MARKUS, GYORGY (1978), *Marxism and Anthropology*, Assen: Van Gorcum.

MARSTRAND, PAULINE (1984), *New Technology and the Future of Work and Skills*, London: Frances Pinter.

MARTIN, ROSS M. (1980), *Trade Unions in Australia*, 2nd edn., Melbourne: Penguin.

MAURICE, MARC, SELLIER, FRANÇOIS, and SILVESTRE, JEAN-JACQUES (1986), *The Social Foundations of Industrial Power*, Cambridge, Mass.: MIT Press.

MARX, KARL (1973), *Grundrisse*, Harmondsworth: Penguin.

—— (1975), *Early Writings*, Harmondsworth: Penguin.

—— (1976), *Capital, Volume One*, Harmondsworth: Penguin.

—— and ENGELS, FREDERICK (1976), *The German Ideology*, Moscow: Progress.

MATHEWS, JOHN (1988), *A Culture of Power: Rethinking Labour Movement Goals for the 1990s*, Sydney: Pluto Press.

MEADE, JAMES (1988), 'Different Forms of Share Economy', in Susan Howson, ed., *The Collected Papers of James Meade: Volume Two*, London: Unwin Hyman.

MEIDNER, RUDOLF (1978), *Employee Investment Funds*, London: George Allen and Unwin.

METAL TRADES FEDERATION OF UNIONS (1988), *The Metal Unions' Handbook for Delegates*, MTFU.

METAL TRADES INDUSTRY ASSOCIATION OF AUSTRALIA (1986), *Proposals for a Compact with the Metal Unions*, December.

METCALF, DAVID (1989), 'Water Notes Dry Up: The Impact of Donovan Reform Proposals and Thatcherism at Work on Labour Productivity in British Manufacturing Industry', *British Journal of Industrial Relations*, 27, no. 1, March.

MILL, J. S. (1972), *Considerations on Representative Government*, London: Dent.

MILLER, DAVID (1981), 'Market Neutrality and the Failure of Cooperatives', *British Journal of Political Science*, 11.

—— (1983), 'Constraints on Freedom', *Ethics*, 9, no. 1, October.

MILLER, SUSANNE, and POTTHOFF, HEINRICH (1986), *A History of German Social Democracy*, Leamington Spa: Berg.

MILLWARD, NEIL, STEVENS, MARK, SMART, DAVID, and HAWES, W. R. (1992), *Workplace Industrial Relations in Transition*, Aldershot: Dartmouth.

MINTZ, SIDNEY W. (1978), 'Was the Plantation Slave a Proletarian?', *Review*, 2, no. 1, Summer.

MONTGOMERY, DAVID (1979), *Workers' Control in America*, Cambridge:

Cambridge University Press.

MORAWSKI, WITOLD (1987), 'Self-Management and Economic Reform', in J. Koralewicz, I. Bialecki, and M. Watson, eds., *Crisis and Transition*, Oxford: Berg.

MOSES, JOHN A. (1982), *Trade Unionism in Germany from Bismarck to Hitler 1869–1933*, vol. 2, *1919–1933*, London: George Prior.

MUELLER, DENNIS C. (1979), *Public Choice*, Cambridge: Cambridge University Press.

MULLER, EDWARD N., and OPP, KARL-DIETER (1986), 'Rational Choice and Rebellious Collective Action', *American Political Science Review*, 80, no. 2, June.

MULVEY, CHARLES (1978), *The Economic Analysis of Trade Unions*, Oxford: Martin Robertson.

MURRAY, ROBIN (1985), 'Benetton Britain: The New Economic Order', *Marxism Today*, 29, no. 11, November.

NATIONAL INSTITUTE OF ECONOMIC AND INDUSTRY RESEARCH (1988), 'Restructuring Australia', *National Economic Review*, no. 8, March, Melbourne.

NATIONAL LABOUR CONSULTATIVE COUNCIL (1987), *Labour Market Flexibility in the Australian Setting*, Canberra: AGPS.

NEGRELLI, SERAFINO (1988), 'Management Strategy: Towards New Forms of Regulation', in Hyman and Streeck, eds. (1988).

NEWELL, ANDREW, and SYMONS, JAMES (1987), 'Corporatism, *Laissez-Faire* and the Rise in Unemployment', *European Economic Review*, 31, April.

NEWMAN, OTTO (1981), *The Challenge of Corporatism*, London: Macmillan.

NICHOLLS, DAVID (1974), *Three Varieties of Pluralism*, London: Macmillan.

NORMAN, RICHARD (1987), *Free and Equal: A Philosophical Examination of Political Values*, Oxford: Oxford University Press.

NOVE, ALEC (1983), *The Economics of Feasible Socialism*, London: George Allen and Unwin.

NOZICK, ROBERT (1974), *Anarchy, State and Utopia*, Oxford: Blackwell.

NUTI, DOMENICO MARIO (1987), 'Profit-Sharing and Employment: Claims and Overclaim', *Industrial Relations*, 26, no. 1, Winter.

NUTZINGER, H. G. (1983), 'Empirical Research into German Codetermination: Problems and Perspectives', *Economic Analysis and Workers' Management*, XVII.

ODIORNE, GEORGE S. (1979), *MBO II: A System of Managerial Leadership for the 80's*, Belmont, Calif.: Fearon Pitman.

OECD (1986a), *Labour Market Flexibility*, Report by a high-level group of experts to the Secretary-General, Paris: OECD.

—— (1986b), *Flexibility in the Labour Market: The Current Debate*, Paris: OECD.

—— (1987), *Structural Adjustment and Economic Performances*, Paris: OECD.

OECD (1988), *Economic Outlook*, 43, June, Paris: OECD.
—— (1989), *Economic Transition: Structural Adjustment in OECD Countries*, Paris: OECD.
—— (1990a), *Economic Outlook*, 47, Paris: OECD.
—— (1990b), *Historical Statistics 1960–1988*, Paris: OECD.
—— (1993), *Economic Outlook*, 54, December, Paris: OECD.
OFFE, CLAUS (1981), 'The Attribution of Public Status to Interest Groups: Observations on the West German Case', in Berger, ed. (1981).
—— (1985a), *Disorganised Capitalism*, Cambridge: Polity.
—— (1985b), 'The Future of the Labour Market', in Offe (1985a).
—— and WIESENTHAL, HELMUT (1985), 'Two Logics of Collective Action', in Offe (1985a).
OHMAN, BERNDT (1983), 'The Debate on Wage-Earner Funds in Scandinavia', in Crouch and Heller, eds. (1983).
OLLMAN, BERTELL (1971), *Alienation*, Cambridge: Cambridge University Press.
OLSON, MANCUR (1965), *The Logic of Collective Action*, Cambridge, Mass.: Harvard University Press.
—— (1982), *The Rise and Decline of Nations*, New Haven, Conn.: Yale University Press.
OSWALD, ANDREW (1985), 'The Economic Theory of Trade Unions: An Introductory Survey', *Scandinavian Journal of Economics*, 87.
PALOHEIMO, HEIKKI (1988), 'The Effect of Trade Unions and Governments on Economic Peformance', unpublished paper, Helsinki: WIDER.
PANITCH, LEO (1977), 'The Development of Corporatism in Liberal Democracies', in Panitch (1986).
—— (1986), *Working Class Politics in Crisis*, London: Verso.
PANNEKOEK, ANTON (1950), *Workers Councils*, Melbourne.
PATEMAN, CAROLE (1970), *Participation and Democratic Theory*, Cambridge: Cambridge University Press.
—— (1988), *The Sexual Contract*, Cambridge: Polity.
PATTERSON, ORLANDO (1982), *Slavery and Social Death*, Cambridge, Mass.: Harvard University Press.
PEETZ, DAVID (1985), 'The Accord and Low Income Earners', *Wages and Incomes Policy Research Paper*, no. 7, Canberra: Department of Employment and Industrial Relations.
—— PRESTON, ALISON, and DOCHERTY, JIM, eds. (1992), *Workplace Bargaining in the International Context*, Canberra: Department of Industrial Relations.
PEKKARINEN, JUKKA, POHJOLA, MATTI, and ROWTHORN, BOB, eds. (1992), *Social Corporatism—A Superior Economic System?*, Oxford: Oxford University Press.
PELCZYNSKI, Z. A., and GRAY, JOHN, eds. (1984), *Conception of Liberty in Political Philosophy*, London: Athlone.

PETERSON, RICHARD B. (1987), 'Swedish Collective Bargaining—A Changing Scene', *British Journal of Industrial Relations*, XXV, no. 1, March.

PHELPS BROWN, HENRY (1983), *The Origin of Trade Union Power*, Oxford: Oxford University Press.

PIEKALKIEWICZ, JAROSLAV (1972), *Public Opinion Policy in Czechoslovakia, 1968–69*, New York: Praeger.

PIORE, MICHAEL J. (1986a), 'Perspectives on Labour Market Flexibility', *Industrial Relations*, 25, no. 2, Spring.

—— (1986b), 'The Decline of Mass Production and the Challenge to Union Survival', *Industrial Relations Journal*, 19, no. 3, Autumn.

—— and SABEL, CHARLES F. (1984), *The Second Industrial Divide: Possibilities for Prosperity*, New York: Basic Books.

PISSARIDES, C. A. (1987), 'Real Wages and Unemployment in Australia', Centre for Labour Economics, London School of Economics, Discussion Paper no. 286, June.

PIVEN, FRANCES FOX, ed. (1991), *Labour Parties in Postindustrial Societies*, Cambridge: Polity.

PIZZORNO, ALESSANDRO (1978), 'Political Exchange and Collective Identity in Industrial Conflict', in C. Crouch and A. Pizzorno, eds., *The Resurgence of Class Conflict in Western Europe since 1968, Volume 2: Comparative Analyses*, London: Macmillan.

—— (1981), 'Interests and Parties in Pluralism', in Berger, ed. (1981).

PLAMENATZ, JOHN (1973), *Democracy and Illusion*, London: Penguin.

PLOWMAN, DAVID H. (1986), 'Employers and Compulsory Arbitration: The Higgins Era 1907–1920', *The Journal of Industrial Relations*, 28, no. 4, December.

—— (1988), *A Long Haul: The Origins of the Confederation of Australian Industry*, Industrial Relations Research Center Monograph, May, University of New South Wales.

POHJOLA, MATTI (1992), 'Corporatism and Wage Bargaining', in Pekkarinen *et al.*, eds. (1992).

POLANYI, KARL (1957), *The Great Transformation*, Boston: Beacon.

POLLERT, ANNA (1988), 'Dismantling Flexibility', *Capital and Class*, 34, Spring.

PONS, XAVIER (1984), *Out of Eden*, Sydney: Sirius.

PONTUSSON, JONAS (1987), 'Radicalisation and Retreat in Swedish Social Democracy', *New Left Review*, 165, September/October.

POOLE, MICHAEL (1975), *Workers' Participation in Industry*, London: Routledge.

—— and JENKINS, GLENVILLE (1990), *The Impact of Economic Democracy*, London: Routledge.

PRASNIKAR, JANEZ, and SVEJNAR, JAN (1989), 'Employment and Income Determination in Yugoslav Labor-Managed Firms',

unpublished paper.
PRZEWORSKI, ADAM (1985), *Capitalism and Social Democracy*, Cambridge: Cambridge University Press.
PRZEWORSKI, ADAM (1985a), 'Material Bases of Consent', in Przeworski (1985).
—— (1985b), 'Material Interests, Class Compromise, and the State', in Przeworski (1985).
—— and SPRAGUE, JOHN (1986), *Paper Stones: A History of Electoral Socialism*, Chicago: University of Chicago Press.
PUTTERMAN, LOUIS, ed. (1986), *The Economic Nature of the Firm*, Cambridge: Cambridge University Press.
—— (1990), *Division of Labor and Welfare: An Introduction to Economic Systems*, Oxford: Oxford University Press.
RAPOPORT, ANATOL, GUYER, MELVIN J., and GORDON, DAVID G. (1976), *The 2 × 2 Game*, Ann Arbor, Mich.: The University of Michigan Press.
—— and PERNER, J. (1974), 'Testing Nash's Solution of the Cooperative Game', in A. Rapoport, ed., *Game Theory as a Theory of Conflict Resolution*, Dordrecht: Reidel.
RAWLS, JOHN (1972), *A Theory of Justice*, Oxford: Oxford University Press.
RAWSON, D. W. (1986), *Unions and Unionists*, 2nd edn., Sydney: Allen and Unwin.
RAZ, JOSEPH (1986), *The Morality of Freedom*, Oxford: Clarendon.
—— (1987), 'Government by Consent', in J. W. Pennock and J. R. Chapman, eds. (1987), 'Authority Revisited', *Nomos 29*, New York: New York University Press.
REGINI, MARINO (1984), 'The Conditions for Political Exchange: How Concertation Emerged and Collapsed in Italy and Great Britain', in Goldthorpe, ed. (1984a).
—— (1987), 'Social Pacts in Italy', in Ilja Scholten, ed., *Political Stability and Neo-Corporatism*, London: Sage.
—— ed. (1992), *The Future of Labour Movements*, London: Sage.
RIDEOUT, ROGER W., and DYSON, JACQUELINE (1983), *Rideout's Principles of Labour Law*, 4th edn., London: Sweet and Maxwell.
RIDLEY, F. F. (1970), *Revolutionary Syndicalism in France*, Cambridge: Cambridge University Press.
RIMMER, MALCOLM (1985), 'Incomes Policy in Australia, 1975–85', *Working Paper* 85-031, November, Australian Graduate School of Management, University of New South Wales.
ROSEN, COREY, and KLEIN, KATHERINE (1983), 'Job-Creating Performance of Employee-Owned Firms', *Monthly Labor Review*, 106, no. 8, August.
ROSS, A. M. (1948), *Trade Union Wage Policy*, Berkeley, Calif.: University of California Press.
ROWTHORN, BOB (1992), 'Corporatism and Labour Market Performance', in Pekkarinen *et al.*, eds. (1992).
—— and GLYN, ANDREW (1990), 'The Diversity of Unemployment Ex-

perience Since 1973', in Marglin and Schor, eds. (1990).

RYDER, A. J. (1967), *The German Revolution of 1918*, Cambridge: Cambridge University Press.

SABEL, CHARLES F. (1981), 'The Internal Politics of Trade Unions', in Berger, ed. (1981).

—— (1982), *Work and Politics: The Division of Labour in Industry*, Cambridge: Cambridge University Press.

SARTORI, GIOVANNI (1969), 'From the Sociology of Politics to Political Sociology', in Seymour Martin Lipset, ed., *Politics and the Social Sciences*, Oxford: Oxford University Press.

SCHELLING, THOMAS C. (1960), *The Strategy of Conflict*, Cambridge, Mass.: Harvard University Press.

SCHMITTER, PHILIPPE C. (1979a), 'Still the Century of Corporatism', in Schmitter and Lehmbruch, eds. (1979).

—— (1979b), 'Modes of Interest Intermediation and Models of Societal Change in Western Europe', in Schmitter and Lehmbruch, eds. (1979).

—— (1981), 'Interest Intermediation and Regime Governability in Contemporary Western Europe and North America', in Berger, ed. (1981).

—— and LEHMBRUCH, GERHARD, eds. (1979), *Trends Towards Corporatist Intermediation*, Beverly Hills, Calif.: Sage.

SCHOTT, KERRY (1984), *Policy, Power and Order: The Persistence of Economic Problems in Capitalist Societies*, New Haven, Conn.: Yale.

—— 'Consensual Macroeconomic Policies: A Cross Country Study of Economic Performance and Political Arrangements in the 1970s', *Wages and Incomes Policy Research Paper*, no. 2, Canberra: Department of Employment and Industrial Relations.

SCHULLER, TOM (1985), *Democracy at Work*, Oxford: Oxford University Press.

SCHWERIN, DON S. (1980), 'The Limits of Organisation as a Response to Wage-Price Problems', in R. Rose, ed., *Challenge to Governance*, London: Sage.

SEN, AMARTYA (1982), 'Rational Fools: A Critique of the Behavioural Foundations of Economic Theory', in *Choice, Welfare and Measurement*, Oxford: Blackwell.

SIMES, R. M., and HORN, P. M. (1988), 'The Role of Wages in the Australian Macro-economy', paper prepared for the 1988 Australian Economics Congress, 24 August–2 September.

—— and RICHARDSON, C. J. (1987), 'Wage Determination in Australia', *The Economic Record*.

SIMON, HERBERT (1983), *Reason in Human Affairs*, Oxford: Blackwell.

SMITH, PETER, and THOMAS, STEPHEN (1988), 'Wage Dispersion and Inflation', *Discussion Papers in Economics and Econometrics*, no. 8808, University of Southampton, May.

SMITH, STEPHEN (1990), 'On the Economic Rationale for Codetermination Law', *EUI Working Papers*, ECO Number 90/12.

SOPER, PHILIP (1989), 'Legal Theory and the Claim of Authority', *Philosophy and Public Affairs*, 18, no. 3, Summer.

SORGE, ARNDT, and STREECK, WOLFGANG (1988), 'Industrial Relations and Technical Change: The Case for an Extended Perspective', in Hyman and Streeck, eds. (1988).

SOSKICE, DAVID (1990), 'Wage Determination: The Changing Role of Institutions in Advanced Industrialised Countries', *Oxford Review of Economic Policy*, 4, no. 3, Autumn.

STEINER, HILLEL (1974/75), 'Individual Liberty', *Proceedings of the Aristotelian Society*, New Series, LXXV.

STEINMO, SVEN, THELEN, KATHLEEN, and LONGSTRETH, FRANK, eds. (1992), *Structuring Politics: Historical Institutionalism in Comparative Perspective*, Cambridge: Cambridge University Press.

STEPHENS, JOHN D. (1979), *The Transition from Capitalism to Socialism*, London: Macmillan.

STILWELL, FRANK (1986), *The Accord and Beyond*, Sydney: Pluto.

STRAUSS, GEORGE (1988), 'Australian Labour Relations Through American Eyes', *Industrial Relations*, 27, no. 2, Berkeley, Calif.: University of California Press.

STREECK, WOLFGANG (1981), 'Qualitative Demands and the Neo-Corporatist Manageability of Industrial Relations', *British Journal of Industrial Relations*, XX, no. 2.

—— (1984a), *Industrial Relations in West Germany*, London: Heinemann.

—— (1984b), 'Neo-Corporatist Industrial Relations and the Economic Crisis in West Germany', in Goldthorpe, ed. (1984a).

—— (1984c), 'Co-determination: The Fourth Decade', in B. Wilpert and A. Sorge, eds. (1984), *International Yearbook of Organising Democracy*, vol. II.

—— (1989), 'Skills and the Limits of Neo-Liberalism: The Enterprise of the Future as a Place of Learning', *Work, Employment and Society*, 3, no. 1, March.

—— and SCHMITTER, P. C. (1985), 'Community, Market, State—and Associations? The Prospective Contribution of Interest Governance to Social Order', in *Private Interest of Government Beyond Market and State*, Beverly Hills, Calif.: Sage.

SUTCLIFFE, CHARLES (1982), 'Inflation and Prisoner's Dilemmas', *Journal of Post Keynesian Economics*, IV, no. 4, Summer.

SVEJNAR, JAN (1982), 'Codetermination and Productivity and Empirical Evidence from the Federal Republic of Germany', in D. Jones and J. Svejnar, eds., *Participatory and Self-Managed Firms: Evaluating Economic Perfomance*, New York: Lexington Books.

SWEDISH INSTITUTE (1987), 'Labour Relations in Sweden', *Fact Sheets on Sweden*, classification FS 3p Oha, December.

SWEDISH MINISTRY of FINANCE (1984), *Employer Investment Funds*, Stockholm: Ministry of Finance.

TARANTELLI, EZIO (1986), 'The Regulation of Inflation and Unemployment', *Industrial Relations*, 25, no. 1, Winter.

TAWNEY, R. H. (1964), *The Radical Tradition*, London: George Allen and Unwin.

TAYLOR, CHARLES (1985), *Philosophy and the Human Sciences: Philosophical Papers 2*, Cambridge: Cambridge University Press.

—— (1985a), 'Atomism', in Taylor (1985).

—— (1985b), 'What's Wrong with Negative Liberty', in Taylor (1985).

TILTON, TIM (1990), *The Political Theory of Swedish Social Democracy*, Oxford: Oxford University Press.

TOCQUEVILLE, ALEXIS (1990), *Democracy in America*, vol. 1, New York: Vintage.

TRAXLER, FRANZ (1990), 'Political Exchange, Collective Action and Interest Governance: Towards a Theory of the Genesis of Industrial Relations and Corporatism', in Marin, ed. (1990a).

TREASURY (1988a), *Budget Statements 1988–89*, Canberra: AGPS.

—— (1988b), *Economic Round-up*, September, Canberra: AGPS.

—— (1993), *Budget Statements 1 and 2 of Budget Paper No. 1, 1993–94*, Canberra: AGPS.

TREGILLIS, SHANE (1987), 'Uprooted, Ripped-off, Reconstructed', *Australian Society*, September.

TUDOR, H., and TUDOR, J. M., eds. (1988), *Marxism and Social Democracy*, Cambridge: Cambridge University Press.

TURNER, IAN (1983), *In Union Is Strength*, 3rd edn., Melbourne: Nelson.

URSELL, GILL (1983), 'The Views of British Managers and Shop Stewards on Industrial Democracy', in Crouch and Heller, eds. (1983).

VALENZUELA, SAMUEL J. (1992), 'Labour Movements and Political Systems: Some Variations', in Regini, ed. (1992).

VAN DUIJN, J. J. (1983), *The Long Wave in Economic Life*, London: George Allen and Unwin.

VANEK, JAROSLAV (1970), *The General Theory of Labor-Managed Market Economies*, Ithaca, NY: Cornell University Press.

—— (1971), *The Participatory Economy*, Ithaca, NY: Cornell University Press.

VISSER, JELLE (1992), 'The Strength of Union Movements in Advanced Capitalist Democracies', in Regini, ed. (1992).

VON NEUMANN, JOHN, and MORGENSTERN, OSKAR (1947), *Theory of Games and Economic Behaviour*, Princeton, NJ: Princeton University Press.

VON OTTER, CASTEN (1985), 'Employment Attitudes to Worker Participation in Capital Accumulation: A Critical Appraisal', Working Paper, Stockholm: Arbetslivscentrum.

WALTON, RICHARD E. (1985), 'From Control to Commitment in the Workplace', *Harvard Business Review*, 2, March–April.

WALZER, MICHAEL (1983), *Spheres of Justice*, Oxford: Martin Robertson.

WARD, BENJAMIN N. (1967), *The Socialist Economy*, New York: Random House.

WARD, RUSSELL (1965), *The Australian Legend*, Melbourne: Oxford University Press.

WEINTRAUB, ROY E. (1975), *Conflict and Cooperation in Economics*, London: Macmillan.

WEIR, MARGARET, and SKOCPOL, THEDA (1985), 'State Structures and the Possibilities for "Keynesian" Responses to the Great Depresssion in Sweden, Britain, and the United States', in Peter B. Evans, Dietrich Rueschemeyer, and Theda Skocpol, eds., *Bringing the State Back In*, Cambridge: Cambridge University Press.

WHEELWRIGHT, E. L., and BUCKLEY, KEN, eds. (1975), *Essays in the Political Economy of Australian Capitalism: Volume One*, Sydney: Australia and New Zealand Book Co.

WHITFIELD, KEITH (1988), 'The Australian Wage System and Its Labor Market Effects', *Industrial Relations*, 27, no. 2, Berkeley, Calif.: University of California Press.

WILLIAMS, B. A. O. (1962), ' The Idea of Equality', in Peter Laslett and W. G. Runciman, eds., *Philosophy, Politics and Society*, Second Series: Oxford.

WILLIAMSON, OLIVER (1985), *The Economic Institutions of Capitalism*, New York: The Free Press.

—— WACHTER, MICHAEL, and HARRIS, JEFFREY (1986), 'Understanding the Employment Relation: The Analysis of Idiosyncratic Exchange', in Putterman, ed. (1986).

WILLIAMSON, PETER J. (1985), *Varieties of Corporatism*, Cambridge: Cambridge University Press.

WOLFE, JOEL D. (1985), 'Corporatism and Union Democracy: The British Miners and Incomes Policy, 1973–74', *Comparative Politics*, 17, no. 4, July.

—— (1988), 'Workers, Participation, Democracy: Internal Politics in the British Union Movement', *American Political Science Review*, 80.

WOLFF, ROBERT PAUL (1976), *In Defense of Anarchism*, New York: Harper & Row.

WOOD, STEPHEN (1988), 'Between Fordism and Flexibility? The US Car Industry', in Hyman and Streeck, eds. (1988).

WRIGHT, ANTHONY (1986), *Socialism: Theories and Practices*, Oxford: Oxford University Press.

ZIOLKOWSKI, MAREK (1988), 'Individuals and the Social System: Values, Perceptions, and Behavioural Strategies', *Social Research*, 55, nos. 1–2, Summer.

ZYSMAN, JOHN (1985), 'Inflation and the Politics of Supply', in Lindberg and Maier, eds. (1985).

Index

Accord 87–8, 191, 202, 208–9
  and enterprise bargaining 228–9
  Mark II 209, 220
  Mark III 211, 223
  Mark IV 220
  origins 205–7
active labour market policy 178
ACTU (Australian Council of Trade
  Unions) 191, 198, 220
affected non-subjects 29, 30–3
all-affected principle 27–8, 38–9
all-subjected principle 32–3
Anglo-Saxon countries 48, 96, 189,
  192, 194, 229
Arbitration system 202–5, 207, 209,
  226
Asia 232
asset specificity 50–1
associations 24–5
  decision-making 26–34
Australasia 67, 126, 192
Australia 83, 152, 177, 236
  constitution 201–2
  employer organizations 200–1,
    223–4
  ideological traditions 194–6
  Labor party 197, 199–200, 206
  the state 201–5
  unions 196–9, 203, 206, 222–3
  wage-fixing systems 204–5, 207–12,
    228–9
Australia Reconstructed 223
Austria 89, 153 n., 192, 199, 223, 236
Austro-Marxism 8, 106
authority 29–30, 186
  and autonomy 33–4
  of the state 33, 46–7
  see also authority of the firm;
    subjects
authority of the firm:
  over labour 43–4, 45–7
  over shareholders 47–9
  its possible elimination 49–53
  scope 54–5, 58–9
  under Fordism 183–7
autonomy 18–19, 22
awards 202
  award restructuring 226–7

bargaining:
  generalized societal bargaining 99,
    178
  simple bargaining game 121–9,
    137–40
Belgium 236
Berlin, Isaiah 14, 17, 19, 20
Bernstein, Eduard 1 n., 4 n.
bounded rationality 50–3
Branting, Hjalmar 106
Brazil 88
Britain:
  Chartism 3 n.
  Combination Acts 76 n.
  economic democracy 105, 112,
    117 n., 161, 166, 168
  economic performance 117, 170 n.,
    174
  electoral reform 4 n.
  industrial relations system 83, 152,
    183, 192, 194, 221, 223
  labour market flexibility 179, 181
  party–union relations 199
  unions 128 n., 151, 222
  worker morale 82 n.
Bullock Inquiry 105, 126 n.

Cameron, David 78–9
Canada 83, 154
capital, capitalists 42, 47–9
  preferences 108, 120
  vital interests 118
capitalist domination of the state 86,
  87
Carmichael, Laurie 200 n., 225
central planning 3, 4, 5
centralization 72–4, 78, 80–3
  of collective bargaining 235–6
  and economic performance 153–4
  labour centralization 78–9, 88–91,
    129, 151, 154, 181, 191, 233–6
Christian Democracy 113 n., 114 n.,
  236
class analysis 68–9
class collaboration 85–6
class co-operation 74–5, 78, 80–3,
  85–6, 151, 191
class entry and exit 55, 56–8

Coase, Ronald 49
co-determination 105, 142, 156–8, 227
Cole, G. D. H. 4 n., 6, 8, 25, 27, 106, 137
collective action 94–8
collective identity 94–8, 110, 133
colonial socialism 201
commitment (to the firm) 184–5
communism 8, 114 n., 128 n., 200, 225
concentration of power 72–3, 78–9, 90, 198
Conciliation and Arbitration Commission (Australia), *see* arbitration system
consensus 74–5, 85–6
Conservative Party (Britain) 77, 152
constitutive morality 12–13, 35–7
consumers 32 n., 39–41, 70–2, 136 n.
contracts:
  contingent claims contracts 50–3
  sequential spot contracts 50–3
control, *see* direct control; exit control; indirect control; voice control; workers' control
control against ownership 105, 156–8, 162, 168, 189
control through ownership 105, 156, 158–62, 168, 189
control stickiness 141–3
control trade-off (single) 107
  in Australia 220–1, 226–7
  conditions for capitalist agreement 117–21
  conditions for government agreement 113–17
  conditions for labour agreement 111–13
  game theoretic analysis 121–9
  and economic performance 155–62, 183–7
  summary of conditions 132, 162, 187
  and workers' material interests 163–8, 187–9
control trade-offs (series) 107
  conditions for accumulation 134–43
  conditions for instability 133–4
  conditions for repetition 134
  game theoretic analysis 137–40
  summary of conditions 143–4
co-operatives 6, 161
  see also control through ownership
corporatism:
  advantages 87–8, 91–102, 103

conditions for its maintenance 108, 129–32
dangers 85–91
definitions 79–81
and economic performance 148–55, 174–83, 207, 212–19, 222–8
its establishment 129 n., 192
and fascism 80, 86
neo-corporatism 83–4
in the next century 232–6
corporatist trade-off strategy 107, 229
cost-competitive standardized production 172, 185–7
credible commitment 125–9, 131–2, 142–3
  ideological capacity 127–8
  institutional capacity 126–7
Crouch, Colin 74, 80–1, 83, 88 n., 152 n., 193

Dahl, Robert 25, 27, 33, 46
democracy 26–35, 37
  direct participation 28
  and rights 34–5
Denmark 157 n., 158 n., 167, 236
direct control 29, 30–3
  over firms 41–4, 48–9, 54–5, 58–60, 103–6, 186
disagreement point 121, 131, 137
Dworkin, Ronald 12, 35–6

Eastern Europe 67, 112, 232
economic democracy:
  basic model 44–5, 47, 48, 49, 53, 54, 61
  and capitalism 5, 38, 44
  definition 5, 38, 230
  and earlier socialists 6
  and efficiency 63–4
  gradual transition 106–7
  relevant actors 68–72, 109
  summary of the main arguments 230, 231–2
  and worker ownership 45, 105
economic performance, *see* control trade-off (single); corporatism; national economic management
electoral reform 4
electoral theories 114–15
employee investment funds, *see* wage earner funds
employee share ownership 161
  see also control through ownership

employers, *see* capital, capitalists
employment contract 42–3, 55, 68, 92,
   179
Engels, Frederick 1, 62, 94 n.
Enlightenment 1, 2, 3, 7, 8, 12, 36,
   231, 236
environmentalism 5
equal liberty:
  principle of 12, 13–23, 25, 37, 41
equality 22–3
European Union 6 n., 46 n., 236
exchangeable goods 103
exit control 39–41, 44, 48–9
exchange relationship 43, 55–8, 183

feasibility:
  definitions 61–3, 64–5
  and preferences 65, 66
  of a series of control trade-
    offs 133–44
  of a single control trade-off 108–32
  strategic feasibility 2, 65–6
  and viability 63, 155–6
Finland 236
firm entry and exit 55–6, 58
firms:
  as associations 38
flexible specialization 172
Fordism 171–2, 183–5
France:
  le Chapelier laws 76 n.
  economic democracy 112 n.
  industrial relations system 83, 183,
    235
  labour market flexibility 181
  May 1968 147
  party–union relations 199
  training 180
Fraser government 209
fraternity 25–6
free rider problem 95, 96, 133, 161,
   179–80
freedom 13–22, 186, 230–1
  compound concept 13, 14
  democratic freedom 34–5, 54
  see also liberty
freedom of action 13–19
  absence of constraint 14–16, 55
  availability of means 16–18, 56
  and choice 18–19
freedom of choice 15, 19–22
  absence of constraint 19
  availability of means 19
  and self-development 20–2

functional flexibility 178–81

Garrett, Geoffrey 114
Germany:
  Berlin 151
  Christian Democratic party 113 n.
  co-determination 99 n., 105, 117 n.,
    137 n., 156–7, 162, 168
  economic democracy 112 n.
  economic performance 149, 170 n.
  industrial relations system 183, 192,
    223, 229, 235
  labour market flexibility 179, 181
  social democratic party 110 n., 199
  socio-economic parliament 137
  training 180
  tripartism 123 n.
  unions 72, 105, 174
government:
  internal organization 75–6
  regulation 39, 40–1, 171
Greece 235, 236
guild socialism 25

Harsanyi, John 124
Harvester case 202
Hawke, Bob 206 n., 209, 211
Hawke government 191, 222
Higgins, Justice 202
Hirschman, Albert 41, 44
Hungary 137

incomes policy 100, 165–8, 191, 208
incorporation 86–7
indirect control 29, 30–3
  over firms 39–41, 48–9
industrial relations systems:
  defining characteristics 77–8
  games and meta-games 108, 130–2
  laissez-faire 81–2, 130, 150–1, 154,
    182
  neo-liberalism 84, 98, 130, 131,
    151–4, 183
  pluralist free collective
    bargaining 83, 150, 152
  see also corporatism
inflation 146, 149–55, 160, 212–15,
   217, 232
interest ambiguity 95, 96
interest intermediation 88–9
Ireland 83, 236
Italy:
  Christian Democratic party 113 n.,
    114 n.

Italy (*cont.*):
  economic democracy 107 n., 112 n.,
    166, 188
  electoral reform 4 n.
  Hot Autumn 147
  industrial relations system 83, 235
  party–union relations 199

Keating, Paul 191 n., 209, 220, 221
Keynesian economics 149
Kondratiev cycle 189
Korpi, Walter 86 n., 91, 93

Labor Party (Australia) 87–8, 197,
    199–200
labour 42
  fictitious commodity 42–3
  and labour power 43, 183
  power relative to capital 92–100,
    107–8, 190
Labour Market Board (Sweden) 178
labour market flexibility 175, 224
  and corporatism 175–83, 222–8
  and worker control 183–7
labour movement 2, 99, 113
  politically significant 67
labour parties:
  conditions for electoral
    success 113–17
  and corporatism 102 n., 199–200
  in government 99, 101, 132 n., 143,
    149, 154
Labour Party (Britain) 77, 152
laissez-faire 193
  see also industrial relations systems
Lehmbruch, Gerhard 79, 80–1, 85
Leo XIII 80
liberal parenthesis 193
liberalism 1, 14, 37
  English radical liberalism 194–5,
    196
  see also neo-liberalism
liberty:
  and the conditions of liberty 17
  negative liberty 14, 16
  positive liberty 18
  see also freedom
living standards 208, 217–19
LO (Swedish union federation) 115 n.,
    158–60
Lukes, Steven 13–14, 17, 18, 20

Macpherson, C. B. 17, 21, 34 n.
markets:

market coordination 24
Marx, Karl 1, 20–1, 23–4, 43–4, 55–7,
    62, 70, 183
Marxism 25 n., 102 n., 199–200, 234 n.
mateship 194, 195–6
Meidner plan 106, 135 n., 158–9, 166
membership density 73, 78–9, 198,
    228 n.
mergeability of labour and
    capital 93–4
misery index 153
mobility of labour 42, 176, 177–8
Morgenstern, Oskar 124

Nash, John 124, 137–40
National Development funds 166, 221
national economic management:
  as a condition for electoral
    success 115–17, 130
  requirements during
    stagflation 148–50
  requirements during structural
    adjustment 174–5
nationalization 3, 4, 5
neo-liberalism 230–1
  see also industrial relations systems
Netherlands 107 n., 157 n., 158 n., 236
  Amsterdam 147
Norway 157 n., 223, 236
Nove, Alec 61–3

Offe, Claus 80, 93–5, 98
oil shock 147, 157
oligarchy 88–91
Olson, Mancur 150–1, 182
opportunism 50–3, 64
organization of work 103, 171, 181,
    188, 227–8
organizational unity 73, 78–9, 198,
    228

Panitch, Leo 80, 85, 130
parliamentary democracy 3, 5
pelegos 88
pension funds 120, 158, 160, 166–8,
    186 n.
  see also superannuation
Piore, Michael 171–2
pluralism 25
Poland 151
Portugal 235
productivity 120, 157–8, 161, 176 n.,
    208, 221
  productivity bargaining 183, 224

profitability, profits 118–21, 148,
157–8, 161
profit-threatening goods 118–19,
138–9
during stagflation 148
during structural adjustment 173–4
programmatic goals 3–5, 6–7
pro-labour parties, *see* labour parties
Przeworski, Adam 114, 164
public involvement 76–7, 78, 80–4,
86–8, 151, 155, 191

quality-competitive customized
production 172, 185–7

rational choice theory:
assumptions 109–10, 133
application to industrial
relations 110–11, 164
Rawls, John 12 n., 13, 17, 23, 63 n.
restrictive work practices 173–4, 181,
184–5, 189–90, 224
see also organization of work
revolution through reform 106
revolutionary dilemma 135–7, 159 n.

Sabel, Charles 171–2
Scandinavia 86, 229
Schelling, Thomas 125–9, 137–40
skills 94, 179–81, 187–8
and discretion 184
see also training
slave, slavery 14, 55, 58–60
free slave paradox 20
social contracts 77, 87, 221, 235
social democracy 7, 129
Social Democratic Party
(Sweden) 159 n., 160
social democratic parties, *see* labour
parties
social wage 101
socialism:
constitutive morality 12–13, 35–7
and internationalism 5
and liberalism 1, 16 n., 37, 230–1
origin of the term 1 n.
and social democracy 7–8
socialist movement 2, 236
socialist theory 1–2
sociality:
axiom of 12, 23–5
South Africa 99 n.
Soviet socialism 7, 8, 40, 63, 71, 82 n.,
231

Spain 235
stagflation 145–7
in Australia 207–21
causes 147, 179 n.
recurrent problems 168–9, 232
stakeholders 39
standestaat 193
Stephens, John D. 104, 186
Streeck, Wolfgang 179, 182–3
structural adjustment 145, 170–1
in Australia 221–9
causes 171–2
recurrent problems 189–90, 232
subjects 29, 30–3
and exit rights 47
see also authority
superannuation 220
Sweden:
co-determination 105, 157 n.
economic democracy 106, 130 n.,
186, 221
economic performance 149
industrial relations system 183, 192,
223, 235
labour market flexibility 177, 178,
179, 181
nationalization 4
pensions 166
social democratic party 199
unions 91, 115, 159–60
wage earner funds 156, 158–62

Tawney, R. H. 6, 92 n.
Taylor, Charles 21–2
Taylor, Frederick W. 184
technological change 103, 140, 170,
171, 179 n., 188 n.
Thatcher government 151, 222
trade-off:
corporatist trade-off 99–101, 107,
155, 229
see also control trade-off
Trades and Labour Councils 197, 198
tradition-boundness thesis 193–207
training 103, 171, 225–8
see also skills
transaction costs 49, 177, 178
trust 74–5, 184–5

unemployment 100, 146, 149–55, 160,
212–15, 217, 232
unions:
centralization, *see* labour
centralization

unions (*cont.*):
in an economic democracy 136–7
internal democracy 91
metalworkers' union
(Australia) 206, 227
metalworkers' union (Germany) 72,
105
metalworkers' union
(Sweden) 159–60
safety stewards 105
shearers' union (Australia) 196,
198
United States:
consumer durables 171
economic democracy 112, 120 n.,
161, 166
industrial relations system 83, 151,
183
labour market flexibility 177, 178
union label 71
unions 89, 101 n., 158
universal suffrage 3

viability, *see* feasibility

voice control 41, 44
von Neumann, John 124

wage earner funds 156, 158–61
see also Meidner plan
wage restraint 140, 149–50, 155,
164–6, 181
and codetermination 157
and corporatism 150–5, 215–17
and wage earner funds 159
wages 103, 107, 148, 188
aggregate wages 176
differentials 176–7, 218–19
welfare state 4–5, 36–7
Western Europe 67, 126, 165
Wigfoss, Ernst 106
Williamson, Oliver 49–53
Wilson, Harold 174
workers, *see* labour
workers' control:
advantages to capitalists 120–1
degree and level 104–5, 186
desire for more 112, 163
over investment 164, 166–8, 220–1